MURTY CLASSICAL
LIBRARY OF INDIA

THE BUDDHA'S PATH TO AWAKENING

MCLI 40

THE BUDDHA'S PATH TO AWAKENING

Translated by
SARAH SHAW

MURTY CLASSICAL LIBRARY OF INDIA
HARVARD UNIVERSITY PRESS
Cambridge, Massachusetts
London, England
2025

Printed in the United States of America
First printing

SERIES DESIGN BY M9DESIGN

Library of Congress Cataloging-in-Publication Data

Names: Shaw, Sarah, 1955- translator.
Title: The Buddha's path to awakening / translated by Sarah Shaw.
Other titles: Jātakanidāna. (Shaw) |
Murty classical library of India ; 40.
Description: Cambridge, Massachusetts ; London, England :
Harvard University Press, 2025. |
Series: Murty classical library of India ; 40
| "The text in this edition is based on the first volume of the
transliterated six-volume series of the Jātakatthavaṇṇanā ...
published for the first time in the original Pali by V. Fausbøll
in 1877, as The Jātaka Together with its Commentary,
Being Tales of the Anterior Births of Gotama Buddha.
The work translated here, Jātakanidāna (the Cause of the Jatakas),
although independent, forms its introduction"--Page xxxiii |
Includes bibliographical references and index. | In English and Pali.
Identifiers: LCCN 2024003684 |
ISBN 9780674296527 (cloth)
Subjects: LCSH: Gautama Buddha--Pre-existence. |
Jataka stories. | Buddhism--Sacred books.
Classification: LCC BQ1470.J3 B83 2025 |
DDC 294.3/82325--dc23/eng/20240314
LC record available at https://lccn.loc.gov/2024003684

CONTENTS

INTRODUCTION

The life of Gotama Buddha is one of the most renowned narratives in Asia. *The Buddha's Path to Awakening: The Origin of the Birth Stories* (*Jātakanidāna*) translates into English the first complete prose narrative that describes his search for freedom. It starts many eons in the past when the hero of this work, Gotama Buddha, first takes the Bodhisatta (Bodhisattva in Sanskrit) vow to postpone his own awakening until the time he can teach others too. He renews this vow in the presence of Buddhas throughout history. Finally, after a long quest, he achieves his aim and becomes a Buddha. The work closes when he is fully awakened, now a teacher of gods and humans, and it gives us a panoramic frieze of key moments on his extraordinary path.

The Buddha's Path to Awakening was intended primarily as an introduction to the 547 birth stories (*jātakas*). The text, composed in Pali, was apparently authored by a monk at the Great Vihara in Anuradhapura, in what is now Sri Lanka. It dates to around the fifth or sixth century C.E., centuries after the formation of the Pali canon. *The Buddha's Path* describes the many lifetimes that feature the Bodhisatta as hero, developing the skills that will enable him to teach. Jatakas form one of the nine "limbs" of the Buddha's teachings, a genre considered essential to the transmission of the whole Buddhist path.[1] *The Buddha's Path* offers the early background and frame narrative for these ever-popular tales. The work appears to have had a single author—though it should also be noted that for all late-Pali commentarial works, the plural term "authors" is also appropriate, as works written then, even by a single author, collator, or editor, are the result of centuries of glosses, commentary, and add-on stories by monks dedicated to perpetuating the Buddha's teaching.

By modern standards, this is no "biography." In going back to the Buddha's first undertaking of the Bodhisatta vow, this work extends the perspective of what we consider a single life: his last life is preceded by countless others since that moment. It is filled with supposed quotations by the subject—who recollects manifold lifetimes—in what could only be termed, loosely, an "autobiographical" manner. The hero does not keep the same name as he metamorphoses, through his awakening, into a Buddha. The story is a mythic narrative, about multiple lives, that includes both biographical and autobiographical elements. It manages to be both typological and personal, transcending the usual boundaries and limitations of a human life span. It moves between first and third person, the far past and "present" comments on the action of the past. It describes endless cycles of time acting within and yet somehow outside linear chronology. It suggests, through constant shifts of voice, and through the ages of time it evokes, an authoritative narration that arises precisely from its embodiment of a kind of "nonself," the resolve of the Bodhisatta who has undertaken the vow, operating throughout the contradictions of human history and constant rebirths. The hero starts with one identity, a human called Sumedha, who becomes a Bodhisatta—one "attached to awakening," with many names and in many species and spheres of existence—and finally completes his work in human form once more. With his last identity, as a Buddha, there is no more rebirth. Throughout, the work is unified by one resolve: it shows how the doctrine of nonself can still sustain a heroic quest through time, space, and constant change. Once the goal has been achieved, the hero becomes a Buddha. He is described with epithets that apply to all Buddhas: blessed one (Bhagava), "one with ten powers" (Dasabala), a Great Being (Mahasatta), a teacher (Sattha), and a "Thus-Gone" (Tathagata), literally one who has "gone thus."

The Story and Its Structure

"The Far Origin," the first section, starts with the ascetic Sumedha taking the Bodhisatta vow at the feet of a Buddha, long ago. He renews the vow before a succession of many Buddhas, who predict that he will indeed become a Buddha in his final life. As Buddhas come and go, the hero gains experience, skills, and wisdom in many kinds of rebirths. Through renewed effort, he cultivates in many lives the qualities he will need to teach others. This great quest constitutes the drama of the birth stories, described in the 547 tales of the main collection.

The second section, "The Near Origin," opens in the Tusita heaven, where the Bodhisatta has been reborn and awaits his final rebirth, after enacting the dramas described in the Jatakas. Persuaded by the gods to take human form one last time, in one particular time and place, it tells of his conception and describes the events of his birth and renunciation, culminating in his awakening and rediscovery of the path to freedom, which so many Buddhas had found and taught him in the first section.

The third section, "The Recent Origin," is the finale, the "recent" past, and for Buddhist audiences it presents the very familiar events of Gotama's teaching, and hence the world of his discourses (*suttas*) and the creation of a Sangha, or community, the means by which his teaching will be perpetuated.

Each of the three sections is called a *nidāna,* or cause, foundation, origin. All three "origins" are needed for the complete fulfillment of a Bodhisatta vow. The vow and the decision of the hero to postpone his own awakening until he has acquired the skills needed for Buddhahood are the seeds of everything that follows; one moment of inspired insight contains all the stories that follow. The second section, with the steps that lead to the awakening, is also an "origin" for the stories. It provides the perspective of the enlightenment moment, in which all past lives can be recollected and the teaching (Dhamma) is known. The third section, which describes the dissemination of that teaching to others, establishes the Sangha, the monastic community.

The Buddha's Path to Awakening, with its description of the three primary origins of Buddhahood and full awakening, has an inherent literary integrity arising from its function. It gives the origin of the birth stories in the vow and tells how the awakened being, the purported "omniscient" narrator, came to the wisdom that allowed him to remember these lives and turn them into stories. It also sets the scene for the establishment of an audience, the laity, and the Sangha, the listeners necessary for birth stories to be told, who can themselves participate in the larger Buddhist narrative. The basic structure of this short work invites the ongoing interaction of listeners and readers; it offers a template for everyone, Buddhist or not, to tell their own "story" in a new way, with themselves as part of a vast web of interdependencies in time and space. So, while it has a linear narrative, it is really a story about cycles: about recurrent Buddhas; about the repetition of key events in the lives of these Buddhas; and about the possibility that readers—or in ancient times, listeners—can themselves go through cycles of existence while trying to perfect their own spiritual paths.

Traditions and Purpose

The story is a paean to the great beauty and power of the aspiration to dedicate one's life and subsequent lives to the service of all sentient beings. The notion of the Bodhisatta, one who finds a path and teaches it to others, had a revolutionary effect on Indian and Asian philosophy, art, and religion. The vast spatial and temporal perspectives of this work invite us to reassess our own place in time and space and to see ourselves as potential participants in this endeavor. It seems intended as an entryway to the teachings of early Buddhism. Many people, we are told, become awakened on hearing a birth story, if it is accompanied by a teaching on the four noble truths: the suffering to be understood, the craving to be abandoned, the goal to be realized, and the path to be cultivated. The Jatakas, although subject to many evolutions, were considered from the outset to have been told by the Buddha. At the end of many, we are told of the people who heard the story and immediately became enlightened. No such account is related about *The Buddha's Path.* While it describes the many people who did achieve awakening through being in the presence of a Buddha, it has no pretensions to being itself a means of effecting that transformation.

This work is the product of the teaching of the Theriyas, the "elders"; its author seems anxious to stress its great antiquity.[2] So while *The Buddha's Path,* like so much Buddhist literature in the years of the first millennium, includes marvels, wondrous events, and intimations of vast reaches of space and time, and while its preface is also the introduction to the Jatakas as a whole, through which people do become enlightened, it tends toward an appreciation of what is already present in the long-established tradition: enjoyment of and reflection on the great achievement of past Buddhas, the "present" Buddha, and his Sangha. The opening *mangala,* the formal homage and preliminary to a Buddhist text, is made simply to a few fellow monks at the Great Vihara of Anuradhapura who have been encouraging the author to write it in accordance with the Theriya traditions. This is rather a homely and low-key statement, comparable to those that precede other Pali commentaries written at this time.[3] From the evidence of the *mangala,* this work, while collected from many sources, has been assembled and finally written by one person, an unknown monk who is clearly *bahussuto,* one who has heard much.[4] Tradition held that this author was Buddhaghosa, although that appears unlikely.[5]

While not itself intended as an awakening text, *The*

Buddha's Path seems intent on creating the space where awakening can take place. There is so much rich visual imagery in *The Buddha's Path,* as well as scenes familiar from monuments, that its role is most naturally explained by a sight one often sees in South and Southeast Asia: Buddhist monasteries and temple complexes that are so immense they are almost like their own town or village. Their overall structure appears to be of the kind described at the end of this work, built on ground donated by the lay follower Anathapindika to the Buddha and the Sangha. Filled with stupas, small temples, sometimes ancient shrines, shrine halls, and living quarters, these religious sites are also open to the public. At the entrance, a building, perhaps new, offers a way in to the whole. This is the public face of the monastery and temple, through which visitors can find their way to the other parts and look around. *The Buddha's Path to Awakening* feels like this spacious, well-lit entrance hall. Some doors open out to the Jatakas, scattered around like ancient shrines and stupas that have perhaps changed and been added to over the years. Some open out to the whole of the Pali canon, by this time ancient, like the far older shrines, intact, studded around the temple grounds. The text is an introduction to these structures too, with directions, to help one look around the large complex and explore Pali Buddhist teaching and the Buddha's teaching career. *The Buddha's Path* is a fresh construction, but in its retellings and quotations it uses the stones, as it were, of older buildings, and its doorways open to ancient ones deeper within. Verses from and allusions to a range of older texts, such as the *Cariyapiṭaka* (The Basket of Deeds), the *Dhammapada*

(The Steps of the Teaching), and the *Buddhavaṃsa* (The Lineage of the Buddhas), as well as *suttas* and the *Vinaya,* abound.[6]

The taking of the Bodhisatta vow, the key event near the outset of this work, is not simply a narrative linking device. It also serves as a gateway, or an opening, for a heroic search that can be undertaken by anyone. The practitioners who reflect on the lives of the Bodhisatta and the Buddha can find in themselves the possibilities of an awakened mind. Whether as an aspirant Buddha, a disciple, or a being who finds awakening for themselves (*paccekabuddha*), the combined stories invite the listener or practitioner to see their own journey as following a comparable trajectory. This story opens the doors and invites us to walk around and explore the larger whole.

The ancients linked art, text, and story in ritual. Scenes from both earlier lives and the last ones are remembered and contemplated by those who regard them as objects of faith and emulation, in a practice known as the recollection of the qualities of the Buddha (*buddhānussati*). This meditation is still undertaken today, often by walking around, paying homage to, and reflecting on such scenes. This is said to allow one to attain a state of calm, faith, mindfulness, understanding, happiness, and the capacity to endure pain.[7] The subject matter helps such reflections: one of the most popular scenes in early Indian art is that of an aspirant to Buddhahood, an ascetic with matted hair, paying homage at the feet of another Buddha. It is frequently depicted in Gandharan art and can be seen among the ancient monuments at Sanchi and Nagarjunakonda.[8] The Jatakas are like outflows from that one moment, endlessly diverse objects of recollection and meditation.

Two complementary stories wind around countless stupas and decorate lintels, murals, and friezes, flanking, echoing, and responding to each other, and interacting with local legends, folktales, and myths. The first one is the life of Gotama Buddha described in the last section of *The Buddha's Path,* with the birth, the awakening, and the teaching career of the Buddha. The entry into nibbana (nirvana in Sanskrit), though not described in *The Buddha's Path,* also features. The second story is that of the quest, embodied in the Jatakas with their many genres and styles. These two narratives exist alongside each other, each constantly connected and associated with key events in the other. In countries and regions where Buddhism is practiced, they are depicted everywhere and have become the warp on which the rest of the Buddhist teaching can be woven. The last life, and the many lives that contribute to it, form an enveloping Buddhist *imaginaire,* filled with stories, heroism, and glimpses of the possibility of freedom. The meditation on the recollection of the Buddha includes and encompasses all of the many individual tales involved.

The writer of *The Buddha's Path* clearly felt it necessary to write down, for the first time perhaps, a simple, sequential story about the earlier lives and last life of the Buddha: the great temple complex of the Pali canon needed to be opened to the public and to posterity. The fact that the commentary sometimes discusses the merits of different versions of the life story in terms of their investigative, discursive, and even interactive styles suggests that different reciters in various regions embraced the many ways of telling the story. This work pulls them together into a distinctive and authoritative panorama along the walls of one "building" that everyone can visit and feel at home in. If the *mangala* at the beginning is correct, one person has supervised its adaptation into this easily accessed atrium. But, as would have been the case for a great monastery complex, many generations of builders, authors, and editors have contributed to the larger construction.

Audience

While it presents itself as an introduction to the Jatakas, this book also seems to be a little manual for the teller of stories, the monk, or perhaps nun, who would be recounting them to the people who came to visit a temple. People would have viewed the associated temple art while practicing not just the recollection of the Buddha but also the recollections of the Dhamma (teaching) and the Sangha, all core meditations in Pali Buddhism. They would have heard many of these stories again and again. Asides in the birth stories, as well as in this introduction to them, suggest that they were intended to be read by a monastic—who would then tell them in the manner they saw fit, rather as is the case in South and Southeast Asia today. Perhaps the poetic sections were intended to be recited, too, another custom in Buddhist Southeast Asia, where monastic and lay practitioners historically learned Pali and vernacular versions of texts by heart. The way *The Buddha's Path* ends, with the laudatory appreciation of the layman Anathapindika for donating a large monastery, suggests an audience of lay followers; but monastics, of course, would want to know this story, and they would be the ones most likely to recount it, in temples, perhaps in the evening when people had finished their daily business. The stories would support the listeners, enlivening and informing their appreciation of the art and Buddhist practice in the very places where they would most likely be told.

Commentaries and Genre

Like the birth stories, this work is what is technically known as a commentary, a modern term for some ancient forms compiled for the purpose of making original texts clear. Prose is often mixed with original verse in explaining older Buddhist texts from the Pali canon. Pali commentaries from this time reveal many historical layers of adaptation to the needs and responses of listeners, long before texts were written down. The English word "commentary," however, does not cover the range of genres, often grouped together in different ways, that we find in these various works. Commentaries on verse collections, in particular, are often composed of extended and riveting narratives describing the lifetimes and experiences of the people who heard, or uttered, the verse concerned. The commentaries on the *Dhammapada,* for instance, *Theragāthā* (The Elder Monks' Verses) and *Therīgāthā* (The Elder Nuns' Verses), tell magnificent and complicated backstories, lasting lifetimes, for each verse. They allow the law of karma to be seen enacted, and reveal how each individual life is part of a far greater process of spiritual development. Such writing seems itself a kind of genre, with patterns and cycles that repeat as the practitioner reaches their final goal.

So, while termed a commentary, the birth stories are in practice multiple biographies—stories of the different lifetimes of the Bodhisatta on his path. Each usually involves just one life of the Bodhisatta. From the beginning, the birth stories cannot have been told in verse alone: many do not make sense without the prose narration, which suggests either that it was there at the start in some form, or that the verses were always intended simply as cues for the storyteller.[9] Each story carries the layers of plot, explanation, and description that have accreted around older verses, wrapping themselves around the original kernel. The stories thus appear to have developed over centuries, with the old verses retained at their core.

The Buddha's Path follows these older traditions and is most akin to Jatakas. But despite having many comparable features, it feels different. Like the Jatakas, it tells a story in greater detail than the verse summaries. It too is supported by early verse content, performing roles that include straightforward storytelling, the lyrical expression of emotion, and quotes from the teaching. It also includes, in a manner peculiar to Jatakas, plentiful comments on the action from the Buddha "in the present," offering the perspective of the fully awakened mind on events long past. Like the commentaries on the elders' verses, this is an extended biography of a type that seems to be applied to most of the major Buddhist figures.

The "biography" in *The Buddha's Path,* however, is far more wide-ranging, appropriate to the founder of the tradition. The story has clearly had a slightly different evolution from other birth stories. The first section, the account of Sumedha and his aspiration, is in some ways an extended Jataka that takes the *Buddhavaṃsa,* the story of the many Buddhas that have preceded Gotama, as its core. Events described in its verses are explained, elaborated, and made into story form, just as Jataka prose expands on the verses and makes them into a continuous whole. There is a crucial difference, though, deriving perhaps from the style of the *Buddhavaṃsa.* Although told in the third person, the story also includes the Buddha's own first-person reminiscences in verse—a feature quite different from Jatakas, where the narrator in the verses is usually "the Teacher" or "the awakened one," not the "I" of the present Buddha, until right at the end of each tale. After the Sumedha story and the account of the earlier Buddhas, the narrative acquires a life of its own. Sections two and three draw on verses from all sorts of different early works.

The Buddha's Path is the most important multiple-life biography of the tradition, that of the teacher himself, and as such it has its own power: as an inspirational story, as a meditation, in encouraging meditative recollection of the Buddha, and as a lineage history spanning eons. The result is a coherent story that distills all the "things needed for Buddhahood" and for the teaching to be perpetuated; its continuity is ensured by the central figure, the Bodhisatta, who becomes a Buddha. The effect is curiously multidimensional. It presents doorways to all the different times in the past, set out in the birth stories and the rest of the Pali canon, but it makes a unified whole.

Accessibility and the attempt to tell a good, engaging tale from multiple sources are key to this work's role as the introduction to the birth stories. These features suggest how it may have been compiled and used in the early days. As the Pali canon was delivered entirely orally for so long, the reciters for each collection, male and sometimes female, seem to have developed their own theories and stories about its origins. The first texts could have been written down very early on—the Sri Lankan tradition says around the beginning of the first millennium. But a strong predisposition to orality continued, as it did until well into the twentieth century in Southeast Asian Buddhist countries. All kinds of stories must have been circulating about the Buddha's life events. The editor would have committed to writing those he selected as the most authoritative.[10] He would have been deeply influenced both by traditional oral delivery and the fact that his work would thereafter shape new oral traditions. Most people would not have been literate but probably would have known the Buddha's most important texts and life events reasonably well. They would want to hear this compelling story as a whole, with all its details.

The Bodhisatta Vow and the Ten Perfections

The notion that lifetimes may be spent developing supreme spiritual qualities is an unusually capacious and adventurous literary device. The aspirant Bodhisatta must be reborn as animal, god, and human, in all kinds of castes and situations: the vow generates and encompasses manifold stories. By the time *The Buddha's Path* was written, the vow had also long been an animating principle of what we now know as Theravada Buddhism. Indeed, in many ways the power of the Bodhisatta vow is the true subject of this story. The vow is presented as transcending a conventional sense of self; it participates in some way with the "deathless." From its perspective, any lifetime can be radically transformed. For the fully awakened mind to develop, it must fulfill many causally interrelated conditions, over many lives. In Pali Buddhism the Bodhisatta needs to cultivate the ten perfections (*pāramī*): generosity (*dāna*), morality (*sīla*), renunciation (*nekkhamma*), wisdom (*paññā*), vigor or heroic effort (*viriya*), forbearance (*khanti*), truthfulness (*sacca*), resolve (*adhiṭṭhāna*), loving-kindness (*mettā*), and equanimity (*upekkhā*). The perfections, this work asserts, do not die with a person's death, even while the one developing them may suffer endless rounds of birth and death in cyclical existence; rather, they flourish like a plant. By resolving to develop them, the Bodhisatta, in the one moment described at the beginning of this work, the first taking of his vow, creates the "seed" of the whole story. Throughout ages of cyclical existence, "our" Bodhisatta transforms himself to become "our" Buddha. But even Buddhas are not permanent: the goal involves freedom from that kind of thinking.

The many Jatakas, historically from an earlier date, also anticipate the vow. Their verses are slightly later than the major texts but are still constituents of the early Pali canon. In the last life in the Jataka collection, in which the Bodhisatta gives away all his possessions for the sake of his vow, Prince Vessantara asks both his son and his daughter to help him on his path to fulfilling his "perfection."[11] There is no mention of the Bodhisatta, but the word "perfection" gives an indication of the direction the Jatakas are about to take, and of the impulse that animates his repeated births in samsara, the cycle of karmic death and rebirth. By the first or second century B.C.E., with the composition of the *Buddhavaṃsa,* the ideal is fully developed. The perfections appear in the *Buddhavaṃsa* and in later prose parts of various Jatakas, which are often attributed to one or another of them. At the end of the first section of *The Buddha's Path,* some of the major Jatakas are cited as times when the Bodhisatta was developing a particular perfection. And there is always a special emphasis on the last and historically most pervasive story, *Vessantara Jātaka* (The Vessantara Birth Story). Anyone from one of the Buddhist regions of the world, ancient or modern, who heard the accounts given in *The Buddha's Path* would know at least a few. The Bodhisatta's undertaking is thus immediately imbued with meaning, as listeners attune themselves to the stories whose depictions they may have walked past in the temple, or have heard, or seen painted or performed in dramas, dances, and processions.[12]

Orality and Imagery

Orality lends itself to certain features we find in the oral heroic and bardic literatures of the world, such as catalogues. Lists of names and lineages, for example, are key to both Homeric epics and the bardic poems of Europe. This work lists all the Buddhas that have preceded the historical one, and their key attributes, appearances, and attendants.

People in cultures without reading have always liked to imagine and hear tales of their long-distant antecedents, of heroic figures and wonderful mythical origins, as they place them and their own culture in an inspiring historical tradition. Such works delight in long roll calls of names and accounts of extraordinary heroic attributes, larger-than-life figures, great achievements, and a sense of grandeur. Oral epics, poems, and other accounts encourage family and community meetings, a sense of the festive, and a feeling of belonging to something larger than oneself.

One aspect of this is the collective evocation of shared images. Many of the incidents in this work have been so often described that they have become emblems with a life of their own, part of the emotional and imaginative landscape for Buddhists throughout the world. In Sri Lanka, temple friezes everywhere show the Bodhisatta in different forms, taking and renewing his vow before successive Buddhas: as a naga before the Buddha Sumana, a lion in front of the Buddha Paduma, a king, an ascetic. Indian Buddhist art from the early centuries of the first millennium subverts temporality: scenes from the Buddha's life flank those from the far past, so that one act of generosity is seen echoed in past existences, and the cultivation of the perfections participates in timelessness.[13] In other Buddhist regions, incidents such as the entry of the Buddha into nirvana are found everywhere. Scenes from the text have been part of ritual and devotional life for centuries. Visualization is also a feature of the text itself, as the listener is invited to imagine the Buddhas described. All the Buddhas in the first part are splendid; many are vast, and many have special magnificences. Some of their qualities are evoked in detail: in this text, this appears to be invited. One Buddha, for example, is described as so radiant that it is impossible to tell whether it is night or day. Presumably those present would have imagined this vividly and felt it to be so.

Orality, Numbers, and Enumeration

The oral nature of lists brings us to the surprisingly related theme of number. A striking feature of *The Buddha's Path* is the great ease with which it encompasses breathtakingly large numbers and expanses of time while cheerfully expecting the reader or listener to envisage such numbers too, as we are encouraged to "build" around numerical time schemes of dazzling vastness. Ancient Indians, it seems, had a highly sophisticated ability to play with enormous numbers in ways apparently undreamed of in the West. Indic culture was unusual in its enjoyment of vast, painstakingly defined measurements of space and time, as well as its openness to the complete absence of such parameters: measurelessness and the infinite form a constant background. Ancient Buddhists saw the universe not as created but "beginningless": whole universes emerge, grow, and fall apart, endlessly, throughout what we can still call, simply, "time." And within finite time schemes there is still plenty of creative play.

The Buddha's Path starts, precisely, four incalculable epochs and a hundred thousand eons ago. A Pali eon, *kappa,* is calculated at about sixteen million years. An "incalculable" epoch (*asaṅkheyya*) is a great *kappa,* the time it takes for the universe to come into being and collapse four times, to the power of sixty.[14] It was certainly a very long time ago when the first vow took place, in the incident described near the opening of this work. As listeners, and now readers, we are encouraged to venture into this exploration of deep time.

It is not just time schemes that are large. With painstaking care, *The Buddha's Path* goes through a concertina-like diminishment of time schemes, life spans, and size, with only an occasional expansion as the movement goes down. The first Buddha described, Dipankara, had three assemblies, the first of a hundred thousand crore, which is one trillion. His life span was a hundred thousand rainy seasons, or years, and his body, 80 forearm lengths long—about 120 feet. After that, assembly numbers, sizes, and life spans diminish gradually, in irregular but gentle waves, as successive Buddhas come and go in deep time. Clearly there is a meditative element to this; as noted, the recollections of the Buddha, the Dhamma, and the Sangha are calm meditations. Here, listeners are invited to extend their imaginative range apparently endlessly. The divine abidings of loving-kindness, compassion, sympathetic joy, and equanimity are *aparimana,* boundless, and the listeners are, it seems, encouraged to include a sense of deep time in opening their imaginative scope as worlds stretch back. There is something calming in the gentle rhythm of the leisured repetition of Buddha after Buddha, their coming into being and passing away like a humming pulse, as each one teaches and then enters nirvana. The great act of generosity the Bodhisatta makes under the Buddha Suruci requires him to find space for a hundred thousand crore of monks. The pavilion the king of the gods makes for him is explicitly created as a kind of jeweled mandala and is compared to a vast meditation device (*kasina*), usually constructed as a circle to be seen in the mind's eye.[15] We are invited to imagine this wonderful phenomenon and to enjoy the exercise.

But there is a twist. For however great the achievement or the person, even those who become Buddhas, the law of impermanence still operates. As the verses about the first Buddha, Dipankara, say after their descriptions of his great miraculous powers and his entrance into nirvana: "Are not all constructed things empty?"[16] This insight is built into an understanding of the succession of Buddhas. As the Bodhisatta notes while he contemplates where and how to be born: "Dhamma teachings by Buddhas are never without these three signs: of impermanence, unsatisfactoriness, and nonself."[17]

Finally, we come to our Buddha, who chooses to teach at a time when people have life spans that are neither too long nor too short, for if people live too long, they do not notice death; if life is too short, they cannot focus. His assembly is going to be large but not inordinately so. Though unspecified, his height will be what we call normal. He will live in a world where things are not so wonderful but not too bad. People will be able to practice his teachings.

The effect of all these imaginary enumerations, vast time schemes, and the visualization of the gentle rise and fall of Buddhas gradually decreasing in power and size is that we focus on "our" Buddha, who, in the midst of this wonder, is called in a friendly and proprietary way "our" Bodhisatta. As the Buddhas come and go in a tidal ebb and flow of impermanence, his growth in the perfections matures. He will be extraordinary. Miracles and marvelous events will happen around him. But he will be like us—a normal human being, of reasonable height, a reasonable life span, and with a reasonable number of followers. It is rather like those films that start with a vision of infinite space and galaxies, then zoom in to smaller galaxies, then to a small one, then one sun, one solar system, and a familiar planet. Zooming in further, we find ourselves in a playroom in Denver or an office in Hong Kong: the "here and now" of the film's heroes, and the world they live in. And we see that it is, broadly speaking, just like "ours."

The Natural World and Miracles

From the outset, the natural world responds, heaves, and quivers in sympathy with the Bodhisatta's resolve. Miracles and earthquakes dramatize the great events in his final life: his conception, birth, awakening, and first teaching. Buddhism is sometimes thought of as life denying but the natural world, with all its riches, is his constant ally and supporter throughout his ventures. Flowers pour from the sky at momentous times; the earth itself tries to stop him from looking back when he takes the renunciation.

Many heavenly deities appear in this work who, at that time, would have been considered part of the natural world. Many of them support the Bodhisatta's quest and the attainment of Buddhahood by witnessing, commenting on, and aiding the action. The gods are of various kinds, according to the heaven they inhabit. There are sense-sphere devas who have bodies that can be seen by humans. Devas muffle the sounds of the prince's horse's hooves, for instance, so that the family will not hear him leave the palace. Gods of deep meditation, from the Brahma heavens, also feature. They rarely visit humans, but the lord of these, Brahma himself, encourages the new Buddha to teach after enlightenment. Another kind of god is the formless being, reborn without a physical body after practicing formless meditations. These beings have life spans lasting eons and have no contact with humans. Kala Devala, the seer who predicts Gotama's Buddhahood, knows that he is going to be reborn as such a god. With great sadness, he predicts that his own death and rebirth without bodily form will occur before Gotama becomes enlightened: he will miss the teachings of this new Buddha.

The perfections are the only type of growth that survives the rise and fall of death, for even the gods are impermanent, with a definite life span. The aspirant Buddha is several times called a "Buddha sapling"; his vow is frequently said to "ripen" and "blossom" through time, like the perfections. The perfections strengthen and mature as Buddhas come into being and pass away. When Gotama comes to human birth, it is the right season, when all causes have come to ripeness. He also returns to his family when, the text says, the "season" is right for him to do so. The Bodhisatta path is long, but its fruition will take place when the moment is right, and when the natural world, which supports him throughout, has come to the time and place for its harvest.

Words like "hagiographic" are often applied to the fabular, wondrous elements of the Pali and Sanskrit accounts of the Buddha. Something more precise is going on, however.

Certainly Buddhahood brings marvels. But they are things, the text suggests, that can also happen in a "real" world, with "real" people; marvels are perceived as natural in the natural world. Small details among the stories' mythical elements feel approachably human. We are being invited to admire the hero but also to see him as a human being. The fact that the Buddha, though welcomed, does not receive alms when he returns to his family after the awakening seems convincing. The way the Buddha faces his challenges on the night before the enlightenment—the clouds of darkness, fog, and burning doubt hurled at him by Mara, the god of delusion—feels metaphorically true. So does his final struggle before his attainment. As his final attack, Mara challenges Gotama's right even to sit in meditation at the spot he has chosen. This touch of inspired psychological accuracy evokes the hidden fears and lack of self-worth that can prevent meditative progress for anyone, at any stage. Only the recollection of generosity offers armor against this: the earth bears witness to all the countless acts of giving the Bodhisatta has performed in the past. At this, Mara admits defeat and Gotama can attain his goal. We then have the detail of Mara gloomily drawing lines on the ground, listing his own deficiencies, like a comically thwarted baddie in a children's film. "Evil" is tragic and problematic but ultimately ludicrous. Such details are not simply hagiographic or mythical embellishments; they are the lifeblood of the larger story. *The Buddha's Path* is a heroic, miraculous tale, but one intended for humans who, it suggests, might like to explore its inspiring possibilities themselves.

Acknowledgments

I would like to thank Professor Sheldon Pollock for his patient reading and editing; friends Professor Jas Elsner and Dr. Julia Shaw for conversations about Indian art, archaeology, and the environment; and many friends in India, Myanmar, Sri Lanka, and Thailand who have shown me around temples and shrines, explaining their beauties to me. I would also like to thank Professor Rupert Gethin, chair of the Pali Text Society, for his help and encouragement, and Professor Maria Heim for our many conversations and her helpful input and editing. In recent unhappy times, Maria has demonstrated unswerving scholarly integrity and loyalty to the aims of this series. Thank you also to Julie Hagen, Heather Hughes, Samantha Mateo, Professor Beatrice Chrystall, Dr. Katherine Ulrich, and diligent proofreaders for their painstaking work. Lastly, gratitude to Charles.

NOTES

1 Jatakas were not confined to Southern or Theravada Buddhism. The story of the vow taking before Dipankara is found throughout Pali literature. Some versions call him Megha; the *Divyavadāna* calls the hero Sumati. *Bodhisattvapiṭaka* (The Bodhisattva Collection) has fourteen Jatakas, including the story of the future Gotama Buddha and his undertaking the vow with Dipankara, the twenty-fourth Buddha before him (Skilling 2008: 64). See also Matsumura 2010.

2 For the complex history of the self-conscious emergence of this tradition, see Gethin 2012.

3 See von Hinüber 2015.

4 The date of the first prose "biography" of the Buddha's last life is unknown. It has been suggested that one emerged a hundred years after his death (see Reynolds and Hallisey 1987: 323). There seem to have been "floating oral traditions" from early times (Harvey 2013: 14). The author of *The Buddha's Path* sees his work as new,

presumably for its scope in covering the Bodhisatta's progress from the vow up to the last life, although he cites other versions of events.

5 See Geiger 1943: 25–32; von Hinüber 2015. For a close examination of Jataka commentarial method, see Gombrich's discussion of the subject (Cone and Gombrich 2011: xxvii–xxxv).

6 The *suttas* are the discourses of the Buddha. This "basket" of the teaching also includes Jatakas, songs by monks and nuns, and poems, including lineage chronicles. The *Vinaya* delineates the monastic code.

7 Ñāṇamoli 2009: VII.67; Nyanatusita 2021: 1.386–405.

8 Neelis gives 129 examples of Gandharan depictions of what is often known as "Dipankara Jataka" (Neelis 2019: 175–177); see also Jongeward 2018: 35; Huntington 2012. In southern India the scene appears at Nagarjunakonda (Longhurst 1938: 34–35). Only 10 percent of Amaravati art survives; there are no extant depictions of this scene, but we can assume some may have been there. The recitation of Buddha lineages remains strong in South and Southeast Asia (Skilling 1996).

9 See von Hinüber 1996: 54–57.

10 See, for instance, traditions of Buddhist learning and recitation in Thailand (Seeger 2018: 181–213).

11 Fausbøll 1877–1896: I.546.

12 See Shaw 2006: i–xxi.

13 Elsner 2021: 544–546.

14 On *kappa* (*kalpa*), see Buswell and Lopez 2014.

15 *The Buddhist Path,* [32–34].

16 *The Buddhist Path,* [39, vv. 220–221].

17 *The Buddhist Path,* [40].

NOTE ON THE TEXT AND TRANSLATION

The text in this edition is based on the first volume of the transliterated six-volume series of the *Jātakatthavaṇṇanā,* which, literally translated, means "The Exposition of the Jatakas." It was published for the first time in the original Pali by V. Fausbøll in 1877, as *The Jātaka Together with Its Commentary, Being Tales of the Anterior Births of Gotama Buddha.* The work translated here, *Jātakanidāna* (The Origin of the Jatakas), although independent, forms its introduction. Fausbøll used three sources, the Ck, Cs, and Cv manuscripts, found in Ceylon (now Sri Lanka), which he felt originally derived from a single original; the *C* denotes Ceylon. His work is now known as the Pali Text Society standard edition. Fausbøll's text has also been formatted for online dissemination on the Göttingen Register of Electronic Texts in Indian Language (GRETIL) website.

Because this Murty Classical Library of India volume is not a critical edition, I have made only a small number of editorial changes in the Pali text: there are now no inverted commas, for instance, and there is no capitalization. Minor adjustments have been made with regard to formatting. The few textual emendations are outlined in the Notes to the Text.

Fausbøll was dissatisfied with the Burmese recension of the Jataka corpus and felt more work was needed on examining its variants before all versions could be integrated into one standard text. A Burmese edition, however, is now online as the *Chaṭṭha Saṅgāyana,* published by the Vipassana Research Institute and freely available on the institute's Pali Tipitaka website. Its Jataka text is a little longer than the standard edition, as it incorporates some glosses as part of the text and simplifies some archaic language. It also avoids following "the more difficult reading" principle, that an unusual wording or term is more likely to be authentic (*lectio difficilior potior,* "the more difficult reading is the stronger"). I have made one or two emendations in this volume following the *Chaṭṭha Saṅgāyana,* having first corroborated them in either the Ck, Cs, or Cv manuscript, or all three. There are, however, few significant differences from the Pali Text Society edition in this section of the text. A small number of emendations have been made when the *Buddhavaṃsa* or the *Cariyapiṭaka,* from which the text quotes, gives a different reading. Those texts may be found in translation in I. B. Horner's Pali Text Society edition.

A few Pali terms are used frequently in this translation. Some are translated into English and some are left in Pali. Corresponding endnotes offer brief explanations at their first use and refer readers to the Glossary in the back of the book. Apart from the text's three main section titles, headings in the translation are my own and are provided as helpful reference points: the account of every early Buddha, for instance, is under each respective name. Numbers in square brackets refer to the page number in Fausbøll's edition, which, as the Pali Text Society text, is usually used for citations. For citation purposes, the whole text is called Ja I.1–94 (with the volume and page number used by Fausbøll).

I cite Jataka stories by number in the notes: for instance, I refer to the *Apaṇṇaka jātaka,* the first story in Fausbøll's *The Jātaka,* as *J* 1. The prose parts of a story follow the Jataka pattern of mixing usually older verses with the story that has developed around them. The words "it is said" often preface quoted verse. The *Buddhavaṃsa* (Lineage of the Buddhas) is quoted throughout the early part of the text. Alternative translations to many of these verses are found in Horner's *Chronicle of the Buddhas.*[1] The Pali text does not use inverted commas for speech, but a single one (') is used for elisions.

NOTES

1 Horner 1975: 1–99.

dūrenidāna

namo tassa bhagavato arahato
sammāsambuddhassa

1 jātikoṭisahassehi pamāṇarahitaṃ hitaṃ
lokassa lokanāthena kataṃ yena mahesinā
2 tassa pāde namassitvā katvā dhammassa c' añjalim
saṅghañ ca patimānetvā sabbasammānabhājanaṃ
3 namassanādino[1] assa puññassa ratanattaye
pavattassānubhāvena bhetvā sabbe upaddave
4 taṃ taṃ kāraṇam āgamma desitāni jutīmatā
apaṇṇakādīni purā jātakāni mahesinā
5 yāni yesu ciraṃ satthā lokanittharaṇatthiko
anante bodhisambhāre paripācesi nāyako
6 tāni sabbāni ekajjhaṃ āropentehi saṃgahaṃ
jātakaṃ nāma saṃgītaṃ dhammasaṃgāhakehi yaṃ
7 buddhavaṃsassa etassa icchantena ciraṭṭhitiṃ
yācito abhigantvāna therena atthadassinā
8 asaṃsaṭṭhavihārena sadā saddhivihārinā
tath' eva buddhamittena santacittena viññunā

THE FAR ORIGIN

Homage to the Bhagavan, the enlightened one,
the fully awakened Buddha

For many hundreds of thousands of births, 1
immeasurable benefit to the world has been brought
about by the leader of the world: the great sage.[1]
At his feet I pay homage, cupping my hands in 2
reverence to the teaching, and bowing down to
the Sangha, the vessel of all honor!
I have cut through obstacles by the great power 3
resulting from the merit of this homage to the
three jewels:
For the birth stories, starting with "The True Story 4
Jataka," taught long ago by the brilliant sage, act
by act,[2]
births in which, for a long time, the Teacher, the guide 5
dedicated to the salvation of the world, brought the
ingredients for awakening to ripeness—
for acquiring all these birth stories, long recited 6
together under the name of "Jataka" by the chanters
and compilers of the Buddha's teaching,
the Elder Atthadassina approached me and inquired, 7
hoping to preserve this lineage story of the Buddha.
Atthadassina lives apart from the world, always in the 8
company of other monks; I was also asked in the same
way by the wise and calm Buddhamitta,

9 mahiṃsāsakavaṃsamhi sambhūtena nayaññunā
buddhadevena ca tathā bhikkhunā suddhabuddhinā
10 mahāpurisacariyānaṃ ānubhāvaṃ acintiyaṃ
tassa vijjotayantassa jātakass' atthavaṇṇanaṃ
11 mahāvihāravāsīnaṃ vācanāmagganissitaṃ
bhāsissaṃ bhāsato tam me sādhu gaṇhantu sādhavo.

1 sā panāyaṃ jātakassa atthavaṇṇanā dūrenidānaṃ avidūrenidānaṃ santikenidānan ti imāni tīṇi nidānāni dassetvā vaṇṇiyamānā ye naṃ suṇanti tehi samudāgamato paṭṭhāya viññātattā yasmā suṭṭhu viññātā nāma hoti tasmā taṃ tīṇi nidānāni dassetvā vaṇṇayissāma. tattha ādito tāva tesaṃ nidānānaṃ paricchedo veditabbo. dīpaṃkarapādamūlasmiṃ hi katābhinīhārassa mahāsattassa yāva vessantarattabhāvā cavitvā tusitapure nibbatti tāva pavatto kathāmaggo dūrenidānaṃ nāma. tusitabhavanato pana cavitvā yāva bodhimaṇḍe sabbaññutappatti tāva pavatto kathāmaggo avidūrenidānaṃ nāma. santikenidānaṃ pana tesu tesu ṭhānesu viharato tasmiṃ tasmiṃ yeva ṭhāne labbhatī ti. tatr' idaṃ dūrenidānaṃ nāma:

who was born in the lineage of *mahimsasaka,* and 9
is knowledgable in method; and in the same way by
Buddhadeva, also a wise monk.[3]
So, this commentary on the birth stories, which 10
illustrates the splendor of the inconceivable actions of
a great man,
I will recite, in the way those who live in the Great 11
Monastery explain it.[4] May good people grasp fully
what I am saying!

And this commentary on the birth stories will be compre- 1
hensible to listeners when I have explained the far origin, the near origin, and the recent origin—so long as they have understood it from its beginning. So, I will recount it, after explaining and making clear the three origins.

The division into these three origins from the beginning should be understood as follows: The course of the story of the Great Being's existence, from the time that he made a resolution to become a Buddha at the feet of Dipankara to his appearance in the Tusita heaven after falling away from his life as Vessantara, is called the far origin.[5]

The course of the story from his falling away from the Tusita to his attainment of awakening on the ground by the Bodhi Tree is called the near origin.

And the recent origin is found in all the various places at which he stayed on his travels, in this place and that.

Now follows the far origin.

2 ito kira kappasatasahassādhikānaṃ catunnaṃ asaṃkheyyānaṃ matthake amaravatī nāma nagaraṃ ahosi. tattha sumedho nāma brāhmaṇo paṭivasati ubhato sujāto mātito ca pitito ca saṃsuddhagahaṇiko yāva sattamā kulaparivaṭṭā akkhitto anupakkuṭṭho jātivādena abhirūpo dassanīyo pāsādiko paramāya vaṇṇapokkharatāya samannāgato. so aññaṃ kammaṃ akatvā brāhmaṇasippam eva uggaṇhi. tassa daharakāle yeva mātāpitaro kālam akaṃsu. ath' assa rāsivaḍḍhako amacco āyapotthakaṃ āharitvā suvaṇṇarajatamaṇimuttādibharite gabbhe vivaritvā ettakaṃ te kumāra mātusantakaṃ ettakaṃ pitusantakaṃ ettakaṃ ayyakapayyakānan ti yāva sattamā kulaparivaṭṭā dhanaṃ ācikkhitvā etaṃ paṭijaggāhī ti āha. sumedhapaṇḍito cintesi: imaṃ dhanaṃ saṃharitvā mayhaṃ pitupitāmahādayo paralokaṃ gacchantā ekaṃ kahāpaṇam pi gahetvā na gatā mayā pana gahetvā gamanakāraṇaṃ kātuṃ vaṭṭatī ti rañño ārocetvā nagare bheriñ carāpetvā mahājanassa dānaṃ datvā tāpasapabbajjaṃ pabbaji. imassa pan' atthassa āvibhāvatthaṃ imasmiṃ ṭhāne sumedhakathā kathetabbā. sā pan' esā kiñcā 'pi buddhavaṃse nirantaraṃ āgatā yeva gāthābandhanena pana āgatattā na suṭṭhu pākaṭā tasmā taṃ antarantarā gāthābandhadīpakehi vacanehi saddhiṃ kathessāma.

kappasatasahassādhikānaṃ hi catunnaṃ asaṃkheyyānaṃ matthake dasahi saddehi avivittaṃ amaravatīti ca amaran ti ca laddhanāmaṃ nagaraṃ ahosi yaṃ sandhāya buddhavaṃse vuttaṃ:

The Story of Sumedha

They say that a hundred thousand eons and four incalculable 2
epochs ago, there was a city called Amaravati. In that city lived a Brahman called Sumedha. He was respected, being of irreproachable birth, completely pure descent on both mother's and father's side for seven generations: a man of a noble line, of handsome appearance, good-looking, friendly, and endowed with an excellent, lotus-like complexion. He applied himself only to his Brahmanic studies, not taking on anything else. While he was still young, his parents died. Then, a minister who was in charge of his wealth brought the accounts book and opened the rooms filled with gold, silver, jewels, pearls, and other valuables. He said: "Young man, so much belonged to your mother, so much to your father, so much to your grandparents and great-grandparents." Pointing out to him the wealth inherited from seven generations, he said: "Guard this well."

The wise Sumedha reflected, "When my parents and all the rest of my ancestors passed on to another world, they could not take even one little coin with them. Is it right for me to try to take it with me?" So, after telling the king, he had a drum beaten around the city, gave his wealth to the people at large, and went out into homelessness as an ascetic.

To make this matter clear, the story of Sumedha needs to be told. Although it is given in full in the *Buddhavamsa,* it is not so clearly explained because it is in verse.[6] I will tell it here, with sentences at intervals explaining the verses. Four incalculable epochs and a hundred thousand eons ago, there was a city, resounding with ten sounds, called Amaravati or Amara, about which this is said in the *Buddhavamsa*:

12 kappe ca satasahasse ca caturo ca asaṃkhiye
amaraṃ nāma nagaraṃ dassaneyyaṃ manoramaṃ
dasahi saddehi avivittaṃ annapānasamāyutan ti.

tattha dasahi saddehi avivittan ti hatthisaddena assasaddena rathasaddena bherisaddena muṭiṅgasaddena vīṇāsaddena gītasaddena sammasaddena saṃkhasaddena tāḷasaddena asanātha pivatha khādathā ti dasamena saddenā ti imehi dasahi saddehi avivittaṃ ahosi. tesaṃ pana saddānaṃ ekadesam eva gahetvā

13 hatthisaddaṃ assasaddaṃ bherisaṃkharathāni ca
khādatha pivatha c'-eva annapānena ghositan ti

buddhavaṃse vuttagāthaṃ vatvā

14 nagaraṃ sabbaṅgasampannaṃ
sabbakammam upāgataṃ
sattaratanasampannam nānājanasamākulaṃ
samiddhaṃ devanagaraṃ ā 'va āvāsaṃ
puññakamminaṃ.
15 nagare amaravatiyā sumedho nāma brāhmaṇo
anekakoṭisannicayo pahūtadhanadhaññavā
16 ajjhāyako mantadharo tiṇṇaṃ vedāna pāragū
lakkhaṇe itihāse ca sadhamme pāramim gato ti

3 vuttaṃ hi. ath' ekadivasaṃ so sumedhapaṇḍito uparipāsādavaratale rahogato hutvā pallaṃkaṃ ābhujitvā nisinno cintesi: punabbhave paṇḍita paṭisandhigahaṇaṃ nāma dukkhaṃ tathā nibbattanibbattaṭṭhāne sarīrabhedanaṃ ahañ ca jātidhammo jarādhammo vyādhidhammo maraṇa-

A hundred thousand eons and four incalculable 12
epochs ago, there was a city called Amara—
Deathless—beautiful and delightful. It was filled with
the ten sounds and was abundant in food and drink
combined:[7]
The trumpeting of elephants, the neighing of horses, 13
drums, conches, carriages, and the shouting of offers
of food and drink: "Eat! Drink!"

This piece of verse is in *The Lineage of the Buddhas:*[8]

It was a city supplied with everything that is needed, 14
and engaged in every sort of activity,
endowed with the seven treasures and crowded with
all sorts of different people.[9]
It was prosperous, like the city of the gods, and a
dwelling place for people who make merit.
In the city of Amaravati there was a Brahman named 15
Sumedha, who had accumulated vast amounts of
wealth, possessing great riches and grain.
He was a chanter of texts, knew the mantras by heart, 16
and had mastered the three Vedas; he was proficient
in the art of divination of the marks, in history, and in
following teachings.[10]

So, it is said: And then, one day, wise Sumedha went up to 3
the upper courtyard in his house, sat down, and folded his
legs into the cross-legged position, and reflected: "Wise one,
taking rebirth in a new bodily form is suffering and so too
is the breakup of the body in whatever place one is born.[11]
I am subject to birth, old age, sickness, and death. Being the

dhammo evaṃbhūtena mayā ajātiṃ ajaraṃ avyādhiṃ adukkham asukhaṃ sītalaṃ amatamahānibbānaṃ pariyesituṃ vaṭṭati avassam bhavato muñcitvā nibbānagāminā ekena maggena bhavitabban ti tena vuttaṃ:

17 rahogato nisīditvā evaṃ cintes' ahan tadā:
dukkho punabbhavo nāma sarīrassa ca bhedanaṃ.
18 jātidhammo jarādhammo vyādhidhammo c' ahan tadā
ajaraṃ amaraṃ khemaṃ pariyesissāmi nibbutiṃ
19 yan nūn' imaṃ pūtikāyaṃ nānākuṇapapūritaṃ.
chaḍḍayitvāna gaccheyyaṃ anapekkho[2] anatthiko.
20 atthi hehiti so maggo na so sakkā na hetuye.
pariyesissāmi taṃ maggaṃ bhavato parimuttiyā ti.

4 tato uttarim pi evaṃ cintesi: yathā hi loke dukkhassa paṭipakkhabhūtaṃ sukhaṃ nāma atthi evaṃ bhave sati tappaṭipakkhena vibhavenā 'pi bhavitabbaṃ yathā ca uṇhe sati tassa vūpasamabhūtaṃ sītam pi atthi evaṃ rāgādīnaṃ vūpasamena nibbānenā 'pi bhavitabbaṃ. yathā ca pāpakassa lāmakassa dhammassa paṭipakkhabhūto kalyāṇo anavajjadhammo pi atthi yeva evam eva p'kāya jātiyā sati sabbajātikkhepanato ajātisaṃkhātena nibbānenā 'pi bhavitabbam evā ti.

sort of person I am, I should seek the absence of birth, the absence of old age, the absence of sickness, and the absence of either suffering or pleasure: the great deathless state, nibbana, the cool.[12] There must be a way to be followed that, by a single path, gives release from becoming and leads inevitably to nibbana."

About this, it is said:

"Being alone, sitting, this thought then came up for 17
me:[13] 'Taking rebirth and the breakup of the body are
certainly suffering.
I am subject to birth, old age, and sickness, so I will 18
look for the secure refuge that does not age and is
without death: nibbana.
Why don't I just discard this putrid body, with all 19
its various things that are foul, and just go, without
looking back or wanting things?
There is, there will be, a path. It wouldn't be possible 20
for that not to be so. I'll seek that path for the sake of
release from becoming!'"

And then he thought some more, "Just as, in the world, 4
happiness arises as an opposite to suffering, so where there is becoming, the opposite must occur, nonbecoming.[14] And just as where there is heat, there is cool to allay that, so, where there is desire and the other passions, there must be nibbana, to allay that. For, just as bad, inferior, teaching has as its opposite, the beautiful, faultless teaching, in just this way where is a bad rebirth, there must be its opposite, nibbana. This is termed the birthless, as it is without birth and is not compounded."

tena vuttaṃ:

21 yathā 'pi dukkhe vijjante sukhaṃ nāma pi vijjati
evaṃ bhave vijjamāne vibhavo pi icchitabbako.
22 yathā 'pi uṇhe vijjante aparaṃ vijjati sītalaṃ.
evaṃ tividhaggi vijjante nibbānaṃ icchitabbakaṃ.
23 yathā 'pi pāpe vijjante kalyāṇaṃ pi vijjati
evam eva jāti vijjante ajātiṃ pi icchitabbakan ti.

5 aparam pi cintesi: yathā nāma gūtharāsimhi nimuggena purisena dūrato pañcavaṇṇapadumasañchannaṃ mahātaḷākaṃ disvā katarena nu kho maggena ettha gantabban ti taṃ taḷākaṃ gavesituṃ yuttaṃ yaṃ tassa agavesanaṃ na so taḷākassa doso evaṃ kilesamaladhovane amatamahānibbānataḷāke vijjante tassa agavesanaṃ na amatanibbānamahātaḷākassa doso yathā ca corehi samparivārito puriso palāyanamagge vijjamāne pi sace na palāyati na so maggassa doso purisass' eva doso evam eva kilesehi parivāretvā gahitassa purisassa vijjamāne yeva nibbānagāmimhi sive magge maggassa agavesanaṃ nāma na maggassa doso puggalass' eva doso yathā ca vyādhipīḷito puriso vijamāne vyādhitikicchake vejje sace taṃ vejjaṃ gavesitvā vyādhin na tikicchāpeti na so vejjassa

This is what is said about that:
"Just as where happiness is found, suffering is, too, 21
so where becoming is found, we should wish for
nonbecoming.
And just as where there is heat, there is also cold, so 22
where there is the threefold fire, there we should wish
for nibbana.[15]
And just as the bad exists, the good does too, then 23
where there is birth, we should wish for the state
without birth."

Then he pondered further: "It is just like a man, sunk into 5
a heap of excrement, who sees far off a magnificent lake, filled with lotuses of five colors. He says to himself, 'Surely there is a path whereby I can get there?' And if he does not search for it, it is not the fault of the lake that he does not find it! In the same way, if one does not look for the lake of the deathless, the magnificent nibbana, for the washing away of defilements, it is not the fault of the magnificent lake of the deathless, nibbana, if it is not reached.[16] And again, if a man is surrounded by thieves, and there is an escape route, it is the fault of the man, not the escape route, if he does not get away. In the same way, if a man has been taken, and is encircled by defilements, even though there is a route to nibbana, it is the fault of the man, not the route that it is not taken. And it is like a man afflicted with a disease, when there is a doctor for the disease available and able to treat the disease: if he does not seek out the doctor and get him to cure the disease, it is not the fault of the doctor. So for the one who is afflicted with the defilements, who does not seek

doso evam eva yo kilesavyādhipīḷito kilesavūpasamamagga-
kovidaṃ vijjamānam eva ācariyaṃ na gavesati tass' eva doso
na kilesavināsakassa ācariyassā ti tena vuttaṃ:

24 yathā gūthagato puriso taḷākaṃ disvāna pūritaṃ
na gavesati taṃ taḷākaṃ na doso taḷākassa so
25 evaṃ kilesamaladhove vijjante amatantale
na gavesati taṃ taḷākaṃ na doso amatantale.
26 yathā arīhi pariruddho vijjante gamane pathe
na palāyati so puriso na doso añjasassa so
27 evaṃ kilesapariruddho vijjamāne sive pathe
na gavesati taṃ maggaṃ na doso sivamañjase.
28 yathā 'pi vyādhito puriso vijjamāne tikicchake
na tikicchāpeti taṃ vyādhim na so doso tikicchake
29 evaṃ kilesavyādhīhi dukkhito patipīḷito
na gavesati taṃ ācariyaṃ na so doso vināyake ti.

6 aparam pi cintesi: yathā maṇḍanakajātiko puriso kaṇṭhe
āsattaṃ kuṇapaṃ chaḍḍetvā sukhaṃ gacchati evaṃ mayā
'pi imaṃ pūtikāyaṃ chaḍḍetvā anapekhena nibbānanaga-

out a Teacher when there is one at hand who is experienced in the path that allays the defilements, the fault is his own, not that of the Teacher who can put an end to the defilements."

This is what is said about this:

"It is as if a man, who has fallen into excrement, sees a 24
brimming lake and does not search for it, it is not the
fault of the lake.
In the same way, when the lake of the deathless, which 25
washes away defilements, is available, and he does not
search for that, it is not the fault of the lake of
the deathless.
It is like a man hemmed in by enemies, who does not 26
get away even though there is an escape route; it is not
the fault of the road.
In the same way, when a man is obstructed by the 27
defilements, even though there is a way ahead and he
does not take it, it is not the fault of the auspicious
path.
In the same way, if a man, being sick, does not get a 28
doctor to treat him, even though there is one at hand,
it is not the fault of the doctor.
In the same way, if someone afflicted with the various 29
diseases of the defilements is suffering and does not
seek out that Teacher, it is not the fault of
the instructor."

And he thought some more: "Just as when a man who is used 6
to getting himself up in really smart clothes walks easily when
he has thrown off any dirt clinging to his neck, so should I,
throwing off this putrid body with equanimity, seek out the

raṃ pavisitabbaṃ yathā ca naranāriyo ukkārabhūmiyaṃ uccārapassāvaṃ katvā na taṃ ucchaṅgena vā ādāya dasantena vā veṭhetvā gacchanti jigucchamānā pana anapekhā 'va chaḍḍetvā gacchanti evaṃ mayā 'pi imaṃ pūtikāyaṃ anapekhena chaḍḍetvā amataṃ nibbānanagaraṃ pavisituṃ vaṭṭati yathā ca navikā nāma jajjaraṃ nāvaṃ anapekhā chaḍḍetvā gacchanti evaṃ aham pi imaṃ navahi vaṇamukhehi paggharantaṃ kāyaṃ chaḍḍetvā anapekho nibbānanagaraṃ pavisissāmi yathā ca puriso nānāratanāni ādāya corehi saddhim maggaṃ gacchanto attano ratananāsabhayena te chaḍḍetvā khemaṃ maggaṃ gaṇhāti evaṃ ayam pi karajakāyo ratanavilopakacorasadiso sac' āhaṃ ettha taṇhaṃ karissāmi ariyamaggakusaladhammaratanam me nassissati tasmā mayā imaṃ corasadisaṃ kāyaṃ chaḍḍetvā nibbānanagaraṃ pavisituṃ vaṭṭatī ti tena vuttaṃ:

30 yathā 'pi kuṇapaṃ puriso kaṇṭhe baddhaṃ jigucchiya
mocayitvāna gaccheyya sukhī serī sayaṃvasī
31 tath' ev' imaṃ pūtikāyaṃ nānākuṇapasañcayaṃ
chaḍḍayitvāna gaccheyyaṃ anapekho anatthiko.
32 yathā uccāraṭṭhānamhi karīsan naranāriyo
chaḍḍayitvāna gacchanti anapekhā anatthikā
33 evam eva imaṃ kāyaṃ nānākuṇapapūritaṃ
chaḍḍayitvāna gacchissaṃ vaccaṃ katvā yathā kuṭiṃ.

city of nibbana. And just as men and women excreting feces on a dung heap do not pick it up and take it with them on their laps or in the fold of their clothes, but without regret leave it behind in disgust, so it would be right for me to seek out the deathless city of nibbana, discarding this putrid body without regret. It is like sailors who abandon a boat that is broken down with age and do not look back. In the same way, I will abandon this body, which oozes with pollutants from its nine woundlike openings and, without looking back, enter the city of nibbana.[17] Or it is as if a man, carrying various kinds of jewels, is traveling on the same road as some thieves and takes a safe road, avoiding them out of fear of losing his treasure; in the same way, this disgusting body is like a jewel thief. And if I form any craving for it, the precious jewel of the good teaching that leads to the noble path will be lost to me. Because of this it is right that I abandon this body, which is just like a thief, and enter the city of nibbana."

So it is said:

"Just as a man who has freed himself in disgust from 30
any dirt around his neck would walk on, happy, just as
he likes, and his own master,

so I will throw off this putrid body, with all its various 31
kinds of foul things, and go on without looking back or
wishing for it.

Men and women leave behind their feces on the dung 32
hill and move on without looking back or wishing
for it,

so, like someone leaving a hut after evacuating 33
excrement, I will throw off this body, filled with all
kinds of dung, and move on.

34 yathā 'pi jajjaraṃ nāvaṃ paluggaṃ udakagāhiniṃ
sāmī chaḍḍetvā gacchanti anapekhā anatthikā
35 evam eva imaṃ kāyaṃ navacchiddaṃ dhuvassavaṃ
chaḍḍayitvāna gacchissaṃ chinnaṃ nāvaṃ 'va sāmikā.
36 yathā 'pi puriso corehi gacchanto bhaṇḍam ādiya
bhaṇḍacchedabhayaṃ disvā chaḍḍayitvāna gacchati
37 evam eva ayaṃ kāyo mahācorasamo viya
pahāy' imaṃ gamissāmi kusalacchedanābhayā ti.

7 evam sumedhapaṇḍito nānāvidhāhi upamāhi imaṃ nekkhammūpasaṃhitaṃ atthaṃ cintetvā sakanivesane aparimitaṃ bhogakkhandhaṃ heṭṭhāvuttanayena kapaṇaddhikādīnaṃ vissajjetvā mahādānaṃ datvā vatthukāme ca kilesakāme ca pahāya amaranagarato nikkhamitvā ekako 'va himavante dhammakaṃ nāma pabbataṃ nissāya assamaṃ katvā paṇṇasālañ ca caṃkamañ ca māpetvā pañcahi nīvaraṇadosehi vivajjitaṃ evaṃ samāhite citte ti ādinā nayena vuttehi aṭṭhahi kāraṇaguṇehi samupetaṃ abhiññāsaṃkhātaṃ balaṃ āharituṃ tasmiṃ assamapade navadosasamannāgataṃ sāṭakaṃ pajahitvā dvādasaguṇasamannāgataṃ vākacīraṃ nivāsetvā isipabbajjaṃ pabbaji evaṃ pabba-

Owners abandon a boat that is old, broken down and 34
waterlogged, without looking back or wishing for it.
So too I will abandon this body, with its nine openings, 35
always leaking, and, like the owners of a leaking boat,
move on.
A man who carries goods and travels along when there 36
are thieves around, seeing the danger of being parted
from his goods, leaves the thieves behind and goes on.
In the same way, this body is like a really powerful 37
thief: Leaving it behind, I'll go with no fear of being
separated from what is good."

When the learned Sumedha had reflected in these various 7
similes on the great advantage connected with renunciation, he gave away the riches in his own house—which were unlimited in the way we have just mentioned—to beggars and people of the road. He made a great gift of generosity. Abandoning desire for material goods and desire for sensual pleasures, he left the city of Amara. In the Himalayan region, he settled on a mountain called Dhammaka and made a hermitage. He had a leaf hut and walking area constructed, without the five faults that can be a hindrance to such places.[18]

In order to cultivate the power of higher knowledge that is endowed with the development of the eight qualities, whose method is explained in the phrase, "With the mind concentrated in this way," he renounced the world in that hermitage as an ascetic.[19] He put away his outer garment, which had nine disadvantages, and put on a bark garment, which possessed the twelve advantages.[20] He settled down as a sage

jito aṭṭhadosasamākiṇṇaṃ taṃ paṇṇasālaṃ pahāya dasaguṇasamannāgataṃ rukkhamūlaṃ upagantvā sabbaṃ dhaññavikatiṃ pahāya pavattaphalabhojano hutvā nisajjaṭṭhānacaṅkamavasen' eva padhānaṃ padahanto sattāhabbhantare yeva aṭṭhannaṃ samāpattīnaṃ pañcannañ ca abhiññānaṃ lābhī ahosi evan taṃ yathāpatthitaṃ abhiññābalaṃ pāpuṇi tena vuttaṃ:

38 evāhaṃ cintayitvāna nekakoṭisataṃ dhanaṃ
nāthānāthānaṃ datvāna himavantaṃ upāgamiṃ.
39 himavantassa avidūre dhammako nāma pabbato
assamo sukato mayhaṃ paṇṇasālā sumāpitā.
40 caṅkamaṃ tattha māpesiṃ pañcadosavivajjitaṃ
aṭṭhaguṇasamūpetaṃ abhiññābalam āhariṃ.
41 sāṭakaṃ pajahim tattha navadosamupāgataṃ
vākacīraṃ nivāsesiṃ dvādasaguṇamupāgataṃ.
42 aṭṭhadosasamākiṇṇaṃ pajahiṃ paṇṇasālakaṃ.
upāgamiṃ rukkhamūlaṃ guṇe dasah' upāgataṃ
43 vāpitaṃ ropitaṃ dhaññaṃ pajahiṃ niravasesato
anekaguṇasampannaṃ pavattaphalam ādiyiṃ.
44 tattha-ppadhānaṃ padahiṃ nipajjaṭṭhānacaṅkame
abbhantaramhi sattāhe abhiññābala pāpuṇin ti.

and renouncer. In this way he gave up the leaf hut, filled with the eight faults, and went to the foot of a tree, which has ten advantages.[21] He gave up all food made with grain and lived on a diet of fruit found naturally. He applied great effort in sitting, standing, and walking, and within a week, achieved the eight attainments of the fivefold higher knowledge.[22] In this way, in accordance with his vow, he reached to the power of higher knowledge.

About this it is said:

"So, after reflecting, I gave away many millions to the 38
rich and the poor, and came to the Himalayan region.
Not far from the Himalayas there is a mountain called 39
Dhammaka. Here I made a well-built ashram,
a carefully constructed leaf hut.
There was a walking place there, without the five 40
defects; it possessed the eight good qualities, and
I attained to higher knowledge.
Then I threw away my cloak, with its nine disadvant- 41
ages, and put on a bark garment, with its twelve
advantages.
I gave up the leaf hut, since it was crowded with eight 42
faults, and went to the foot of a tree, a place to live that
is endowed with ten excellences.
I completely turned my back on grain, sown and 43
planted, and lived off fruit imbued with all kinds of
advantages, found naturally.
Then I made a great effort, while sitting, standing, and 44
walking, and within seven days I found the powers of
higher knowledge."[23]

8 evam abhiññābalaṃ patvā sumedhatāpase samāpattisukhena vītināmente dīpaṃkaro nāma satthā loke udapādi. tassa paṭisandhijātibodhidhammacakkappavattanesu sakalā 'pi dasasahassīlokadhātu saṃkampi sampakampi sampavedhi mahāviravaṃ viravi dvattiṃsa pubbanimittāni pāturahaṃsu. sumedhatāpaso samāpattisukhena vītināmento n' eva taṃ saddam assosi na tāni nimittāni addasa tena vuttaṃ:

45 evaṃ me siddhippattassa vasībhūtassa sāsane
dīpaṃkaro nāma jino uppajji lokanāyako.
46 uppajjante ca jāyante bujjhante dhammadesane
caturo nimitte nāddasaṃ jhānaratisamappito ti.

9 tasmiṃ kāle dīpaṃkaradasabalo catuhi khīṇāsavasatasahassehi parivuto anupubbena cārikaṃ caramāno rammakaṃ nāma nagaraṃ patvā sudassanamahāvihāre paṭivasati. rammanagaravāsino dīpaṃkaro kira samaṇissaro paramābhisambodhiṃ patvā pavattavaradhammacakko anupubbena cārikaṃ caramāno rammanagaraṃ patvā sudassanamahāvihāre paṭivasatī 'ti sutvā sappinavanītādīni c' eva bhesajjāni vatthacchādanāni ca gāhāpetvā gandhamālādihatthā yena buddho yena dhammo yena saṅgho tanninnā tappoṇā tappa-

Now, when the ascetic Sumedha had attained the power 8
of higher knowledge and was enjoying the happiness of his attainments, a Teacher called Dipankara arose in the world. At the moments of his conception, birth, awakening, and at his first setting in motion the wheel of the Dhamma, the whole universe with its ten thousand world systems quivered,[24] trembled, shook, and gave out a mighty roar. The thirty-two auspicious signs appeared. But the ascetic Sumedha, enjoying the happiness of his attainments, did not hear the noise and did not see the signs.

So, it is said about this:

"When I had attained the powers and mastery in 45
the holy life, a leader for the world, called Dipankara,
appeared.
Because I was meditating and delighting in *jhāna*, 46
I did not see the four signs, at his conception, his birth,
his awakening, and at his teaching of the Dhamma."[25]

At that time, Dipankara, with ten powers, was going on his 9
wanderings stage by stage, surrounded by four hundred thousand arhats, and reached the city of Rammaka. He took up residence in the Beautiful Monastery. The people who lived in Ramma got to talking: "They say the foremost lord has reached the highest awakening. He has set in motion the noble wheel of the Dhamma, is going on his wanderings in stages, and has arrived at the Beautiful Monastery." When the citizens heard about this, they took ghee and butter, medicines, and various kinds of clothes and garments and perfumes and garlands in their hands. The people of the city were stretching out their arms, inclining, and harboring a

bbhārā hutvā satthāraṃ upasaṃkamitvā vanditvā gandhādīhi pūjetvā ekamantaṃ nisinnā dhammadesanaṃ sutvā svātanāya nimantetvā uṭṭhāyāsanā pakkamiṃsu. te punadivase mahādānaṃ sajjetvā nagaraṃ alaṃkaritvā dasabalassa āgamanamaggaṃ alaṃkarontā udakabhinnaṭṭhānesu paṃsuṃ pakkhipitvā samaṃ bhūmitalaṃ katvā rajatapaṭṭavaṇṇaṃ vālukaṃ ākiranti lājāni c' eva pupphāni ca vikiranti nānāvirāgehi vatthehi dhajapaṭāke ussāpenti kadaliyo c' eva puṇṇaghaṭapantiyo ca patiṭṭhāpenti. tasmiṃ kāle sumedhatāpaso attano assamapadā uggantvā tesaṃ manussānaṃ uparibhāgena ākāsena gacchanto te haṭṭhatuṭṭhe manusse disvā kin nu kho kāraṇan ti ākāsato oruyha ekamantaṃ ṭhito manusse pucchi: hambho kassa tumhe imaṃ maggaṃ alaṃkarothā ti tena vuttaṃ:

47 paccantadesavisaye nimantetvā tathāgataṃ
tassa āgamanaṃ maggaṃ sodhenti tuṭṭhamānasā
48 ahan tena samayena nikkhamitvā sakassamā
dhunanto vākacīrāni gacchāmi ambare tadā.
49 vedajātaṃ janaṃ disvā tuṭṭhahaṭṭhaṃ pamoditaṃ
orohitvāna gaganā manusse pucchi tāvade:

yearning for the Buddha, the Dhamma, and the Sangha. They approached the Teacher, honored him, made offerings of perfumes and things like that, and sat to one side. After listening to a teaching from him and inviting him for a meal on the following day, they rose from their seats and left. The next day, when they had prepared a magnificent banquet, they decorated the city and got the road ready for the approach of the one with ten powers. They carefully laid earth in places broken by water erosion, making the ground's surface even. They strewed sand that had the appearance of a fine sheet of silver. They scattered puffed grain and flowers around. They put up banners and streamers with cloths in various colors, and even set out plantain trees and brimming bowls. At that time, Sumedha the ascetic rose from his hermitage and traveled through the air until he was above these people. When he saw them excited and rejoicing, he wondered, "What is the reason for this?" Descending from the sky he stood to one side and asked them, "Friends, in whose honor are you decorating the road?"

So, it is said:

"Men from the borderlands have invited the Tatha- 47
gata. Delighted at heart, they clear the approach road.
At that time I left my own hermitage. I traveled 48
through the air, with my bark garment flapping.
When I saw the fervent crowd, excited, rejoicing, 49
and filled with gladness, I came down from the air
and straightway asked people:

50 tuṭṭhahaṭṭho pamodito vedajāto mahājano
kassa sodhīyatī maggo añjasaṃ vaṭumāyanan ti.

10 manussā āhaṃsu: bhante sumedha na tvaṃ jānāsi: dīpaṃkaradasabalo sammāsambodhiṃ patvā pavattavaradhammacakko cārikaṃ caramāno amhākaṃ nagaraṃ patvā sudassanamahāvihāre paṭivasati mayan taṃ bhagavantaṃ nimantayimha tass' etaṃ buddhassa bhagavato āgamanamaggaṃ alaṃkaromā ti. sumedhatāpaso cintesi: buddho ti kho ghosamattam pi loke dullabhaṃ pag eva buddhuppādo mayā 'pi imehi manussehi saddhiṃ dasabalassa maggaṃ alaṃkarituṃ vaṭṭatī ti. so te manusse āha: sace bho tumhe etaṃ maggaṃ buddhassa alaṃkarotha mayham pi ekaṃ okāsaṃ detha aham pi tumhehi saddhiṃ maggaṃ alaṃkarissāmī ti. te sādhū ti sampaṭicchitvā sumedhatāpaso iddhimā ti jānantā udakabhinnokāsaṃ sallakkhetvā tvaṃ imaṃ ṭhānaṃ alaṃkarohī ti adaṃsu. sumedho buddhā rammaṇaṃ pītiṃ gahetvā cintesi: ahaṃ imaṃ okāsaṃ iddhiyā alaṃkarituṃ pahomi evaṃ alaṃkato pana maṃ na paritosessati ajja mayā kāyaveyyāvaccaṃ kātuṃ vaṭṭatī ti paṃsuṃ āharitvā tasmiṃ padese pakkhipi. tassa tasmiṃ padese analaṃkate yeva dīpaṃkaro dasabalo mahānubhāvānaṃ chaḷabhiññakkhīṇāsavānaṃ catuhi satasahassehi parivuto devatāsu dibbamālāgandhādīhi pūjayantesu dibbasaṃgītesu pavattantesu manussehi mānusakagandhehi c' eva mālādīhi ca pūjayantesu anantāya buddhalīḷhāya manosilātale vijambhamāno sīho viya taṃ alaṃkatapaṭiyattamaggaṃ paṭipajji. sumedhatāpaso akkhīni ummīletvā

> 'The fervent crowd is excited, rejoicing and filled with gladness. For whom is the road being cleared, a path that goes straight ahead?'"

The people replied: "Venerable Sumedha, don't you know? The Buddha Dipankara has attained complete awakening. Setting in motion the excellent wheel of the Dhamma and traveling on a journey, he has come to our city and is staying at the Beautiful Monastery. We have invited the Bhagavan and are getting the approach road ready for this blessed Buddha." Sumedha the ascetic pondered: "The very sound of the word 'Buddha' is hard to find in this world; how much more so the appearance of one. It is important for me to join in with these people too and prepare the road for the one with ten powers." He spoke to these people: "Friends, if you are preparing this road for the Buddha, hand me a section too, and I will make the road ready with you." "Of course," they said, agreeing. Bearing in mind that Sumedha the ascetic had miraculous powers, they gave him a section that had been broken up by water erosion. "You clear this area," they said.

Sumedha was filled with joy at the thought of the Buddha "I am quite capable of making this area ready with my psychic powers. But it would not make me happy to prepare it that way. Today it is right for me to do the job with service, with my body." He brought earth and laid it over that area. But just as he was preparing this spot, along came Dipankara, with ten powers, attended by a retinue of four hundred thousand arhats; they were powerful, with pollutants exhausted, and had attained the six higher knowledges. While the gods were paying homage with heavenly garlands and perfumes,

alaṃkatamaggena āgacchantassa dasabalassa dvattiṃsamahāpurisalakkhaṇapatimaṇḍitaṃ asītiyā anubyañjanehi anubyañjitaṃ byāmappabhāya samparivāritaṃ maṇivaṇṇagaganatale nānappakārā vijjullatā viya āveḷāveḷabhūtā c' eva yugaḷayugaḷabhūtā ca chabbaṇṇaghanabuddharasmiyo vissajjentaṃ rūpaggappattaṃ attabhāvaṃ oloketvā ajja mayā dasabalassa jīvitapariccāgaṃ kātuṃ vaṭṭatī ti mā bhagavā kalale akkami maṇiphalakasetuṃ pana akkamanto viya saddhiṃ catuhi khīṇāsavasatasahassehi mama piṭṭhiṃ maddamāno gacchatu taṃ me bhavissati dīgharattaṃ hitāya sukhāyā 'ti kese mocetvā ajinajaṭāvākacīrāni kāḷavaṇṇe kalale pattharitvā maṇiphalakasetuṃ viya kalalapiṭṭhe nipajji

tena vuttaṃ:

51 te me puṭṭhā vyākariṃsu: buddho loke anuttaro
dīpaṃkaro nāma jino uppajji lokanāyako
tassa sodhīyatī maggo añjasaṃ vaṭumāyanaṃ'.

52 buddho ti mama sutvāna pīti uppajji tāvade
buddho buddho ti kathayanto somanassaṃ
pavedayiṃ.

accompanied by divine songs, and humans were paying homage with human perfumes and garlands, Dipankara stepped onto the decorated area made ready for him, with the infinite grace of a Buddha, like a lion rousing himself on a flat rock the color of red arsenic. As the one with ten powers approached on the decorated road, the ascetic Sumedha, with unblinking eyes, regarded that form, of the highest excellence of beauty, adorned with the thirty-two marks of a great man, and characterized by the eighty minor marks.[26] It was surrounded by a halo to the depth of a fathom, sending out streams of six-colored Buddha rays, linked in pairs of different colors, wreathed like diffuse streaks of lightning flashing in jewel-lit heavens.

Then Sumedha exclaimed: "Today it is right for me to offer up my life for the one with ten powers. Don't let the Bhagavan walk in the mud! Instead, let him come, with his four hundred thousand arhats trampling on my back, as if walking on a bridge of jeweled boards. This will be a long-lasting blessing and happiness for me." Untying his hair, he spread his black antelope skin, tangled ascetic's locks, and bark garment on the black ground and lay down in the mud like a bridge of jeweled boards.

For this is what is said:

"When I asked them, they said: 'A victor, called 51
Dipankara, a leader for the world, an incomparable
Buddha, has appeared in the world. The road,
the common highway, is being cleared up for him.'
'Buddho!' Hearing this name, joy rose up at once; 52
'Buddho, Buddho': I felt great happiness at repeating
this.

53 tattha ṭhatvā vicintesiṃ tuṭṭho saṃviggamānaso:
idha bījāni ropissaṃ khaṇo ve mā upaccagā
54 yadi buddhassa sodhetha ekokāsaṃ dadātha me
aham pi sodhayissāmi añjasaṃ vaṭumāyanaṃ.
55 adaṃsu te mam' okāsaṃ sodhetuṃ añjasaṃ tadā.
buddho buddho ti cintento maggaṃ sodhem' ahan
tadā.
56 aniṭṭhite mam' okāse dīpaṃkaro mahāmuni
catūhi satasahassehi[3] chaḷabhiññehi tādihi
khīṇāsavehi vimalehi paṭipajji añjasaṃ jino.
57 paccuggamanā vattanti vajjanti bheriyo bahū
āmoditā naramarū sādhukāraṃ pavattayuṃ.
58 devā manusse passanti manussā 'pi ca devatā
ubho pi te pañjalikā anuyanti tathāgataṃ.
59 devā dibbehi turiyehi manussā mānusakehi ca
ubho pi te vajjayantā anuyanti tathāgataṃ.
60 dibbaṃ mandāravaṃ pupphaṃ padumaṃ
pāricchattakaṃ
disodisaṃ okiranti ākāsanabhagatā marū.
61 campakaṃ salaḷaṃ nīpaṃ nāgapunnāgaketakaṃ
disodisaṃ ukkhipanti bhūmitalagatā narā.
62 kese muñcitv' ahaṃ tattha vākacīrañ ca cammakaṃ
kalale pattharitvāna avakujjo nipajj' ahaṃ.

Standing there, delighted, and moved with urgency, 53
I thought about it like this: 'I will sow the seed right
here; don't let the moment pass me by.'
'If you are clearing it for the Buddha, hand one 54
section over to me. I will clear the road, the common
highway!'
They gave me a section of the road to clear. 'Buddho, 55
Buddho': I reflected on this, and cleared the road.
I still hadn't finished when Dipankara, the great 56
Teacher, along with four hundred thousand arhats
with the six higher knowledges, who had destroyed
the pollutants and were pure, entered on the road.
People went out to greet him, many drums were 57
beaten, Humans and gods were delighted and rushed
to meet him.
The gods saw humans; humans saw the gods. Both 58
cupped their hands together in reverence and
followed the Tathagata.
Gods with heavenly instruments, humans with earthly 59
ones: both were playing these as they followed the
Tathagata.
Gods hovering in the clouds of the sky showered down 60
heavenly coral flowers, lotuses, and *pārichattaka*
flowers in all directions.[27]
People standing on the surface of the ground threw 61
yellow champaca, *salala,* burflower, ironwood,
punnaga, and screw-pine flowers in all directions.[28]
I untied my hair, spread the bark garment out on the 62
mud and the deerskin, and lay out flat right there:

63 akkamitvāna maṃ buddho saha sissehi gacchatu
mā kalale akkamittho hitāya me bhavissatī ti.

11 so kalalapiṭṭhe nipannako 'va puna akkhīni ummīletvā dīpaṃkaradasabalassa buddhasiriṃ sampassamāno evaṃ cintesi: sace ahaṃ iccheyyaṃ sabbakilese jhāpetvā saṅghanavako hutvā rammanagaraṃ paviseyyaṃ aññātakavesena pana me kilese jhāpetvā nibbānapattiyā kiccaṃ n' atthi yan nūnāhaṃ dīpaṃkaradasabalo viya paramābhisambodhiṃ patvā dhammanāvaṃ āropetvā mahājanaṃ saṃsārasāgarā uttāretvā pacchā parinibbāyeyyaṃ idaṃ mayhaṃ patirūpan ti. tato aṭṭha dhamme samobhānetvā buddhabhāvāya abhinīhāraṃ katvā nipajji tena vuttaṃ:

64 pathaviyaṃ nipannassa evam me āsi cetaso:
icchamāno ahaṃ ajja kilese jhāpaye mama.
65 kim me aññātavesena dhammaṃ sacchikaten' idha
sabbaññutaṃ pāpuṇitvā buddho hessaṃ sadevake.
66 kim me ekena tiṇṇena purisena thāmadassinā
sabbaññutaṃ pāpuṇitvā santāressaṃ sadevake.
67 iminā me adhikārena purisena thāmadassinā
sabbaññutaṃ pāpuṇāmi tāremi janataṃ bahuṃ.

'May the Buddha, and all his disciples, walk right over 63
me! Don't let him tread on the mud. It will be a great
blessing to me.'"

As he lay in the mud, he opened his eyes and, considering the 11
great Buddha glory of Dipankara, with ten powers, thought: "If I wished it, I could enter the city of Ramma and burn away all the defilements as a new member of the Sangha. But it does not suit me to burn away all the defilements and enter nibbana, wearing the clothes of any old person. Why don't I, like Dipankara, with ten powers, enter upon supreme awakening? I could lead people aboard the ship of the Dhamma, and encourage them across the ocean of existence, and afterward they can attain nibbana. This would be right for me." Then, with the coming together of the eight conditions, he lay down and made the aspiration to become a Buddha.

Thus, it is said:

"As I lay upon the earth this thought arose in my 64
heart: 'I could burn away the defilements today if
I wanted to.

Why should I find the truth of the Dhamma wearing 65
the clothes of a nobody? I will attain omniscience and
become a Buddha, in the world of the gods.

Why should I, steadfast in my vision, cross the ocean 66
alone? I will attain omniscience and enable many
people to cross the ocean too.

With this resolve, as someone with steadfast vision, 67
I will attain omniscience and ensure many people
cross the ocean too.

68 saṃsārasotaṃ chinditvā viddhaṃsitvā tayo bhave
dhammanāvaṃ samāruyha santāressaṃ sadevake ti.

yasmā pana buddhattaṃ patthentassa:

69 manussattaṃ liṅgasampatti hetu satthāradassanaṃ
pabbajjā guṇasampatti adhikāro ca chandatā
aṭṭhadhammasamodhānā abhinīhāro samijjhati.

12 manussatthabhāvasmiṃ yeva hi ṭhatvā buddhattaṃ patthentassa patthanā samijjhati nāgassa vā supaṇṇassa vā devatāya vā patthanā no samijjhati manussattabhāve pi purisaliṅge ṭhitass' eva patthanā samijjhati itthiyā vā paṇḍakanapuṃsakaubhatobyañjanakānaṃ vā no samijjhati purisassa pi tasmiṃ attabhāve arahattappattiyā hetusampannass' eva patthanā samijjhati no itarassa hetusampannena pi sace jīvamānakabuddhass' eva santikā patthentassa patthanā

> Cutting off the stream of existence, and destroying the 68
> three types of becoming,[29] I will embark on the ship of
> the Dhamma and ferry humans and gods across.'"

Because of this, for the one who resolves on Buddhahood there are these factors:

> The resolution succeeds through the coming together 69
> of eight conditions: birth as a human being, the
> advantage of sex, a root cause, seeing a great Teacher,
> becoming a monk, an innate capacity for the eight
> attainments, the dedication of one's life, and resolve.[30]

Then the Bhagavan Dipankara arrived and stood near the 12
place where the ascetic Sumedha was laying his head. He opened his eyes, which possessed the fivefold grace, as if opening a jeweled window. Seeing the ascetic Sumedha lying in the mud he said: "This ascetic, lying here, has made an aspiration to Buddhahood: will what he wishes be fulfilled or will it not?" He directed his attention to knowledge of the future and realized: "Yes, after the passing of four

samijjhati parinibbute buddhe cetiyasantike vā bodhimūle vā patthentassa na samijjhati buddhānaṃ santike patthentassā 'pi pabbajjāliṅge ṭhitass' eva samijjhati no gihiliṅge ṭhitassa pabbajitassā 'pi pañcābhiññassa aṭṭhasamāpattilābhino yeva samijjhati na imāya guṇasampattiyā virahitassa guṇasampannenā 'pi yena attano jīvitaṃ buddhānaṃ pariccattaṃ hoti tassa iminā adhikārena adhikārasampannass' eva samijjhati na itarassa adhikārasampannassā 'pi yassa buddhakāradhammānaṃ atthāya mahanto chando ca mahanto ussāho ca vāyāmo ca pariyeṭṭhi tass' eva samijjhati na itarassa tatth' idaṃ chandamahantatāya opammaṃ: sace hi evam assa yo sakalacakkavāḷagabbhaṃ ekodakībhūtaṃ attano bāhubalena pataritvā pāraṃ gantuṃ samattho so buddhattaṃ pāpuṇāti yo vā pana sakalacakkavāḷagabbhaṃ veḷugumbasañchannaṃ viyūhitvā madditvā padasā gacchanto pāraṃ gantuṃ samattho so buddhattaṃ pāpuṇāti yo vā pana sakalacakkavālagabbhaṃ sattiyo ākoṭetvā nirantaraṃ sattiphalasamākiṇṇaṃ padasā akkamamāno pāraṃ gantuṃ samattho so buddhattaṃ pāpuṇāti yo vā pana sakalacakkavāḷagabbhaṃ vītaccikaṃgārabharitaṃ pādehi maddamāno pāraṃ gantuṃ samattho so buddhattaṃ pāpuṇātī ti yo etesu ekam pi attano dukkaraṃ na maññati ahaṃ etam pi taritvā vā gantvā vā pāraṃ gahessāmī ti evaṃ mahantena chandena ca ussābena ca vāyāmena ca pariyeṭṭhiyā ca samannāgato hoti tassa patthanā samijjhati na itarassa. sumedhatāpaso pana ime aṭṭha dhamme samodhānetvā buddhabhāvāya abhinīhāraṃ katvā nipajji.[4] dīpaṃkaro pi bhagavā āgantvā sumedhatāpasassa sīsabhāge ṭhatvā maṇisīhapañjaraṃ ugghāṭento viya pañcavaṇṇapasādasampannāni akkhīni ummīletvā kalalapiṭṭhe nipannaṃ sumedhatāpasaṃ disva

incalculable epochs and a hundred thousand eons from now, he will become a Buddha called Gotama." Realizing this, standing there, he made a prophecy to the assembly: "Look at this ascetic, who has practiced the highest asceticism, lying down in the mud."

—"Yes, sir."

—"This person lying down has made an aspiration to Buddhahood. His wish will be fulfilled. Indeed, four incalculable epochs and a hundred thousand eons from now, he will become a Buddha, called Gotama. He will live in the city of Kapilavatthu, his mother will be Queen Maya, his father the king Suddhodana, his chief disciple the elder Upatissa, his second chief disciple, Kolita.[31] His personal attendant will be Ananda, his chief female disciple the nun Khema,

ayaṃ tāpaso buddhattāya abhinīhāraṃ katvā nipanno ijjhissati nu kho imassa patthanā udāhu no ti anāgataṃ saññāṇaṃ pesetvā upadhārento ito kappasatasahassādhikāni cattāri asaṃkheyyāni atikkamitvā gotamo nāma buddho bhavissatī ti ñatvā ṭhitako 'va parisamajjhe vyākāsi: passatha no tumhe imaṃ uggatapaṃ tāpasaṃ kalalapiṭṭhe nipannan ti. evaṃ bhante. ayaṃ buddhattāya abhinīhāraṃ katvā nipanno samijjhissati imassa patthanā ito kappasatasahassādhikānaṃ catunnaṃ asaṃkheyyānaṃ matthake gotamo nāma buddho bhavissati tasmiṃ pan' assa attabhāve kapilavatthu nāma nagaraṃ nivāso bhavissati māyā nāma devī mātā suddhodano nāma rājā pitā aggasāvako upatisso nāma thero dutiyasāvako kolito nāma buddhupaṭṭhāko ānando nāma aggasāvikā khemā nāma therī dutiyasāvikā uppalavaṇṇā nāma therī bhavissati paripakkañāṇo mahābhinikkhamanaṃ katvā mahāpadhānaṃ padahitvā nigrodhamūle pāyāsam paṭiggahetvā nerañjarāya tīre paribhuñjitvā bodhimaṇḍaṃ āruyha assattharukkhamūle abhisambujjhissatī ti tena vuttaṃ:

70 dīpaṃkaro lokavidū āhutīnaṃ paṭiggaho
ussīsake maṃ ṭhatvāna idaṃ vacanam abravi:

71 passatha imaṃ tāpasaṃ jaṭilaṃ uggatāpanaṃ
aparimeyye ito kappe buddho loke bhavissati.

72 aho kapilavhayā rammā nikkhamitvā tathāgato
padhānaṃ padahitvāna katvā dukkarakāriyaṃ

73 ajapālarukkhamūle nisīditvā tathāgato
tattha pāyasam aggayha nerañjaram upehiti.

74 nerañjarāya tīre pāyāsaṃ ādāya so jino
paṭiyattavaramaggena bodhimūlamhi ehiti.

and his second chief female disciple Uppalavanna. When his knowledge is ripe, he will make the great renunciation. He will engage in great exertion, and after accepting milk-rice under a banyan tree, and eating it on the banks of the river Neranja, he will sit down and attain the finest awakening, at the root of the Bodhi Tree."

For it is said:
"Dipankara, the knower of all worlds, the receiver of 70
offerings, stood by the place that held my head, as I lay
down, and made this declaration:
'See this ascetic with matted hair, who practices the 71
highest asceticism? After countless eons he will be a
Buddha in the world.
Ah! The Tathagata will leave the city named after 72
Kapila. He will engage in the greatest exertion and
practice severe austerities.
Sitting at the root of the banyan tree, the Tathagata 73
will accept milk-rice and make his way to the banks of
the Neranja.
Taking the milk-rice on the banks of the Neranjara, 74
this conqueror will walk along a decorated path to the
roots of the Bodhi Tree.

75 tato padakkhiṇaṃ katvā bodhimaṇḍaṃ anuttaro
assattharukkhamūlamhi[5] bujjhissati mahāyaso.
76 imassa janikā mātā māyā nāma bhavissati
pitā suddhodano nāma ayaṃ hessati gotamo.
77 anāsavā vītarāgā santacittā samāhitā
kolito upatisso ca aggā hessanti sāvakā.
78 ānando nām' upaṭṭhāko upaṭṭhissati taṃ jinaṃ
khemā uppalavaṇṇā ca aggā hessanti sāvikā
79 anāsavā vītarāgā santacittā samāhitā.
bodhi tassa bhagavato assattho ti pavuccati.

13 sumedhatāpaso mayhaṃ kira patthanā samijjhissatī ti somanassappatto ahosi. mahājano dīpaṃkaradasabalassa vacanaṃ sutvā sumedhatāpaso kira buddhabījaṃ buddhaṃkuro ti haṭṭhatuṭṭho ahosi. evaṃ c' assa ahosi: yathā nāma puriso nadiṃ taranto ujukena titthena uttarituṃ asakkonto heṭṭhātitthena uttarati evam evaṃ mayaṃ dīpaṃkaradasabalassa sāsane maggaphalaṃ alabhamānā anāgate yadā tvaṃ buddho bhavissasi tadā tava sammukhā maggaphalaṃ sacch-

Then he will circle around it in homage and attain the 75
finest awakening, at the roots of the Bodhi Tree.
His natural mother will be called Maya, his father will 76
be called Suddhodana, and he will be called Gotama.
Kolita and Upatissa will be his chief disciples: free 77
from pollutants, free from desire, with peaceful
hearts, composed.
Ananda will be the attendant who looks after the 78
conqueror. Khema and Uppalavanna will be the chief
female disciples:
Free from pollutants, free from desire, with peaceful 79
hearts, composed.The tree of awakening for the
Bhagavan will be called the Bodhi Tree.'"

Sumedha the ascetic cried out in great delight, "My wish will 13
indeed be granted!" People heard the declaration of Dipankara, with ten powers: "They say that Sumedha the ascetic is indeed the seed of a Buddha, the seedling of a Buddha!" And they were overjoyed. Then this occurred to them: "Just as a man who is about to cross a river cannot cross over to the landing place straight opposite him and goes across at a landing place lower down, so we may not be able attain the paths and the fruits in the dispensation of Dipankara, who has ten powers. But we may be able to realize the paths and fruits for ourselves, in your presence, when you become a Buddha in the future!" And they all made their aspiration firm.

ikātuṃ samatthā bhaveyyāmā 'ti patthanaṃ ṭhapayiṃsu. dīpaṃkaradasabalo pi bodhisattaṃ pasaṃsitvā aṭṭhahi pupphamuṭṭhīhi pūjetvā padakkhiṇaṃ katvā pakkāmi. te pi catusatasahassasaṃkhā khīṇāsavā bodhisattaṃ gandhehi ca mālehi ca pūjetvā padakkhiṇaṃ katvā pakkamiṃsu. devamanussā pana tath' eva pūjetvā vanditvā pakkantā. bodhisatto sabbesaṃ paṭikkantakāle sayanā vuṭṭhāya pāramiyo vicinissāmī ti puppharāsimatthake pallaṃkaṃ ābhujitvā nisīdi. evaṃ nisinne bodhisatte sakaladasasahassacakkavāḷe devatā sannipatitvā sādhukāraṃ katvā ayya sumedhatāpasa porāṇakabodhisattānaṃ pallaṃkaṃ ābhujitvā pāramiyo vicinissāmā 'ti nisinnakāle yāni pubbanimittāni nāma paññāyanti tāni sabbāni pi ajja pātubhūtāni nissaṃsayena tvaṃ buddho bhavissasi mayam etaṃ jānāma: yass' etāni nimittāni paññāyanti ekantena so buddho hoti tvaṃ attano viriyaṃ daḷhaṃ katvā paggaṇhā ti bodhisattaṃ nānappakārehi thutīhi abhitthuniṃsu tena vuttaṃ:

80 idaṃ sutvāna vacanaṃ asamassa mahesino
āmoditā naramarū: buddhabījaṃkuro ayaṃ.
81 ukkuṭṭhisaddā vattanti appoṭhenti hasanti ca
katañjalī namassanti dasasahassī sadevakā.
82 yad' imassa lokanāthassa virajjhissāma sāsanaṃ
anāgatamhi addhāne hessāma sammukhā imaṃ.

Dipankara, with ten powers, praised the Bodhisatta, the one intent on awakening.[32] Honoring him with eight handfuls of flowers, he circled him in homage and went on his way. Gods and humans honored him right there, paid their respects to him, and went their way too. When they had all gone, the Bodhisatta got up from where he was lying. "I will examine the perfections!" He sat down cross-legged on the heap of flowers. And as the Bodhisatta was sitting there, the gods of the entire ten-thousand-world system met together and shouted, "Well done! Well done!" "Ascetic Sumedha, sir, when all the bodhisattas of long ago sat cross-legged and said, 'We will examine the perfections!' signs could be seen then: they are all manifest today. There is no doubt at all that you will become a Buddha. We know this. For the one on whose account these signs can be seen becomes a Buddha. Make your effort strong and work hard!"

With these words the gods showered the Bodhisatta with praises.

So, it is said:

"When they heard the words of the incomparable, 80
magnificent sage, humans and gods were delighted:
'This is the seedling of a Buddha!'

The gods of the ten thousand worlds raised cheers 81
and clapped; laughing with joy, they cupped their
hands in reverence and paid homage.

'If we do not attain the teaching of this lord of the 82
world, Dipankara, in future times, we'll be face to face
with this one.

83 yathā manussā nadiṃ tarantā paṭititthaṃ virajjhiya
hetthātitthe gahetvāna uttaranti mahānadiṃ
84 evam evaṃ mayaṃ sabbe yadi muñcem' imaṃ jinaṃ
anāgatamhi addhāne hessāma sammukhā imaṃ.
85 dīpaṃkaro lokavidū āhutīnaṃ paṭiggaho
mama kammaṃ pakittetvā dakkhiṇaṃ padam
uddhari.
86 ye tattha āsuṃ jinaputtā sabbe padakkhiṇam akaṃsu
maṃ
narā nāgā ca gandhabbā abhivādetvāna pakkamuṃ.
87 dassanam me atikkante sasaṅghe lokanāyake
haṭṭho haṭṭhena cittena āsanā vuṭṭhahiṃ tadā.
88 sukhena sukhito homi pāmujjena pamodito
pītiyā ca abhissanno pallaṃkaṃ ābhujiṃ tadā.
89 pallaṃkena nisīditvā evaṃ cintes' ahan tadā:
vasībhūto ahaṃ jhāne abhiññāsu pāramiṃ gato
90 sahassikamhi lokamhi isayo n' atthi me samā
asamo iddhidhammesu alabhiṃ īdisaṃ sukhaṃ.
91 pallaṃkābhujane mayhaṃ dasasahassādhivāsino
mahānādaṃ pavattesuṃ: dhuvaṃ buddho bhavissasi.
92 Yāni[6] pubbe bodhisattānaṃ pallaṃkavaram ābhuje
nimittāni padissanti tāni ajja padissare.

Just as people crossing a river go further down the 83
river and cross the great waters there if they fail to
reach the landing place in front,
just so, we'll all come before him in future times if we 84
miss out on this conqueror's teaching.'
Dipankara, the knower of the worlds, the receiver of 85
offerings, praised my action and, lifting his right foot,
went on his way.
All the sons of the conqueror who were present 86
walked in a reverential circle around me. Humans,
nagas, and heavenly minstrels paid homage to me, and
went on their way.[33]
When the leader of the world, together with his 87
followers, was out of sight, I got up from my seat,
filled with joy and with a delighted heart.
I was happy with happiness, and glad with gladness! 88
Flooded with joy, I sat cross-legged.
While I was sitting there cross-legged, I reflected: 89
'I am master of the *jhānas* and have reached the
perfection of the higher knowledges.
In the thousand world systems there are no sages 90
equal to me. I am unchallenged in psychic powers and
in the happiness I have attained.'
While I was sitting cross-legged, the lords of the ten 91
thousand worlds raised a great cheer: 'You will surely
become a Buddha!
Signs that were seen by bodhisattas in the past when 92
they were sitting cross-legged—these are seen today.[34]

93 sītaṃ vyapagataṃ hoti uṇhañ ca upasammati
tāni ajja padissanti dhuvaṃ buddho bhavissasi.
94 dasasahassīlokadhātu nissaddā hoti nirākulā
tāni ajja padissanti dhuvaṃ buddho bhavissasi.
95 mahāvātā na vāyanti na sandanti savantiyo
tāni ajja padissanti dhuvaṃ buddho bhavissasi.
96 thalajā dakajā pupphā sabbe pupphanti tāvade
te p' ajja pupphitā sabbe dhuvaṃ buddho bhavissasi.
97 latā vā yadivā rukkhā phalabhārā honti tāvade
te p' ajja phalitā sabbe dhuvaṃ buddho bhavissasi.
98 ākāsaṭṭhā ca bhummaṭṭhā ratanā jotanti tāvade
te p' ajja ratanā jotanti dhuvaṃ buddho bhavissasi.
99 mānusakā ca dibbā ca turiyā vajjanti tāvade
te p' ajj' ubho abhiravanti dhuvaṃ buddho bhavissasi.
100 vicittapupphā gaganā abhivassanti tāvade
te p' ajja padissanti dhuvaṃ buddho bhavissasi.
101 mahāsamuddo ābhujati dasasahassī pakampati
te p' ajj' ubho abhiravanti dhuvaṃ buddho bhavissasi.
102 niraye pi dasasahassī aggī nibbāyi tāvade
te p' ajja nibbutā aggī dhuvaṃ buddho bhavissasi.

Cold was dispelled, and heat allayed. These signs are 93
seen today. Surely you will become a Buddha!
The ten thousand world systems fell silent and 94
motionless. These signs are seen today. Surely you will
become a Buddha!
Strong winds did not blow; streams became still. 95
These signs are seen today. Surely you will become a
Buddha!
All flowers bloomed, those growing on land and in 96
water. These signs are seen today too. Surely you will
become a Buddha!
Vines and trees bore fruit all at once, 97
Today they are all fruitful. Surely you will become a
Buddha!
In the sky and on earth jewels sparkled all at once, 98
Today they sparkle all at once. Surely you will become
a Buddha!
Human and divine musical instruments resounded in 99
harmony. They both sound out together today. Surely
you will become a Buddha!
Flowers of all colors showered down from the sky. 100
Today they shower down continuously. Surely you will
become a Buddha!
The vast ocean ebbed in its flow; the ten thousand 101
world systems quaked. They both resound today.
Surely you will become a Buddha!
Even the fire in the ten thousand hells was quenched, 102
all at once. Today fires are quenched. Surely you will
become a Buddha!

103 vimalo hoti suriyo sabbe dissanti tārakā
te pi ajja padissanti dhuvaṃ buddho bhavissasi.
104 anovaṭṭena udakena mahiyā ubbhijje tāvade
taṃ p' ajj' ubbhijjate mahiyā dhuvaṃ buddho
bhavissasi.
105 tārāgaṇā virocanti nakkhattaṃ gaganamaṇḍale
visākhā candimāyuttā dhuvaṃ buddho bhavissasi.
106 bilāsayā darīsayā nikkhamanti sakāsayā
te p' ajja āsayā chuddhā dhuvaṃ buddho bhavissasi.
107 na hoti arati sattānaṃ santuṭṭhā honti tāvade
te p' ajja sabbe santuṭṭhā dhuvaṃ buddho bhavissasi.
108 rogā tad' ūpasammanti jighacchā ca vinassati
tāni ajja padissanti dhuvaṃ buddho bhavissasi.
109 rāgo tadā tanu hoti doso moho pi nassati
te p' ajja vigatā sabbe dhuvaṃ buddho bhavissasi.
110 bhayaṃ tadā na bhavati ajja p' etaṃ padissati
tena liṅgena jānāma: dhuvaṃ buddho bhavissasi.
111 rajo n' uddhaṃsati uddhaṃ ajja p' etaṃ padissati
tena liṅgena jānāma: dhuvaṃ buddho bhavissasi.
112 aniṭṭhagandho pakkamati dibbagandho pavāyati
so p' ajja vāyatī gandho dhuvaṃ buddho bhavissasi.

The sun shone in a cloudless sky, and all the stars were 103
clearly seen. Today they all are seen. Surely you will
become a Buddha!
Water gushed from the earth, all at once, even where 104
it was not seen before. Today it gushes from the earth.
Surely you will become a Buddha!
A myriad of stars and constellations sparkle in the 105
circle of the heavens. The constellation of Visakha is
conjunct to the moon. Surely you will become
a Buddha![35]
Creatures of the caves and creatures of the hollows 106
emerged from their dens. Today they are winkled out
of their haunts. Surely you will become a Buddha!
There was no discontent among living beings; they 107
were all delighted. Today too they are all glad. Surely
you will become a Buddha!
Illnesses were allayed, and hunger disappeared. 108
Today too the same is seen. Surely you will become a
Buddha!
Desire was diminished; hatred and delusion vanished. 109
Today too these have all gone. Surely you will become
a Buddha!
Fear did not exist then; the same is seen today. We 110
know by this sign: surely you will become a Buddha!
Dust was not stirred upward; today too the same is 111
seen. We know by this sign: surely you will become a
Buddha!
Foul smell departed; heavenly scent pervaded. Today 112
too such scent suffuses: surely you will become a
Buddha!

113 sabbe devā padissanti ṭhapayitvā arūpino
te p' ajja sabbe dissanti dhuvaṃ buddho bhavissasi.
114 yāvātā nirayā nāma sabbe dissanti tāvade
te p' ajja sabbe dissanti dhuvaṃ buddho bhavissasi.
115 kuḍḍā kavāṭā selā ca na hont' āvaraṇan tadā
ākāsabhūtā te p' ajja dhuvaṃ buddho bhavissasi.
116 cutī ca upapattī ca khaṇe tasmiṃ na vijjati
tāni ajja padissanti dhuvaṃ buddho bhavissasi.
117 daḷhaṃ paggaṇha viriyaṃ mā nivatta abhikkama
mayaṃ p' etaṃ vijānāma: dhuvaṃ buddho bhavissasī
ti.

14 bodhisatto dīpaṃkaradasabalassa ca dasasahassacakkavāḷe devatānañ ca vacanaṃ sutvā bhiyyoso mattāya sañjātussāho hutvā cintesi: buddhā nāma amoghavacanā n' atthi buddhānaṃ kathāya aññathattaṃ yathā hi ākāse khittaleḍḍussa patanaṃ jātassa maraṇaṃ aruṇe uggate suriyass' uṭṭhānaṃ āsayā nikkhantasīhassa sīhanādanadanaṃ garugabbhāya itthiyā bhāramocanaṃ dhuvaṃ avassabhāvi evam evaṃ buddhānaṃ vacanaṃ nāma dhuvaṃ amoghaṃ addhā ahaṃ buddho bhavissāmīti tena vuttaṃ:

All the gods were seen—except the formless gods.[36] 113
Today too they are all seen: surely you will become
a Buddha!
As many hells as there are were all seen at once. 114
Today too they are all seen: surely you will become
a Buddha!
All at once, walls and doors and rocks create no 115
obstacles. They dissolve into empty space: surely
you will become a Buddha!
Death and birth did not occur at that time. 116
Today too this is seen. Surely you will become a
Buddha!
Make your effort strong; do not go back. Go forward. 117
We know this indeed: surely you will become
a Buddha!'"

When the Bodhisatta heard the declaration from Dipankara, 14
with ten powers, and that of the gods of the ten thousand
world systems, he was filled with resolve, and he reflected:
"Those who are Buddhas do not make empty statements.
There is nothing at variance in the words of a Buddha. Just as a clod of earth thrown right up in the air will certainly fall down, and just as death comes to those who are born, and as sunrise follows the break of dawn, and as a lion roars when he leaves his lair, and as a woman delivers her child when she is in an advanced state of pregnancy: even so the words of the Buddhas are certain and cannot fail. Certainly, I shall become a Buddha.

118 buddhassa vacanaṃ sutvā dasahassina[7] c' ūbhayaṃ
tuṭṭhahaṭṭho pamudito evaṃ cintes' ahan tadā:
119 advejjhavacanā buddhā amoghavacanā jinā
vitathaṃ n' atthi buddhānaṃ dhuvaṃ buddho
bhavām' ahaṃ.
120 yathā khittaṃ nabhe leḍḍu dhuvaṃ patati bhūmiyaṃ
tath' eva buddhaseṭṭhānaṃ vacanaṃ dhuvasassataṃ.
121 yathā 'pi sabbasattānaṃ maraṇaṃ dhuvasassataṃ
tath' eva buddhaseṭṭhānaṃ vacanaṃ dhuvasassataṃ.
122 yathā rattikkhaye patte suriyass' uggamanaṃ dhuvaṃ
tath' eva buddhaseṭṭhānaṃ vacanaṃ dhuvasassataṃ.
123 yathā nikkhantasayanassa sīhassa nadanaṃ dhuvaṃ
tath' eva buddhaseṭṭhānaṃ vacanaṃ dhuvasassataṃ.
124 yathā āpannasattānaṃ bhāramoropanaṃ dhuvaṃ
tath' eva buddhaseṭṭhānaṃ vacanaṃ dhuvasassatan
ti.

15 so dhuv' āhaṃ buddho bhavissāmī ti evaṃ katasanniṭṭhāno buddhakārake dhamme upadhāretuṃ kahan nu kho buddhakārakadhammā kiṃ uddhaṃ udāhu adho disāsu vidisāsū' ti. anukkamena sakaladhammadhātuṃ vicinanto porāṇakabodhisattehi āsevitanisevitaṃ paṭhamaṃ dānapāramiṃ disvā evaṃ attānaṃ ovadi: sumedhapaṇḍita tvaṃ

"Rejoicing in heart and gladdened at the declaration 118
both of the Buddha and the gods of the ten thousand
worlds, I reflected in this way:
'There is nothing at variance in the ways of Buddhas; 119
nothing empty in the words of the conquerors. There
is no falsehood in the Buddhas: surely, I will become
a Buddha.
As a clod thrown into the air is sure to fall right down 120
to the ground, just so, the words of the glorious
Buddhas are infallible and sure.
As the death of all living beings is infallible and sure, 121
just so, the words of the glorious Buddhas are
infallible and sure.
As sunrise is certain when night fades into day, just 122
so, the words of the glorious Buddhas are infallible
and sure.
As the lion, leaving his lair, is sure to roar, just so, the 123
words of the glorious Buddhas are infallible and sure.
As delivery is certain to those about to give birth, just 124
so, the words of the glorious Buddhas are infallible
and sure.'"

The Ten Perfections

"I will surely be a Buddha," he said. And, searching for the 15
conditions that lead to Buddhahood, he thought: "So, what are the things that make a Buddha: are they above or below, in the ten directions, or in the minor directions?" Investigating the entire element of things as they are, systematically, he saw the first perfection, of generosity, practiced

ito paṭṭhāya paṭhamaṃ dānapāramiṃ pūreyyāsi yathā hi nikkujjito udakumbho nissesaṃ katvā udakaṃ vamati yeva na paccāharati evam evaṃ dhanaṃ vā yasaṃ vā puttadāraṃ vā aṅgapaccaṅgaṃ vā anoloketvā sampattayācakānaṃ sabbaṃ icchiticchitaṃ nissesaṃ katvā dadamāno bodhirukkhamūle nisīditvā buddho bhavissasī ti paṭhamaṃ dānapāramiṃ daḷhaṃ katvā adhiṭṭhāsi tena vuttaṃ:

125 handa buddhakare dhamme vicināmi ito c' ito
uddhaṃ adho dasadisā yāvatā dhammadhātuyā.
126 vicinanto tadā dakkhiṃ paṭhamaṃ dānapāramiṃ
pubbakehi mahesīhi anuciṇṇaṃ mahāpathaṃ.
127 imaṃ tvaṃ paṭhamaṃ tāva daḷhaṃ katvā samādiya
dānapāramitaṃ gaccha yadi bodhiṃ pattum icchasi.
128 yathā 'pi kumbho sampuṇṇo yassa kassaci adhokato
vamate udakaṃ nissesaṃ na tattha parirakkhati
129 tath' eva yācake disvā hīnamukkaṭṭhamajjhime
dadāhi dānaṃ nissesaṃ kumbho viya adhokato ti.

and followed by bodhisattas long ago. And he urged himself: "Wise man, Sumedha: starting off, you should fulfill the first perfection, of generosity. Just as a water jar that has been toppled over pours its water, keeping back nothing and not taking the water back, so, regardless of money, fame, wife, or child, or one or another limb of your body, give everything in generosity to people that ask you, each according to their wish, keeping back nothing and without taking anything back: then you will become a Buddha, seated at the foot of the Bodhi Tree!" He made his resolve for the first perfection, of generosity, strong.

So, it is said:

"So, I search for all the things that make a Buddha, 125
above, below, in the ten directions, right to the very
element of things.

Searching, I saw the first perfection, of generosity, a 126
magnificent highway, followed by the great Teachers
of old.

'If you wish to find awakening, go, make firm, and take 127
upon yourself this first perfection, of generosity, if
you want to attain awakening.

Just as a jar filled to the brim, toppled by someone, 128
pours out water, and does not hold onto anything that
remains there,

So you, when you see people asking, low, middling, 129
or high, practice generosity, like a toppled jar, with
nothing held back.'"

16 ath’ assa na ettakeh’ eva buddhakārakadhammehi bhavitabban ti uttarim pi upadhārayato dutiyaṃ sīlapāramiṃ disvā etad ahosi: sumedhapaṇḍita tvaṃ ito paṭṭhāya sīlapāramiṃ pūreyyāsi yathā hi camaramigo nāma jīvitam pi anoloketvā attano vālam eva rakkhati evaṃ tvam pi ito paṭṭhāya jīvitam pi anoloketvā sīlam eva rakkhanto buddho bhavissasī ti dutiyaṃ sīlapāramiṃ daḷham katvā adhiṭṭhāsi tena vuttaṃ:

130 na h’ ete ettakā yeva buddhadhammā bhavissare
aññe pi vicinissāmi ye dhammā bodhipācanā.
131 vicinanto tadā dakkhiṃ dutiyaṃ sīlapāramiṃ
pubbakehi mahesīhi āsevitanisevitaṃ.
132 imaṃ tvaṃ dutiyaṃ tāva daḷhaṃ katvā samādiya
sīlapāramitaṃ gaccha yadi bodhiṃ pattum icchasi.
133 yathā ‘pi camarī vālaṃ kismiṃ ci[8] paṭilaggitaṃ
upeti maraṇaṃ tattha na vikopeti vāladhiṃ.
134 tath’ eva catusu bhūmīsu sīlāni paripūraya[9]
parirakkha sabbadā sīlaṃ camarī viya vāladhin ti.

17 ath’ assa na ettakeh’ eva buddhakārakadhammehi bhavitabban ti uttarim pi upadhārayato tatiyaṃ nekkhammapāramiṃ disvā etad ahosi: sumedhapaṇḍita tvaṃ ito paṭṭhāya nekkhammapāramiṃ pūreyyāsi yathā hi ciram pi bandhanāgāre vasamāno puriso na tattha sinehaṃ karoti atha kho

And he searched some more, saying: "These are not the only 16
things needed for awakening." He saw a second and higher perfection, of virtue, and thought, "Wise Sumedha: from now on you should fulfill the perfection of virtue as well. Just as a yak cow guards her tail, regardless of her life, so you too, from now on, regardless even of your life, guard your virtue and you will become a Buddha." He made his resolve for the second perfection strong.

So, it is said:

"But these are not all the things that lead to Buddha- 130
hood: I will search for other things that ripen
awakening!
Searching, I saw the second perfection, of virtue, 131
followed and practiced by the great Teachers of old.
'If you wish to find awakening, go, making firm and 132
taking upon yourself this second perfection, of virtue.
Just as a yak cow, with her tail caught in something, 133
nears death and still does not harm her tail,
So you, for the fulfillment of the precepts on four 134
levels, continually guard virtue, like a yak cow
her tail.'"[37]

And then he thought: "These are not the only conditions 17
that lead to Buddhahood." And he searched some more and saw a third and higher perfection, of renunciation: "Wise Sumedha: from now on, you should fulfill the perfection of renunciation as well. Just as a man serving a term in prison holds no affection for it but wants only to be away from it, so you make all states of existence as being just like prisons, and be one who turns his face to renunciation, longing to be

ukkaṇṭhati yeva avasitukāmo hoti evam eva tvaṃ sabbabhave bandhanāgārasadise katvā sabbabhave ukkaṇṭhito muñcitukāmo hutvā nekkhammābhimukho 'va hohi evaṃ buddho bhavissasī ti tatiyaṃ nekkhammapāramiṃ daḷhaṃ katvā adhiṭṭhāsi tena vuttam:

135 na h' ete ettakā yeva buddhadhammā bhavissare
aññe pi vicinissāmi ye dhammā bodhipācanā.
136 vicinanto tadā dakkhim tatiyaṃ nekkhammapāramiṃ
pubbakehi mahesīhi āsevitanisevitaṃ.
137 imaṃ tvaṃ tatiyaṃ tāva daḷhaṃ katvā samādiya
nekkhamme pāramiṃ gaccha yadi bodhiṃ pattum
icchasi.
138 yathā andughare puriso ciravuttho dukhaddito
na tattha rāgaṃ abhijaneti muttiṃ yeva gavesati
139 tath' eva tvaṃ sabbabhave passa andughare viya
nekkhammābhimukho hohi bhavato parimuttiyā ti.

18 ath' assa na ettakeh' eva buddhakārakadhammehi bhavitabban ti uttarim pi upadhārayato catutthaṃ paññāpāramiṃ disvā etad ahosi: sumedhapaṇḍita tvaṃ ito paṭṭhāya paññāpāramiṃ pi pūreyyāsi hīnamajjhimukkaṭṭhesu kiñci avajjetvā sabbe pi paṇḍite upasaṃkamitvā pañhaṃ puccheyyāsi yathā hi piṇḍacāriko bhikkhu hīnādibhedesu kulesu kiñci avajjetvā paṭipāṭiyā piṇḍāya caranto khippaṃ yāpanaṃ labhati evaṃ tvam pi sabbapaṇḍite upasaṃkamitvā pañhaṃ pucchanto buddho bhavissasī ti catutthaṃ paññāpāramiṃ

free: this is the way you will become a Buddha." He made his resolve for the third perfection strong.

So, it is said:

"But these are not all the things that lead to Buddha- 135
hood: I will search for other things that ripen
awakening!
Searching, I saw the third perfection, of renunciation, 136
followed and practiced by the great Teachers of old.
'If you wish to find awakening, go, make firm and take 137
upon yourself this third perfection, of renunciation.
Just as a man who has stayed a long time, painfully 138
afflicted, in a jail does not feel desire for it but wishes
only for release,
So you too, see all states of becoming like a prison. 139
Be someone who turns their face to renunciation, for
the complete release from becoming.'"

And then he thought: "These are not the only things that 18
lead to Buddhahood." And he searched some more and saw a fourth and higher perfection, of wisdom: "Wise Sumedha: from now on, you should fulfill the perfection of wisdom as well. You should approach and ask questions of teachers, whether they are poor, middling, or very good. Just as someone on alms round does not avoid any families that he visits, whether poor, middling, or rich, and going for alms from place to place, quickly gets the sustenance to keep him going, in that way you should approach and ask questions of all teachers: this is the way you will become a Buddha." He made his resolve for the fourth perfection strong.

daḷhaṃ katvā adhiṭṭhāsi tena vuttam:

140 na h' ete ettakā yeva buddhadhammā bhavissare
aññe pi vicinissāmi ye dhammā bodhipācanā.
141 vicinanto tadā dakkhiṃ catutthaṃ paññāpāramiṃ
pubbakehi mahesīhi āsevitanisevitaṃ.
142 imaṃ tvaṃ catutthaṃ tāva daḷhaṃ katvā samādiya
paññāpāramitaṃ gaccha yadi bodhiṃ pattum icchasi.
143 yathā 'pi bhikkhu bhikkhanto hīnamukkaṭṭhamajjhime
kulāni na vivajjento evaṃ labhati yāpanaṃ
144 tath' eva tvaṃ sabbakāle paripucchanto budhaṃ janaṃ
paññāpāramitaṃ gantvā sambodhiṃ pāpuṇissasī ti.

19 ath' assa na ettakeh' eva buddhakārakadhammehi bhavitabban ti uttarim pi upadhārayato pañcamaṃ viriyapāramiṃ disvā etad ahosi: sumedhapaṇḍita tvaṃ ito paṭṭhāya viriyapāramiṃ pūreyyāsi yathā sīho migarājā sabbairiyāpathesu daḷhaviriyo hoti evaṃ tvaṃ sabbabhavesu sabbairiyāpathesu daḷhaviriyo anolīnaviriyo samāno buddho bhavissasī ti pañcamaṃ viriyapāramiṃ daḷhaṃ katvā adhiṭṭhāsi tena

So, it is said:

"But these are not all the things that lead to Buddha- 140
hood: I will search for other things that ripen
awakening!

Searching, I saw the fourth perfection, of wisdom, 141
followed and practiced by the great Teachers of old.

'If you wish to find awakening, go, making firm and 142
taking upon yourself this fourth perfection,
of wisdom.

Just as a monk, begging for alms, avoids neither poor, 143
middling, nor rich families, and takes his sustenance
in this way,

So you too, at all times ask questions of wakeful 144
people, and, going to the perfection of wisdom, you
will attain full awakening.'"

And then he thought: "These are not the only things that 19
lead to Buddhahood." And he searched some more and saw a fifth and higher perfection, of heroic strength: "Wise Sumedha: from now on, you should fulfill the perfection of heroic strength as well. Just as a lion, the king of wild creatures, exercises powerful strength without flagging, in all postures, so you, in all states of existence, should exercise heroic strength without flagging, in all postures: this is the way you will become a Buddha." He made his resolve for the fifth perfection strong.

vuttaṃ:

145 na h' ete ettakā yeva buddhadhammā bhavissare
aññe pi vicinissāmi ye dhammā bodhipācanā.
146 vicinanto tadā dakkhiṃ pañcamaṃ viriyapāramiṃ
pubbakehi mahesīhi āsevitanisevitaṃ.
147 imaṃ tvaṃ pañcamaṃ tāva daḷhaṃ katvā samādiya
viriyapāramitaṃ gaccha yadi bodhiṃ pattum icchasi.
148 yathā 'pi sīho migarājā nisajjaṭṭhānacaṅkame
alīnaviriyo hoti paggahītamano sadā
149 tath' eva tvam pi sabbabhave paggaṇha viriyaṃ daḷhaṃ
viriyapāramitaṃ gantvā sambodhiṃ pāpuṇissasī ti

20 ath' assa na ettakeh' eva buddhakārakadhammehi bhavitabban ti uttarim pi upadhārayato chaṭṭhaṃ khantipāramiṃ disvā etad ahosi: sumedhapaṇḍita tvaṃ ito paṭṭhāya khantipāramiṃ pūreyyāsi sammānane pi avamānane pi khamo 'va bhaveyyāsi yathā 'pi paṭhaviyaṃ nāma sucim pi pakkhipanti asucim pi na tena paṭhavi sinehaṃ na paṭighaṃ karoti khamati sahati adhivāseti yeva evam evaṃ tvam pi sammānanāvamānanesu khamo 'va samāno buddho bhavissasī ti chaṭṭhaṃ khantipāramiṃ daḷhaṃ katvā adhiṭṭhāsi tena vuttaṃ:

150 na h' ete ettakā yeva buddhadhammā bhavissare
aññe pi vicinissāmi ye dhammā bodhipācanā.

So, it is said:
"But these are not all the things that lead to Buddha- 145
hood: I will search for other things that ripen
awakening!
Searching, I saw the fifth perfection, of heroic 146
strength, followed and practiced by the great Teachers
of old.
'If you wish to find awakening, go, making firm, and 147
taking upon yourself this fifth perfection, of strength.
Just as a lion, the king of the beasts, whether lying 148
down, standing, or walking, exhibits unabated
strength and is always courageous,
So you too, firmly exerting strength in every state of 149
becoming, going to the perfection of heroic strength,
will attain full awakening.'"

And then he thought: "These are not the only things that 20
lead to Buddhahood." And he searched some more and saw a sixth and higher perfection, of forbearance: "Wise Sumedha: from now on, you should fulfill the perfection of forbearance as well. Be forgiving in the face of honor or contempt. Just as people throw pure and impure things on the earth and the earth does not show favor or disdain, but forgives, endures, and has patience: in this way, be forgiving in the face of honor or contempt: this is the way you will become a Buddha." He made his resolve for the sixth perfection strong.

For it is said:
"But these are not all the things that are needed 150
for Buddhahood: I will search for other things that
ripen awakening!"

151 vicinanto tadā dakkhiṃ chaṭṭhamaṃ khantipāramiṃ
pubbakehi mahesīhi āsevitanisevitaṃ.
152 imaṃ tvaṃ chaṭṭhamaṃ tāva daḷhaṃ katvā samādiya
tattha advejjhamānaso sambodhiṃ pāpuṇissasi.
153 yathā 'pi paṭhavī nāma sucim pi asucim pi ca
sabbaṃ sahati nikkhepaṃ na karoti paṭighaṃ dayaṃ
154 tath' eva tvam pi sabbesaṃ sammānāvamānakkhamo
khantipāramitaṃ gantvā sambodhiṃ pāpuṇissasī ti.

21 ath' assa na ettakeh' eva buddhakārakadhammehi bhavitabban ti uttarim pi upadhārayato sattamaṃ saccapāramiṃ disvā etad ahosi: sumedhapaṇḍita tvaṃ ito paṭṭhāya saccapāramiṃ pi pūreyyāsi asaniyā matthake patamānāya pi dhanādīnaṃ atthāya chandādīnaṃ vasena sampajānamusāvādaṃ nāma mā akāsi yathā hi osadhitārakā nāma sabbautusu attano gamanavīthiṃ jahitvā aññāya vīthiyā na gacchati sakavīthiyā 'va gacchati evam evaṃ tvam pi saccaṃ pahāya musāvādaṃ nāma akaronto yeva buddho bhavissasī ti sattamaṃ saccapāramiṃ daḷhaṃ katvā adhiṭṭhāsi: tena vuttaṃ:

155 na h' ete ettakā yeva buddhadhammā bhavissare
aññe pi vicinissāmi ye dhammā bodhipācanā.

Searching, I saw the sixth perfection, of forbearance, 151
followed and practiced by the great Teachers of old.
'You, with an undivided mind, make firm and take 152
upon yourself the sixth, and you will attain
full awakening.
Just as the earth endures everything thrown upon it, 153
pure and impure alike, and does not show anger
or favor,
So you too, be forgiving in the face of both honor 154
and contempt, and you will go to the perfection of
forbearance and attain full awakening.'"

And then he thought: "These are not the only things 21
that lead to Buddhahood." And he searched some more and saw a higher, seventh perfection, of truthfulness: "Wise Sumedha: from now on, you should fulfill the perfection of truthfulness as well. Even though a thunderbolt might fall on your head, do not tell a conscious lie for the sake of money and suchlike, or through desire or any other motives. Just as the healing star, Venus, in all seasons, follows her own steady course and does not go on any other, in this way you should follow truthfulness, and not make a false statement: this is the way you will become a Buddha." He made his resolve for the seventh perfection strong.

So, it is said:

"But these are not all the things that are needed 155
for Buddhahood: I will search for other things that
ripen awakening!

156 icinanto tadā dakkhiṃ sattamaṃ saccapāramiṃ
pubbakehi mahesīhi āsevitanisevitaṃ.
157 imaṃ tvaṃ sattamaṃ tāva daḷhaṃ katvā samādiya
tattha advejjhavacano sambodhiṃ pāpuṇissasi.
158 yathā 'pi osadhī nāma tulābhūtā sadevake
samaye utuvasse vā na vokkamati vīthito
159 tath' eva tvam pi saccesu mā vokkami vīthito
saccapāramitaṃ gantvā sambodhiṃ pāpuṇissasī ti.

22 ath' assa na ettakeh' eva buddhakārakadhammehi bhavitabban ti uttarim pi upadhārayato aṭṭhamaṃ adhiṭṭhānapāramiṃ disvā etad ahosi: sumedhapaṇḍita tvaṃ ito paṭṭhāya adhiṭṭhānapāramim pi pūreyyāsi yaṃ adhiṭṭhāsi tasmiṃ adhiṭṭhāne niccalo bhaveyyāsi yathā hi pabbato nāma sabbadisāsu pi vāte paharante pi na kampati na calati attano ṭhāne yeva tiṭṭhati evam evaṃ tvam pi attano adhiṭṭhāne niccalo honto 'va buddho bhavissasī ti aṭṭhamaṃ adhiṭṭhānapāramiṃ daḷhaṃ katvā adhiṭṭhāsi tena vuttaṃ:

160 na h' ete ettakā yeva buddhadhammā bhavissare.
aññe pi vicinissāmi ye dhammā bodhipācanā.

Searching, I saw the seventh perfection, of truth- 156
fulness, followed and practiced by the great Teachers
of old.

'Making firm and taking upon yourself the seventh, 157
with undivided speech, you will attain full awakening.

Just as the healing star, Venus, stays balanced for gods 158
and men in all times and seasons and does not deviate
from her course,

So you, do not deviate from the course of the truth, 159
and, going to the perfection of truthfulness, you too
will attain full awakening.'"

And then he thought: "But these are not the only things that 22
lead to Buddhahood." And he searched some more and saw
an eighth and higher perfection, of resolve: "Wise Sumedha:
from now on you should fulfill the perfection of resolve as
well. When you make a resolve, stick to it without waver-
ing. Just as when wind is battering the mountain, facing all
sides, it does not shake or tremble but stands firm; so you
too should be unwavering yourself in your resolve: this is the
way you will become a Buddha." He made his resolve for the
eighth perfection strong.

So, it is said:

"But these are not all the things that are needed for 160
Buddhahood: I will search for other things that ripen
awakening!

161 vicinanto tadā dakkhiṃ aṭṭhamaṃ
adhiṭṭhānapāramiṃ
pubbakehi mahesīhi āsevitanisevitaṃ.
162 imaṃ tvaṃ aṭṭhamaṃ tāva daḷhaṃ katvā samādiya
tattha tvaṃ acalo hutvā sambodhiṃ pāpuṇissasi.
163 yathā 'pi pabbato selo acalo suppatiṭṭhito
na kampati bhusavātehi sakaṭṭhāne 'va tiṭṭhati
164 tath' eva tvam pi adhiṭṭhāne sabbadā acalo bhava
adhiṭṭhānapāramiṃ gantvā sambodhiṃ pāpuṇissasī
ti.

23 ath' assa na ettakeh' eva buddhakārakadhammehi bhavitabban ti uttarim pi upadhārayato navamaṃ mettāpāramiṃ disvā etad ahosi: sumedhapaṇḍita tvaṃ ito paṭṭhāya mettāpāramiṃ pūreyyāsi hitesu pi ahitesu pi ekacitto bhaveyyāsi yathā 'pi udakaṃ nāma pāpajanassa pi kalyāṇajjanassa pi sītabhāvaṃ ekasadisaṃ katvā pharati evam evaṃ tvaṃ sabbasattesu mettacittena ekacitto honto buddho bhavissasī ti navamaṃ mettāpāramiṃ daḷhaṃ katvā adhiṭṭhāsi tena vuttaṃ:

165 na h' ete ettakā yeva buddhadhammā bhavissare
aññe pi vicinissāmi ye dhammā bodhipācanā.
166 vicinanto tadā dakkhiṃ navamaṃ mettāpāramiṃ
pubbakehi mahesīhi āsevitanisevitaṃ.

Searching, I saw the eighth perfection, of resolve, 161
followed and practiced by the great Teachers of old.
'You, making firm and taking upon yourself the 162
eighth, be unwavering there and you will attain
full awakening.
Just as a mountain, a rock, unwavering, is well 163
established, and does not tremble in rough winds but
remains firm in its own place,
So you too, be unwavering at all times in your resolve 164
and, going to the perfection of resolve, you will attain
full awakening.'"

And then he thought: "These are not the only things that lead 23
to Buddhahood." And he searched some more and saw a ninth
and higher perfection, of loving-kindness: "Wise Sumedha:
from now on, fulfill the perfection of loving-kindness as well.
You should have one heart for friends and enemies. Just as
water, with refreshing coolness, suffuses bad and good men
alike, so you too should suffuse all beings with a heart filled
with loving-kindness: doing this, you will become a Buddha."
He made his resolve for the ninth perfection strong.

So, it is said:

"But these are not all the things that are needed for 165
Buddhahood: I will search for other things that
ripen awakening!
Searching, I saw the ninth perfection, of loving- 166
kindness, followed and practiced by the great
Teachers of old.

167 imaṃ tvaṃ navamaṃ tāva daḷhaṃ katvā samādiya
mettāya asamo hohi yadi bodhiṃ pattum icchasi.
168 yathā 'pi udakaṃ nāma kalyāṇe pāpake jane
samaṃ pharati sītena pavāheti rajomalaṃ
169 tath' eva tvam pi ahitahite samaṃ mettāya bhāvaya
mettāpāramitaṃ gantvā sambodhiṃ pāpuṇissasī ti.

24 ath' assa na ettakeh' eva buddhakārakadhammehi bhavitabban ti uttarim pi upadhārayato dasamaṃ upekkhāpāramiṃ disvā etad ahosi: sumedhapaṇḍita tvaṃ ito paṭṭhāya upekkhāpāramiṃ pi pūreyyāsi sukhe pi dukkhe pi majjhatto va bhaveyyāsi yathā 'pi paṭhavī nāma sucim pi asucim pi pakkhippamāne majjhattā 'va hoti evam evaṃ tvam pi sukhadukkhesu majjhatto 'va honto buddho bhavissasī ti dasamaṃ upekkhāpāramiṃ daḷhaṃ katvā adhiṭṭhāsi tena vuttaṃ:

170 na h' ete ettakā yeva buddhadhammā bhavissare
aññe pi vicinissami ye dhammā bodhipācanā.
171 vicinanto tadā dakkhiṃ dasamaṃ upekhāpāramiṃ
pubbakehi mahesīhi āsevitanisevitaṃ.
172 imaṃ tvaṃ dasamaṃ tāva daḷhaṃ katvā samādiya
tulābhūto daḷho hutvā sambodhiṃ pāpuṇissasi.

'You, making firm and taking upon yourself the ninth, 167
be without an equal in loving-kindness if you wish to
attain full awakening.
Just as water suffuses with coolness good and bad 168
people alike, and washes away dust and dirt,
so you too, cultivate loving-kindness for friend 169
and enemy, and, going to the perfection of loving-
kindness, you will attain full awakening.'"

And then he thought: "These are not the only things that 24
lead to Buddhahood." And he searched some more and saw a higher and tenth perfection, of equanimity: "Wise Sumedha: from now on, fulfill the perfection of equanimity as well. Be even, in the middle, in happiness and suffering. Just as the earth remains even, in the middle, when the pure and the impure are thrown at her, in this way stay even, in the middle, in happy events and painful ones: doing this, you will become a Buddha." He made his resolve for the tenth perfection strong.

So, it is said:

"But these are not all the things that are needed 170
for Buddhahood: I will search for other things that
ripen awakening!
Searching, I saw the tenth perfection, of equanimity, 171
followed and practiced by the great Teachers of old.
'You, making firm and taking upon yourself the 172
tenth, be balanced and firm and you will attain
full awakening.

173 yathā 'pi paṭhavī nāma nikkhittaṃ asuciṃ suciṃ
upekkhati ubho p' ete kopānunayavajjitā
174 tath' eva tvam pi sukhadukkhe tulābhūto sadā bhava
upekkhāpāramitaṃ gantvā sambodhiṃ pāpuṇissasī ti

25 tato cintesi: imasmiṃ loke bodhisattehi pūretabbā bodhiparipācanā buddhakārakadhammā ettakā yeva dasa pāramiyo ṭhapetvā aññe n' atthi imā 'pi dasa pāramiyo uddhaṃ ākāse pi n' atthi heṭṭhā paṭhaviyam pi puratthimādisu disāsu pi n' atthi mayhaṃ yeva pana hadayamaṃsantare patiṭṭhitā ti. evaṃ tāsaṃ hadaye patiṭṭhitabhāvaṃ disvā sabbā 'pi daḷhaṃ katvā adhiṭṭhāya punappuna sammasanto anulomapaṭilomaṃ sammasati pariyante gahetvā ādiṃ pāpeti ādimhi gahetvā pariyante ṭhapeti majjhe gahetvā ubhato osāpeti ubhatokoṭisu[10] gahetvā majjhe osāpeti aṅgapariccāgo pāramiyo nāma bāhirabhāṇḍapariccāgo upapāramiyo nāma jīvitapariccāgo paramatthapāramiyo nāmā 'ti dasa pāramiyo dasa upapāramiyo dasa paramatthapāramiyo ti yamakatelaṃ vinivaṭṭento viya mahāmeruṃ manthaṃ katvā cakkavāḷamahāsamuddaṃ āluḷento viya ca sammasi. yassa dasa pāramiyo sammasantassa sammasantassa dhammatejena catunahutādhikāni dve yojanasatasahassāni bahalā ayaṃ mahāpaṭhavī hatthinā akkantanaḷakalāpo viya pīḷiyamā-

Just as the earth looks on unperturbed as both the 173
pure and impure are thrown down upon her, and
avoids both anger and favoritism,
so you too, be balanced at all times to the happy 174
and the painful, and, going to the perfection of
equanimity, you will attain full awakening.'"

Then he thought: "These are all the things in this world that 25
bring awakening to ripeness, that bring about Buddhahood and that have to be fulfilled by bodhisattas. Beyond these ten perfections there are no others. And these ten perfections are not in the sky above. They are not in the earth below. Nor are they in the directions, starting with the east. They are established right in the depths of my heart."

When he saw that they were established in his heart, he made his resolve strong for all of them. Taking hold of them, again and again, he mastered them, forward and backward. Taking them from the end, he went back to the beginning, and taking them from the beginning he went on to the end. Taking them at the middle, he brought them to completion at the ends; taking them from both ends, he brought them to the middle. And he repeated to himself: "The perfections are the giving up of one's limbs: the intermediate perfections are the giving up of one's property; the most excellent perfections are the giving up of one's life."[38] He mastered the ten perfections, the ten intermediate perfections, and the ten most excellent perfections, like someone making an emulsion out of two oils, or like someone churning the great ocean, which is surrounded by mountains, using Mount Meru as the rod.[39] And by the power of his great virtue, as he

naṃ ucchuyantaṃ viya mahāviravaṃ viravamānā saṃkampi sampakampi sampavedhi kulālacakkaṃ viya telayantacakkaṃ viya ca paribbhami tena vuttaṃ:

175 ettakā yeva te loke ye dhammā bodhipācanā
tat' uddhaṃ n' atthi aññatra daḷhaṃ tattha patiṭṭhaha.
176 ime dhamme sammasato sabhāvasarasalakkhaṇe
dhammatejena vasudhā dasasahassī pakampatha.
177 calatī ravatī puthavī ucchuyantaṃ 'va pīḷitaṃ
telayante yathā cakkaṃ evaṃ kampati medinī ti.

26 mahāpaṭhaviyā kampamānāya rammanagaravāsino saṇṭhātuṃ asakkontā yugantavātamhā hatā mahāsālā viya mucchitamucchitā papatiṃsu ghaṭādīni kulālabhājanāni pavaṭṭantāni aññamaññaṃ paharantāni cuṇṇavicuṇṇāni ahesuṃ. mahājano bhītatasito satthāraṃ upasaṃkamitvā kin nu kho bhagavā nāgāvaṭṭo ayaṃ bhūtayakkhadevatāsu aññatarāvaṭṭo ti na hi mayaṃ etaṃ jānāma api ca kho sabbo pi ayaṃ mahājano upadduto kin nu kho imassa lokassa pāpakaṃ bhavissati udāhu kalyāṇaṃ kathetha no etaṃ kāraṇan ti āha. satthā tesaṃ kathaṃ sutvā tumhe mā bhāyatha mā cintayitta n' atthi vo itonidānaṃ bhayaṃ yo so mayā ajja sumedhapaṇḍito anāgate gotamo nāma buddho bhavis-

mastered the ten perfections, the great earth, two hundred forty thousand *yojanas* in thickness, trembled, shook and quaked, and whirled around, like the wheel of a potter or a wheel for grinding out oil.[40]

So, it is said:

"These are all the things in this world that bring 175
awakening to ripeness. Beyond these there are no
others: establish yourself firmly in them."
As he mastered these things, each distinguished by its 176
own taste and character, by the power of this truth the
whole ten thousand worlds shook.
The earth shook and rumbled like a sugarcane mill 177
being pressed, or an oil mill; in this way the earth
herself quaked.

While the great earth was shaking, the people of Ramma 26
could not remain standing: they fell down fainting, like large sal trees felled at the destruction of the world. Water jars and other vessels made by potters, turning on the wheel, knocked against one another and were shattered, ground to pieces. People were terrified and approached the Teacher: "Bhagavan! Is this some kind of naga whirligig? Or a violent shake-up sent by spooks, trolls, or gods? We do not know what is going on. People are just going crazy. Is some disaster about to hit the world, or will it be good? Tell us what is making it happen." The Teacher listened to what they were saying and replied, "Do not be afraid and do not get worried. There is no reason for you to be frightened. Wise Sumedha, about whom I made a prediction today—that he is going to be a Buddha called Gotama—is just acquiring mastery of

sasī ti vyākato so idāni pāramiyo sammasati tassa pāramiyo sammasantassa viloḷentassa dhammatejena sakaladasasahassilokadhātu ekappahārena kampati c' eva ravati cā 'ti āha tena vuttaṃ:

178 yāvatā parisā āsi buddhassa parivesane
pavedhamānā sā tattha mucchitā seti bhūmiyā.
179 ghaṭānekasahassāni kumbhīnañ ca satā bahū
sañcuṇṇamathitā tattha aññamaññ' ūpaghaṭṭitā.
180 ubbiggā tasitā bhītā bhantā vyādhitamānasā
mahājanā samāgamma dīpaṃkaram upāgamuṃ.
181 kim bhavissati lokassa kalyāṇaṃ atha pāpakaṃ
sabbo upadduto loko taṃ vinodehi cakkhumā.
182 tesaṃ tadā saññapesi dīpaṃkaro mahāmuni.
vissatthā hotha mā bhātha imasmiṃ puthavikampane
183 yam ahaṃ ajja vyākāsiṃ buddho loke bhavissati
eso sammasatī dhammaṃ pubbakaṃ jinasevitaṃ.
184 tassa sammasato dhammaṃ buddhabhūmiṃ asesato
tenāyaṃ kampitā pathavī dasasahassī sadevake ti.

27 mahājano tathāgatassa vacanaṃ sutvā haṭṭhatuṭṭho mālāgandhavilepanaṃ ādāya rammanagarā nikkhamitvā bodhisattaṃ upasaṃkamitvā mālādīhi pūjetvā vanditvā

the perfections! And while he masters them, and turns them all around in his mind, by the power of his virtue the entire ten-thousand-world system quakes and rumbles, all at the same time."

So, it is said:

"The assembly, who had come together at the 178
Buddha's eating place, quivered and fainted and lay
flat on the ground.
Thousands of water jars and hundreds of pots 179
crashed against one another and were crushed
to pieces.
People were excited, scared, fearful, veering out of 180
control and out of their senses. They met together and
approached Dipankara.
'Is something good going to happen or something 181
terrible? The whole world is going crazy. Keep harm
away, clear-sighted one.'
Then the great Teacher Dipankara put their minds 182
at rest: 'Take heart. Don't be afraid at this shaking of
the world.
That man, whom I predicted today would be a 183
Buddha, is fully mindful of the field of Buddhahood,
the Dhamma followed by Teachers of old.
And while he is fully mindful of the field of Buddha- 184
hood, with nothing left out, the earth and the ten
thousand world systems tremble.'"

People heard what the Tathagata had to say and were 27
heartened and delighted. Taking garlands, perfumes, and ointments, they left the city of Ramma and approached

padakkhiṇaṃ katvā rammanagaram eva pāvisi. bodhisatto pi dasa pāramiyo sammasitvā viriyaṃ daḷhaṃ katvā adhiṭṭhāya nisinnāsanā vuṭṭhāsi: tena vuttaṃ:

185 buddhassa vacanaṃ sutvā mano nibbāyi tāvade
sabbe maṃ upasaṃkamma puna pi maṃ
abhivandisuṃ.[11]
186 samādiyitvā buddhaguṇaṃ daḷhaṃ katvāna mānasaṃ
dīpaṃkaraṃ namassitvā 'va āsanā vuṭṭhahiṃ tadā ti.

28 atha bodhisattaṃ āsanā vuṭṭhahantaṃ sakaladasasahassacakkavāḷe devatā sannipatitvā dibbehi mālāgandhehi pūjetvā ayya sumedhatāpasa tayā ajja dīpaṃkaradasabalassa pādamūle mahatī patthanā patthitā sā te anantarāyena samijjhatu mā te bhayaṃ vā chambhitattaṃ vā ahosi sarīre appamattako pi rogo mā uppajji khippaṃ pāpamiyo pūretvā sammāsambodhiṃ paṭivijjha yathā pupphūpagaphalūpagā rukkhā samaye pupphanti c' eva phalanti ca tath' eva tvam pi samayaṃ anatikkamitvā khippaṃ bodhim uttamaṃ phusassū 'ti ādīni thutimaṅgalāni payirudāhaṃsu evaṃ payirudāhitvā attano attano devaṭṭhānaṃ eva agamaṃsu.

the Bodhisatta. They made their offerings, paid homage, and honored the Bodhisatta, made a circumambulation, and returned to the city of Ramma. The Bodhisatta, mastering the perfections, made his resolve for them strong and got up from his seat.

So, it is said:

"When they heard what the Buddha had to say, their 185
minds became still there and then. They all came and
paid homage to me once again.
When I had taken on the qualities that lead to 186
Buddhahood, and made my mind firm, I paid homage
again to Dipankara and rose from my seat there."

Then the gods of the ten thousand world systems met 28
together and honored the Bodhisatta with garlands and perfumes as he rose from his seat. They spoke words of praise and offered blessings, saying, "Venerable Sumedha the ascetic: today you have made a great resolution at the feet of Dipankara, who has ten powers. May you succeed in it without obstruction. May no fear or trepidation arise for you. May not even the smallest illness arise in your body. May you quickly fulfill the perfections and penetrate to complete awakening.

Just as flower- and fruit-bearing trees bring out their fruits at the right time, so may you too, without going past the moment, quickly reach the highest awakening."

When they had praised him, they all went right back to their own divine homes.

bodhisatto pi devatāhi abhitthuto ahaṃ dasapāramiyo pūretvā kappasatasahassādhikānaṃ catunnaṃ asaṃkheyyānaṃ matthake buddho bhavissāmī ti viriyaṃ daḷhaṃ katvā adhiṭṭhāya nabhaṃ abbhuggantvā himavantam eva agamāsi tena vuttaṃ:

187 dibbaṃ mānusakaṃ pupphaṃ devā mānusakā ubho
samokiranti pupphehi vuṭṭhahantassa āsanā.
188 vedayanti ca te sotthiṃ devā mānusakā ubho:
mahantaṃ patthitaṃ tuyhaṃ taṃ labhassu yath' icchitaṃ.
189 sabbītiyo vivajjantu sabbarogo vinassatu
mā te bhavatu antarāyo phusa khippaṃ bodhim uttamaṃ.
190 yathā 'pi samaye patte pupphanti pupphino dumā
tath' eva tvaṃ mahāvīra buddhañāṇena pupphasi.
191 yathā ye keci sambuddhā pūrayaṃ dasapāramiṃ
tath' eva tvaṃ mahārīra pūrehi dasapāramiṃ.
192 yathā ye keci sambuddhā bodhimaṇḍamhi bujjhare
tath' eva tvaṃ mahāvīra bujjhassu jinabodhiyaṃ.
193 yathā ye keci sambuddhā dhammacakkaṃ pavattayuṃ
tath' eva tvaṃ mahāvīra dhammacakkaṃ pavattaya.
194 puṇṇamāse yathā cando parisuddho virocati
tath' eva tvaṃ puṇṇamano viroca dasasahassiyaṃ.

The Bodhisatta too, after being praised by the gods, said: "I will fulfill the ten perfections, and a hundred thousand eons and four incalculable epochs from now, I will become a Buddha!" He made his resolve strong and, rising into the clouds, sailed off to the Himalayas.

So, it is said:

As he rose from his seat both gods and men showered 187
him with divine and human flowers.
Both gods and men offered blessings, saying: "You 188
have made a great vow: may you achieve it as you wish!
May all dangers subside, and may all illness disappear. 189
May you too meet no obstruction: and may you
quickly find awakening!
Just as flowering trees flower at the right season: 190
May you too, great hero, blossom, a magnificent hero,
with the knowledge of Buddhas.
Just as all the Buddhas have fulfilled the ten 191
perfections, May you too, great hero, fulfill the
ten perfections.
Just as all Buddhas become awakened on the throne of 192
awakening, May you too, great hero, find awakening
on the seat of enlightenment.
Just as all Buddhas set in motion the wheel of the 193
Dhamma, May you too, great hero, set in motion the
wheel of the Dhamma.
Just as on the full moon day, the moon shines pure. 194
May you too shine, with a full mind, in ten thousand
worlds.

195 rāhumutto yathā suriyo tāpena atirocati
tath' eva lokaṃ muñcitvā viroca siriyā tuvaṃ.
196 yathā yā kāci nadiyo osaranti mahodadhiṃ
evaṃ sadevakā lokā osarantu tav' antikaṃ.
197 tehi thutippasattho so dasa dhamme samādiya
te dhamme paripūrento pavanaṃ pāvisī tadā ti
sumedhakathā niṭṭhitā.

29 rammanagaravāsino pi kho nagaram pavisitvā buddhapamukhassa bhikkhusaṅghassa mahādānaṃ adaṃsu. satthā tesaṃ dhammaṃ desetvā mahājanaṃ saraṇādisu patiṭṭhāpetvā rammanagaramhā nikkhamitvā tato uddhaṃ pi yāvatāyukaṃ tiṭṭhanto sabbaṃ buddhakiccaṃ katvā anukkamena anupādisesāya nibbānadhātuyā parinibbāyi. tattha yaṃ vattabbaṃ taṃ sabbaṃ buddhavaṃse vuttanayen' eva veditabbaṃ vuttaṃ hi tattha:

198 tadā te bhojayitvāna sasaṅghaṃ lokanāyakaṃ
upagañchuṃ saraṇaṃ tassa dīpaṃkarassa satthuno.
199 saraṇāgāmane kañci nivesesi tathāgato
kañci pañcasu sīlesu sīle dasavidhe paraṃ.

Just as the sun, released by Rahu,* blazes with all its 195
fire, May you too, released from the world, shine with
your glory.
Just as all rivers flow into the great ocean, so may 196
all the people of the worlds, and the gods, flow
toward you."
Praised and congratulated by them, the Bodhisatta 197
undertook the ten perfections. Then he entered into
the forest, seeing to their fulfillment.

The story of Sumedha has finished.

The people of Ramma entered the city and gave a magnif- 29
icent meal to the Sangha of monastics, with the Buddha at its head. The Teacher gave them a talk on the Dhamma, and established the crowd in the refuges, and so forth. After leaving the city of Ramma he fulfilled the work of a Buddha until he reached the end of his life. In due course, he entered nibbana, into that element of quenching where there is no more existence.

On this subject all that can be said is explained in the *Buddhavamsa*, for there it is said:

"When they had fed the leader of the world, with the 198
order of monastics, they approached the Teacher,
Dipankara, for refuge.
The Tathagata established some in taking the 199
refuges,some in the five precepts, and others in the
ten precepts.[41]

* God of the eclipse.

200 kassaci deti sāmaññaṃ caturo phalamuttame
kassaci asame dhamme deti so paṭisambhidā.
201 kassaci varasahapattiyo[12] aṭṭha deti narāsabho
tisso kassaci vijjāyo chaḷabhiññā pavecchati.
202 tena yogena janakāyaṃ ovadati mahāmuni
tena vitthārikaṃ āsi lokanāthassa sāsanaṃ.
203 mahāhanu usabhakkhandho dīpaṃkarasanāmako
bahū jane tārayati parimoceti duggatiṃ.
204 bodhaneyyaṃ janaṃ disvā satasahasse pi yojane
khaṇena upagantvāna bodheti taṃ mahāmuni.
205 paṭhamābhisamaye buddho koṭisatam abodhayi
dutiyābhisamaye nātho satasahassaṃ abodhayi.
206 yadā devabhavanaṃhi buddho dhammam adesayi
navutikoṭisahassānaṃ tatiyābhisamayo ahu.
207 sannipātā tayo āsuṃ dīpaṃkarassa satthuno:
koṭisatasahassānaṃ paṭhamo āsi samāgamo.
208 puna nāradakūṭamhi pavivekagate jine
khīṇāsavā vītamalā samiṃsu satakoṭiyo.
209 yadā vasī mahāvīro sudassanasiluccaye
navutikoṭisahassehi pavāresi tadā muni.

To some he gave the way of the recluse, the four fruits 200
of freedom,[42] to some he offered analytic insight,
things beyond compare.[43]
To some the hero among men gave the eight 201
wonderful attainments; he gave the three knowledges
to some, and to some the six higher knowledges.[44]
In this way the great Teacher instructed the people 202
at large: the lord's teaching became widespread in
the world.
With his mighty jaw, and chest like a bull, Dipankara 203
saw many people cross over, and released them from
unhappiness.
If the great Teacher saw people even a hundred 204
thousand *yojanas* away who were capable of
awakening, he went there in an instant and brought
them to awakening.
On the first great moment of illumination, the Buddha 205
brought a hundred crore of people to awakening; at
the second, a hundred thousand.
When he taught the Dhamma in the realms of the 206
gods, he brought nine million people to awakening.
The Teacher Dipankara had three assemblies, 207
The first one was an assembly of a hundred
thousand crore.
Then, when the conqueror went into seclusion on 208
Narada Peak, a hundred crore of spotless arhats met
together.
Again, when the great hero was staying at the 209
Beautiful Peak, the conqueror was surrounded by
ninety thousand crore.

210 ahaṃ tena samayena jaṭilo uggatāpano
antalikkhamhi caraṇo pañcābhiññāsu pāragū.
211 dasavīsaṃsahassānaṃ dhammābhisamayo ahu
ekadvinnaṃ abhisamayo gaṇanāto asaṃkhiyā.
212 vitthārikaṃ bāhujaññaṃ iddhaṃ phītaṃ ahū tadā
dīpaṃkarassa bhagavato sāsanaṃ suvisodhitaṃ.
213 cattāri satasahassāni chaḷabhiññā mahiddhikā
dīpaṃkaraṃ lokaviduṃ parivārenti sabbadā.
214 ye keci tena samayena jahanti mānusam bhavaṃ
appattamānasā sekhā garahitā ‘va bhavanti te.
215 supupphitaṃ pāvacanaṃ arahantehi tādihi
khīṇāsavehi vimalehi upasobhati sadevake.
216 nagaraṃ rammavatī nāma sumedho nāma khattiyo
sumedhā nāma janiyā dīpaṃkarassa satthuno.
217 sumaṅgalo ca tisso ca ahesuṃ aggasāvakā
sāgato nām’ upaṭṭhāko dīpaṃkarassa satthuno.
218 nandā c’ eva sunandā ca ahesuṃ aggasāvikā
bodhi tassa bhagavato pipphalī ti pavuccati.
219 asītihatthamubbedho dīpaṃkaro mahāmuni
sobhati dīparukkho ‘va sālarājā ‘va phullito

At that time, I was an ascetic with matted hair, a 210
man of austere practices, sailing through the sky and
skilled in five higher knowledges.
There was a great moment of illumination for ten, 211
twenty thousands of beings: Of ones, of twos—the
illumination was beyond reckoning!
Then the pure teaching of the Bhagavan Dipankara 212
spread all around, potent and flourishing and known
to so many people.
Four hundred thousand arhats possessing the six 213
higher knowledges surrounded the Bhagavan,
Dipankara, the knower of worlds, at all times.
Anyone who was in training in the path at that time, 214
who left human existence without attaining their goal,
was certainly at fault.
The word of the Buddha irradiates the world of men 215
and the heavens with their gods, made to blossom by
arhats like these, pure and without stain.
Dipankara's city was called Ramma; his father was 216
a Kshatriya, called Sumedha, and his mother was
called Sumedha.
The two chief disciples of the Teacher Dipankara were 217
Sumangala and Tissa; his personal attendant
was Sagata.
Nanda and Sunanda were his two chief female 218
disciples, and the pipal tree was called the awakening
tree of that Bhagavan.
The great Teacher Dipankara was eighty cubits tall; 219
he shone like a magnificent deodar tree or a king
sal tree.[45]

220 satasahassaṃ vassāni āyuṃ tassa mahesino
tāvatā tiṭṭhamāno so tāresi janataṃ bahuṃ.
221 jotayitvāna saddhammaṃ santāretvā mahājanaṃ
jalitvā aggikkhandho 'va nibbuto so sasāvako.
222 sā ca iddhī so ca yaso tāni ca pādesu cakkaratanāni
sabbaṃ samantarahitaṃ nanu rittā sabbasaṃkharā 'ti.

223 dīpaṃkarassa aparena koṇḍañño nāma nāyako
anantatejo amitayaso appameyyo durāsado.

30 dīpaṃkarassa pana bhagavato aparabhāge ekaṃ asaṃkheyyaṃ atikkamitvā koṇḍañño nāma satthā udapādi. tassā 'pi tayo sāvakasannipātā ahesuṃ paṭhamasannipāte koṭisatasahassaṃ dutiye koṭisahassaṃ tatiye navutikoṭiyo. tadā bodhisatto vijitāvī nāma cakkavattī hutvā koṭisatasahassasaṃkhassa buddhapamukhassa bhikkhusaṅghassa mahādānaṃ adāsi. satthā bodhisattaṃ buddho bhavissasī ti vyākaritvā dhammaṃ desesi. so satthu dhammakathaṃ sutvā rajjaṃ niyyādetvā pabbaji. so tīṇi piṭakāni uggahetvā

The great sage lived for a hundred thousand rainy 220
seasons: as long as he remained there, he ferried great
multitudes across.
Having lit up the great Dhamma, and having steered 221
multitudes across, he blazed like a great mass of fire
and, with his disciples, entered into nibbana.
That great power, that glory, those precious jewel- 222
wheels on the feet: all of them have disappeared.
Are not all constructed things empty?"

Kondannya

"After Dipankara, there was a leader called 223
Kondannya, of immeasurable radiance and boundless
glory, limitless and unassailable."

One incalculable epoch passed after the Bhagavan Dipankara, and then a Teacher called Kondannya appeared. He also had three assemblies of disciples: in the first there were a hundred thousand crore of disciples; in the second, a thousand crore; in the third, ninety crore. At that time the Bodhisatta was called Vijitavi, a universal monarch with a hundred thousand crore.[46] He gave a magnificent feast to the order of monastics, with the Buddha at its head. The Teacher predicted, "He will become a Buddha," and gave a talk explaining the Dhamma. The Bodhisatta listened to the Dhamma and, giving up his throne, became a renouncer. He learned the three baskets of the teaching, and developed the eight attainments and five higher knowledges.[47] 30

aṭṭha samāpattiyo pañca ca abhiññāyo uppādetvā aparihīnajjhāno brahmaloke nibbatti.

31 koṇḍaññabuddhassa pana rammavatī nāma nagaraṃ sunando nāma khattiyo pitā sujātā nāma devī mātā bhaddo ca subhaddo ca dve aggasāvakā anuruddho nāma upaṭṭhāko tissā ca upatissā ca aggasāvikā sālakalyāṇi bodhi aṭṭhāsītihatthubbedhaṃ sarīraṃ vassasatasahassaṃ āyuppamāṇaṃ ahosi.

32 tassa aparabhāge ekaṃ asaṃkheyyaṃ atikkamitvā ekasmiṃ yeva kappe cattāro buddhā nibbattiṃsu: maṅgalo sumano revato sobhito ti. maṅgalassa bhagavato tayo sāvakasannipātā ahesuṃ tesu paṭhamasannipāte koṭisatasahassaṃ bhikkhū ahesuṃ dutiye koṭisahassaṃ tatiye navutikoṭiyo. vemātikabhātā kir' assa ānandakumāro navutikoṭisaṃkhāya parisāya saddhiṃ dhammasavanatthāya satthu santikaṃ agamāsi. satthā tassa ānupubbikathaṃ kathesi so saddhiṃ parisāya saha paṭisambhidāhi arahattaṃ pāpuṇi. satthā tesaṃ kulaputtānaṃ pubbacaritaṃ olokento iddhimayapattacīvarassa upanissayaṃ disvā dakkhiṇahatthaṃ pasāretvā

Without falling back from his *jhānas,* he was reborn in a Brahma heaven.

The city of the Buddha Kondannya was called Rammavati, 31
his father was a Kshatriya called Sunanda, his mother was called Queen Sujata, Baddha and Subhadda were his two chief disciples, and Anuruddha his personal attendant. His two chief female disciples were Tissa and Upatissa, and his awakening tree was a beautiful sal. His body was eighty-eight cubits tall, and his life span a hundred thousand rainy seasons.

Mangala

After Vijitavi, at the end of one incalculable epoch, in the very 32
same world cycle, four Buddhas, Mangala, Sumana, Revata, and Sobhita, appeared in one and the same eon. The Buddha Mangala had three assemblies of disciples: in the first there were a hundred thousand crore of monastics, the second a thousand crore, and the third ninety crore. They say that his stepbrother, Ananda, with a retinue of ninety thousand crore, went into the presence of the Teacher to listen to the Dhamma. The Teacher gave a talk that involved a number of stages, and along with his assembly he attained arhatship, and gained the fourfold analytic insight. The Teacher looked at the past behavior of these people of the same clan and saw a strong condition for their receiving bowls and robes made by magical power. He stretched out his right hand: "Come, monks," he said. In one moment, they were wearing robes and carrying bowls made by magical power. Endowed with

etha bhikkhavo ti āha. sabbe taṃ khaṇaṃ yeva iddhimayapattacīvaradharā saṭṭhivassatherā viya ākappasampannā hutvā satthāraṃ vanditvā parivārayiṃsu. ayam assa tatiyo sāvakasannipāto ahosi.

33 Yathā pana aññesaṃ buddhānaṃ samantā asītihatthappamāṇā yeva sarīrappabhā ahosi na evaṃ tassa pana bhagavato sarīrapabhā niccakālaṃ dasasahassilokadhātuṃ pharitvā aṭṭhāsi. rukkhapaṭhavipabbatasamuddādayo antamaso ukkhaliyādīni upādāya suvaṇṇapattapariyonaddhā viya ahesuṃ. āyuppamāṇaṃ pan' assa navutivassasahassāni ahosi. ettakaṃ kālaṃ candasuriyādayo attano pabhāya virocituṃ na sakkhiṃsu rattindivaṃ paricchedo na paññāyittha divā suriyālokena viya sattā niccaṃ buddhāloken' eva vicariṃsu sāyaṃ pupphanakusumānaṃ pāto 'va ravanasakuṇādīnañ ca vasena loko rattindivaṃ paricchedaṃ sallakkhesi. kim pana aññesaṃ buddhānaṃ ayam ānubhāvo n' atthī ti no n' atthi te hi pi ākaṃkhamānā dasasahassī vā lokadhātuṃ tato vā bhiyyo ābhāya phareyyuṃ maṅgalassa pana bhagavato pubbapatthanāvasena aññesaṃ vyāmappabhā viya sarīrappabhā niccam eva dasasahassilokadhātuṃ pharitvā aṭṭhāsi. so kira bodhisattacariyakāle vessantarasadise attabhāve ṭhito saputtadāro vaṃkapabbatasadise pabbate vasi. Ath' eko kharadāṭhiko nāma yakkho mahāpurisassa dānajj-

the carriage of elders of sixty years' experience, they paid homage to the Teacher and encircled him. This was the third assembly of disciples.

The bodily radiance of other Buddhas spreads around for 33
eighty cubits. But it was not so with him, for the radiance of this Bhagavan suffused everywhere, all around, for ten thousand world systems, all the time. Trees, the earth, the mountains and the oceans, and other things, not leaving out cooking pots and pans and things like that, appeared as though covered with a fine sheen of gold. The extent of his life was ninety thousand years. And all this time, the sun, the moon, and the stars could not shine with their own light, so the difference between night and day could not be made out. During the day, people went about in the radiance of the Buddha as if in the perpetual light of the sun; by night, people could tell the difference between night and day only by the flowers and blossoms that come out in the evening, and by the cries of the birds and other creatures who sing at dawn. "But don't other Buddhas possess this power?" someone might ask. It's not that they don't. If they wished it, they could pervade ten thousand world systems with their radiance. But through the power of a vow made by him long ago, the light of the Bhagavan Mangala constantly suffused ten thousand worlds, just as the light of the others constantly suffused the span of both arms stretched out. The story goes that when he was doing the work of a Bodhisatta, in an existence that corresponded to the Vessantara existence, he lived with his wife and children on a mountain just like the Vanka mountain of "The Vessantara Jataka."[48] One

hāsayataṃ sutvā brāhmaṇavaṇṇena upasaṃkamitvā mahāsattaṃ dve dārake yāci. mahāsatto dadāmi brāhmaṇassa puttake ti haṭṭhapahaṭṭho udakapariyantaṃ paṭhaviṃ kampento dve pi dārake adāsi. yakkho caṅkamanakoṭiyaṃ ālambanaphalakaṃ nissāya ṭhatvā passantass' eva mahāsattassa mūlakalāpaṃ viya dārake khādi. mahāpurisassa yakkhaṃ oloketvā mukhaṃvivaṭamatte[13] aggijālā viya lohitadhāraṃ uggiramānaṃ tassa mukhaṃ disvā 'pi kesaggamattam pi domanassaṃ na uppajji sudinnaṃ vata me dānan ti cintayato pan' assa sarīre mahantaṃ pītisomanassaṃ udapādi. so imassa me nissandena anāgate iminā 'va nīhārena rasmiyo nikkhamantū 'ti patthanaṃ akāsi. tassa taṃ patthanaṃ nissāya buddhabhūtassa sarīrato rasmiyo nikkhamitvā ettakaṃ ṭhānaṃ phariṃsu. aparam pi 'ssa pubbacaritaṃ atthi: so kira bodhisattakāle ekassa buddhassa cetiyaṃ disvā imassa buddhassa mayā jīvitaṃ pariccajituṃ vaṭṭatī ti daṇḍakadīpikāveṭhananiyāmena sakalasarīraṃ veṭhāpetvā ratanamakulaṃ satasahassagghaṇakaṃ suvaṇṇapātiṃ sappissa pūrāpetvā tattha sahassaṃ vaṭṭiyo jāletvā taṃ sīsenādāya sakalasarīraṃ jālāpetvā cetiyaṃ padakkhiṇaṃ karonto sakalarattiṃ vītināmesi evaṃ yāva aruṇuggamanā vāyamantassa pi 'ssa lomakūpamattam pi usumaṃ na gaṇhi

day, a bad spirit called Long Fang, hearing about the great man's predisposition to generosity, approached the Great Being disguised as a Brahman and asked for his two children. The Great Being said, "I give my children to the Brahman." Overjoyed, he gave up both children, and the earth, surrounded by the oceans, trembled. The bad spirit, standing by a plank propped up by the walking area, gobbled the two children up like a bundle of roots. As he looked on, not the slightest bit of grief, even so much as a hair tip, arose in the Great Being. As soon as the spirit's mouth had opened, he saw him gushing out streams of blood, like flames of fire; but grief did not arise in him. "This gift was a good gift to give," he said. And as he reflected on this, great joy and contentment welled up in his body.

The Bodhisatta made his vow. "By the merit of this act, may rays emanate from me in this way." Because of this resolution, made by the sapling of a Buddha, rays emanated from him and suffused such a large area.

But there was one more deed done in an earlier existence. They say that while a bodhisatta, he saw a shrine housing relics of an earlier Buddha. He exclaimed: "It would be right for me to offer up my life for this Buddha." So, he wrapped up his whole body as if he were making a torch. He filled a golden bowl with designs on it of flower buds worked in jewels and worth a hundred thousand, and lit a thousand wicks in it. He set fire to his whole body and passed the whole night walking in circumambulation around the shrine, with the bowl on his head. Even though he had been making this effort all night until dawn, not even the root of a hair was singed, but it was as if he were enclosed in the calyx of a lotus.

padumagabbhaṃ paviṭṭhakālo viya ahosi dhammo hi nām' esa attānaṃ rakkhantaṃ rakkhati tenāhā bhagavā:

224 dhammo have rakkhati dhammacāriṃ
dhammo suciṇṇo sukham āvahāti
es' ānisaṃso dhamme suciṇṇe:
na duggatiṃ gacchati dhammacārī ti.

34 imassā 'pi kammassa nissandena tassa bhagavato sarīrobhāso dasasahassilokadhātuṃ pharitvā aṭṭhāsi. tadā amhākaṃ bodhisatto suruci nāma brāhmaṇo hutvā satthāraṃ nimantessāmī ti upasaṃkamitvā madhuradhammakathaṃ sutvā sve mayhaṃ bhikkhaṃ gaṇhatha bhante ti āha. brāhmaṇa kittakehi te bhikkhūhi attho ti. kittakā pana vo bhante parivārabhikkhū ti āha. tadā satthu paṭhamasannipāto yeva hoti tasmā koṭisatasahassan ti āha. bhante sabbehi pi saddhiṃ mayhaṃ gehe bhikkhaṃ gaṇhathā ti. satthā adhivāsesi. brāhmaṇo svātanāya nimantetvā gehaṃ gacchanto cintesi: ahaṃ ettakānaṃ bhikkhūnaṃ yāgubhattavatthādīni dātuṃ no na sakkomi nisīdanaṭṭhānaṃ pana kathaṃ bhavissatī ti. tassa sā cintā caturāsītiyojanasahassamatthake ṭhitassa devarañño paṇḍukambalasilāsanassa uṇhabhāvaṃ janesi. sakko ko nu kho maṃ imasmā ṭhānā cāvetukāmo ti dibbacakkhunā olokento mahāpurisaṃ disvā suruci brāhmaṇo buddhapamukhaṃ bhikkhusaṅghaṃ nimantetvā nisīdanaṭṭhānatthāya cintesi mayā 'pi tattha gantvā puññakoṭṭhāsaṃ gahetuṃ vaṭṭatī ti vaḍḍhakivaṇṇaṃ nimminitvā vāsipharasuhattho mahāsattassa purato pātur ahosi

This is how the Dhamma guards the person who guards it.

Here, the Bhagavan says this:

The Dhamma guards the one who lives in the 224
Dhamma, the Dhamma, followed well, brings
happiness in its train. This reward follows those
who live in the Dhamma: And the one who lives in
the Dhamma does not meet misfortune.[49]

Suruci

So, as the result of that, the bodily radiance of that Bhagavan 34
remained, suffusing the ten thousand world systems all the time. At that time, our Bodhisatta was born as the Brahman Suruci, and, approaching him, heard the Teacher giving a talk of mellow sweetness.

"I will invite him over," he thought."Sir, please take a meal with me."

The Buddha replied: "Brahman, how many monastics would you like?"

—"Sir, how many are there in your retinue?"

At that time there was only the first assembly of disciples, so he replied, "a hundred thousand crore."

—"Sir, please come for a meal at my house, with all of them."

The Teacher accepted the invitation. The Brahman, now he had invited them, thought on his way home: "It is not that I won't be able to give rice gruel, food, clothes, and other gifts to so many monastics. But how will there be space for them all to sit down?"

Now, this thought of his caused the white marble throne

atthi nu kho kassaci bhatiyā kattabban ti āha. mahāpuriso disvā kiṃ kammaṃ karissasī ti āha. mama ajānanasippaṃ nāma n' atthi gehaṃ vā maṇḍapaṃ vā yo yaṃ kāreti tassa taṃ kātuṃ jānāmī ti. tena hi mayhaṃ kammaṃ atthī ti. kiṃ ayyā ti svātanāya me koṭisatasahassabhikkhū nimantitā tesaṃ nisīdanamaṇḍapaṃ karissasī ti. ahaṃ nāma kareyyaṃ sace me bhatiṃ dātuṃ sakkhissathā ti. sakkhissāmi tātā ti. sādhu karissāmī ti gantvā ekaṃ padesaṃ olokesi. dvādasaterasayojanappamāṇo padeso kasiṇamaṇḍalaṃ viya samatalo ahosi. so ettake ṭhāne sattaratanamayo maṇḍapo uṭṭhahatū ti cintetvā olokesi tāvad eva puthaviṃ bhinditvā maṇḍapo uṭṭhahi. tassa sovaṇṇamayesu thambhesu rajata-

of King Sakka, the king of the gods, situated eighty-four thousand *yojanas* above, to become hot.[50] Then, wondering, "Who is it that wants me to leave this place?" he saw the Great Being. So, he thought: "The Brahman Suruci has invited the order of monastics, with the Buddha at its head, to his place, and is wondering about the space to seat them. It is good for me to go there and get a share of this merit!" He then disguised himself as a builder and, carrying an adze and an ax, appeared in front of the Great Being.

He asked: "Has anyone got work to be done for a wage?"

The Great Being saw him and asked: "What work do you do?"

—"Oh, there is no skill I can't put my hand to. If anyone has a house or a pavilion that needs building, I'm the one with the know-how to get it built for him!"

—"If that is the case, I have a job for you."

—"What is it?"

—"I have invited a hundred thousand crore of monastics for tomorrow: you'd make a pavilion for them to sit in."

—"I'll certainly build that . . . if you are you able to pay me."

—"My friend, that I can do."

"All right then," said the builder, and he went and did a survey of the site. Now, there was an area twelve or thirteen *yojanas* long that was completely flat, just like the circle of a meditation disk. He looked intently at that spot and thought: "Let a pavilion, made of the seven precious jewels, be constructed right here."

mayā ghaṭakā ahesuṃ rajatamayesu sovaṇṇamayā maṇitthambhesu pāvālamayā pavālatthambhesu maṇimayā sattaratanamayesu sattaratanamayā ’va ghaṭakā ahesuṃ. tato maṇḍapassa antarantare kiṃkiṇikajālaṃ olambatū ti olokesi. saha olokanen’ eva jālaṃ olambi yassa mandavāteritassa pañcaṅgikass’ eva turiyassa madhurasaddo niggacchati dibbasaṅgītivattanakālo viya hoti. antarā gandhadāmamālādāmāni olambantū ti cintesi dāmāni olambiṃsu. koṭisatasahassasaṃkhānaṃ bhikkhūnaṃ āsanāni ca ādhārakāni ca paṭhaviṃ bhinditvā uṭṭhahantū ti cintesi tāvad eva uṭṭhahiṃsu. koṇe koṇe ekekā udakacāṭiyo uṭṭhahantū ti cintesi udakacāṭiyo uṭṭhahiṃsu. ettakaṃ māpetvā brāhmaṇassa santikaṃ gantvā ehi ayya tava maṇḍapaṃ oloketvā mayhaṃ bhatiṃ dehī ti āha. mahāpuriso gantvā maṇḍapaṃ olokesi olokentass’ eva sakalasarīraṃ pañcavaṇṇāya pītiyā nirantaraṃ phuṭaṃ ahosi. ath’ assa maṇḍapaṃ oloketvā etad ahosi: n’āyaṃ maṇḍapo manussabhūtena kato mayhaṃ pana ajjhāsayaṃ mayhaṃ guṇaṃ āgamma addhā sakkabhavanaṃ uṇhaṃ ahosi tato sakkena devaraññā ayaṃ maṇḍapo kārito bhavissati na kho pana me yuttaṃ evarūpe maṇḍape ekadivasaṃ yeva dānaṃ dātuṃ sattāhaṃ dassāmī ti cintesi. bāhirakadānam hi kittakam pi samānaṃ bodhisattānaṃ tuṭṭhiṃ kātuṃ na sakkoti alaṃkatasīsam pana chinditvā añjitākkhīni uppāṭetvā hadayamaṃsaṃ vā ubbattetvā dinnakāle bodhisattānaṃ cāgaṃ nissāya tuṭṭhi nāma hoti. amhākam pi hi bodhisattassa sivijātake devasikaṃ pañcakahāpaṇammaṇāni vissajjetvā catusu dvāresu majjhe nagare dānaṃ dentassa taṃ dānaṃ cāgatuṭṭhiṃ uppādetuṃ nāsakkhi yadā pan’ assa brāhmaṇavaṇṇena āgantvā sakko devarājā akkhīni yāci tadā tāni uppāṭetvā dadamānass’ eva hāso uppajji kesaggamat-

And in one moment, a pavilion emerged, breaking its way through the earth.

On its golden pillars there were silver capitals, and on its silver pillars golden capitals. On jeweled pillars there were coral capitals, and on coral pillars jeweled capitals. On pillars of the seven kinds of jewel, there were capitals of seven kinds of jewel. Then he looked again. "Let trails of musically jingling bells hang around the pavilion." And just as he was looking, the trails hung there. Their musical tinkling, as they were stirred by the gentle breeze, was like the different instruments in a quintet, or a time when heavenly choirs sing together. And again, he thought: "Let perfumed garlands of flowers hang there too."

And then he pondered more: "Let seats and supports for a hundred thousand crore of monastics appear, breaking through the earth!" Sure enough, they arose. Then he thought, "Let water jars appear at all corners"—and they appeared. Once he had created all of this, he went to the Brahman, and said: "Right, sir. Have a look at your pavilion and pay me your fee." The Great Being went and looked at the pavilion. And as he did so, the five kinds of joy surged up, flowing through him without a break.[51]

As he looked at the hall, he thought: "This pavilion was not created by a human being. Because of my determination today, and my virtue, Sakka's abode became hot, and so this pavilion could have been made by the king of the gods himself. I should not give alms in this pavilion just for one day. I should do it for seven."

However much an external gift may come to, it fails to give satisfaction to bodhisattas: they only feel joy in their

taṃ pi cittaṃ aññathattaṃ n'āhosi. evaṃ dānaṃ nissāya bodhisattānaṃ titti nāma n' atthi. tasmā so 'pi mahāpuriso sattāhaṃ mayā koṭisatasahassasaṃkhānaṃ bhikkhūnaṃ dānaṃ dātuṃ vaṭṭatī ti cintetvā tasmiṃ maṇḍape nisīdāpetvā sattāhaṃ gavapānaṃ nāma dānaṃ adāsi. gavapānan ti mahante mahante kolambe khīrassa pūretvā uddhane āropetvā ghanapākapakke khīre thoke taṇḍule pakkhipitvā pakkaṃ madhusakkaracuṇṇasappīhi abhisaṃkhaṭabhojanaṃ vuccati. manussā yeva pana parivisituṃ n'āsakkhiṃsu devā 'pi ekantarikā hutvā parivisiṃsu. dvādasaterasayojanappamāṇaṭṭhānam pi bhikkhū gaṇhituṃ na-ppahosi yeva te pana bhikkhū attano attano ānubhāvena nisīdiṃsu. pariyosānadivase sabbabhikkhūnaṃ pattāni dhovāpetvā bhesajjatthāya sappinavanītamadhuphāṇitādīni pūretvā ticīvarehi saddhiṃ adāsi. saṅghanavakabhikkhunā laddhacīvarasāṭakā satasahassagghanakā ahesuṃ. satthā anumodanaṃ karonto ayaṃ puriso evarūpaṃ mahādānaṃ adāsi ko nu kho bhavissatī ti upadhārento anāgate kappasatasahassādhikānaṃ dvinnaṃ asaṃkheyyānaṃ matthake gotamo nāma buddho bhavissa tī ti disvā mahāpurisaṃ āmantetvā tvaṃ ettakaṃ nāma kālaṃ atikkamitvā gotamo nāma buddho bhavissasī ti vyākāsi. mahāpuriso vyākaraṇaṃ sutvā ahaṃ kira buddho

offering things up when they cut off their adorned head, or pluck out their collyrium-painted eyes, or tear off the flesh of their heart and give them away. Even when our Bodhisatta, born as Sivi, gave alms in the middle of his city, spending five *amuṇas* of *kahāpanas* every day, this generosity could not give him the satisfaction of letting go completely.[52] When Sakka, king of the gods, arrived disguised as a Brahman and pleaded for Sivi's eyes, only then did joy arise in him, as he pulled them out and gave them to him freely. No regret, not even as much as the tip of a hair, arose for him.

In this way, there is no gift that is enough for a Bodhisatta.

So, the Bodhisatta thought he should give alms for seven days, and he entertained the monastics for a week, giving them the alms called the "cow-milk rice pudding." A cow-milk rice pudding is a dish made of milk in large vessels, to which are added a little rice, some heated honey, crushed palm sugar, and some clarified butter; it simmers slowly over the hearth until it is a thick paste: it is called a cow-milk rice pudding. Humans alone could not wait on them: rather, the gods mingled with them and served the guests. The space of twelve or thirteen *yojanas* was not enough to fit in all of the monastics, but those monastics just seated themselves, each by his own innate power.

On the last day, the Bodhisatta had the bowls of all the monastics washed and he filled them up with clarified and fresh butter, honey, molasses, and other foods to be used as medicines, and handed them back to them, with the three robes. The cloth for the robes of the most junior novices and monastics was worth a hundred thousand.

bhavissāmi ko me gharāvāsena attho pabbajissāmī ti cintetvā tathārūpaṃ sampattiṃ kheḷapiṇḍaṃ viya pahāya satthu santike pabbaji pabbajitvā buddhavacanaṃ uggahetvā abhiññā ca samāpattiyo ca nibbattetvā āyupariyosāne brahmaloke nibbatti.

35 maṅgalassa pana bhagavato nagaraṃ uttaraṃ nāma ahosi pitā 'pi uttaro nāma khattiyo mātā 'pi uttarā nāma sudevo ca dhammaseno ca dve aggasāvakā pālito nāma upaṭṭhāko sīvalī ca asokā ca dve aggasāvikā nāgarukkho bodhi aṭṭhāsītihatthubbedhaṃ sarīraṃ ahosi. navutivassasahassāni ṭhatvā parinibbute pana tasmiṃ ekappahāren' eva dasacakkavāḷasahassāni ekandhakārāni ahesuṃ sabbacakkavāḷesu manussānaṃ mahantaṃ ārodanaparidevanaṃ ahosi.

225 koṇḍaññassa aparena maṅgalo nāma nāyako
tamaṃ loke nihantvāna dhammokkam abhidhārayī ti.

When the Teacher gave his blessings for this merit, he wondered: "This man has hosted such a magnificent feast: what is he going to be in a future lifetime?"

He saw clearly: "In two incalculable epochs and a hundred thousand eons from now, this man will be a Buddha, called Gotama." He addressed the Great Being.

"After the elapse of such and such a period, you are going to be a Buddha." The Great Being heard this declaration and thought: "So, they say I am going to be a Buddha. What have I to do with a householder's life? I'll take the going forth!" He gave up all that wealth, as if it were just a glob of spittle, and took ordination with the Teacher. Grasping the words of the Buddha, he developed the higher knowledges, and at the end of his life he was reborn in a Brahma realm.

The Bhagavan Mangala's city was called Uttara. His father 35
was the Kshatriya Uttara, and his mother, Uttara. His two chief disciples were Sudeva and Dhammasena. His attendant monk was Palita, his two chief female disciples, Sivali and Asoka, and his awakening tree, the ironwood tree. His body was ninety cubits high. When he entered into nibbana after living for ninety thousand years, in one blow all the ten thousand world systems went into darkness, and in all the worlds there was great crying and grief among human beings.

> After Kondannya there was a leader, Mangala. He 225
> held the torch of truth high, dispelling darkness in
> the world.

36 evaṃ dasasahassilokadhātuṃ andhakāraṃ katvā parinibbutassa bhagavato aparabhāge sumano nāma satthā udapādi. tassā 'pi tayo sāvakasannipātā paṭhamasannipāte koṭisatasahassa bhikkhū ahesuṃ dutiye kañcanapabbatamhi navutikoṭisatasahassāni tatiye asītikoṭisatasahassāni. tadā mahāsatto atulo nāma nāgarājā ahosi mahiddhiko mahānubhāvo. so buddho uppanno ti sutvā ñātisaṅghaparivuto nāgabhavanā nikkhamitvā koṭisatasahassabhikkhuparivārassa tassa bhagavato dibbaturiyehi upahāraṃ kāretvā mahādānaṃ datvā paccekaṃ dussayugāni datvā saraṇesu patiṭṭhāsi. so 'pi naṃ satthā anāgate buddho bhavissasī ti vyākāsi. tassa bhagavato nagaraṃ khemaṃ nāma ahosi sudatto nāma rājā pitā sirimā nāma mātā saraṇo ca bhāvitatto ca aggasāvakā udeno nām' upaṭṭhāko soṇā ca upasoṇā ca aggasāvikā nāgarukkho ca bodhi navutihatthubbedhaṃ sarīraṃ navuti yeva vassasahassāni āyuppamāṇaṃ ahosī ti.

226 maṅgalassa aparena sumano nāma nāyako
sabbadhammehi asamo sabbasattānam uttamo.

37 tassa aparabhāge revato nāma satthā udapādi. tassā 'pi tayo sāvakasannipātā paṭhamasannipāte gaṇanā nāma n' atthi dutiye koṭisatasahassaṃ bhikkhū ahesuṃ tathā tatiye. tadā

Sumana

After the Bhagavan's entrance into nibbana sent the ten thousand world systems into darkness, a Teacher called Sumana arose in the world. And he too had three assemblies: one of a hundred thousand crore of monastics, one of ninety hundred thousand at the golden mountain, and a third of eighty hundred thousand crore. At that time, the Great Being was called Atula. He was a naga king of great psychic power and splendor. He heard that a Buddha had arisen. So, he set out from the naga realm with a great retinue from his clan. He made offerings of heavenly music for the Buddha, whose retinue was a hundred thousand crore of monastics, and gave a magnificent feast, as well as offering each monk a pair of robes and establishing himself in the five precepts. The Teacher foretold, "This one will be a Buddha in the future." 36

The city of that Bhagavan was called Khema. His father was a king called Sudatta and his mother was called Sirima. His two chief disciples were Sarana and Bhavittata. His attendant monk was called Udena, his two chief female disciples, Sona and Upasona, and his awakening tree was the ironwood tree. His body was ninety cubits tall, and his life span was ninety thousand years.

> After Mangala, there was a leader called Sumana. He 226
> was unparalleled in all his teachings, the highest of all beings.

After some time, there was a Teacher called Revata. He also 37
had three assemblies: the first was quite beyond reckoning; the second had a hundred thousand crore of monastics, and

bodhisatto atidevo nāma brāhmaṇo hutvā satthu dhammadesanaṃ sutvā saraṇesu patiṭṭhāya sirasi añjaliṃ ṭhapetvā tassa satthuno kilesappahāne vaṇṇaṃ vatvā uttarāsaṃgena pūjaṃ akāsi. so 'pi naṃ buddho bhavissasī ti vyākāsi. tassa pana bhagavato nagaraṃ sudhaññavatī nāma ahosi pitā vipulo nāma khattiyo mātā vipulā nāma varuṇo ca brahmadevo ca aggasāvakā sambhavo nāma upaṭṭhāko bhaddā ca subhaddā ca aggasāvikā nāgarukkho ca bodhi sarīraṃ asītihatthubbedhaṃ ahosi āyuṃ saṭṭhivassasahassānī ti.

227 sumanassa aparena revato nāma nāyako
anūpamo asadiso atulo uttamo jino ti.

38 tassa aparabhāge sobhito nāma satthā udapādi. tassā 'pi tayo sāvakasannipātā paṭhamasannipāte koṭisataṃ bhikkhū ahesuṃ dutiye navutikoṭiyo tatiye asītikoṭiyo. tadā bodhisatto ajito nāma brāhmaṇo hutvā satthu dhammadesanaṃ sutvā saraṇesu patiṭṭhāya buddhapamukhassa bhikkhusaṅghassa mahādānaṃ adāsi. so 'pi naṃ buddho bhavissasī ti vyākāsi. tassa pana bhagavato nagaraṃ sudhammaṃ nāma ahosi pitā sudhammo nāma rājā mātā 'pi sudhammā nāma asamo ca sunetto ca aggasāvakā anomo nāma upaṭṭhāko nakulā ca sujātā ca aggasāvikā nāgarukkho ca bodhi

the third was the same. At that time, the Bodhisatta was a Brahman called Atideva. He heard the Teacher giving a talk on the Dhamma and took refuge.[53] With his palms held together above his head, he praised the Teacher's overcoming of the defilements, and made him an offering of an outer garment. He also said, "You will become a Buddha." The city of that Bhagavan was called Sudhannavati, his father was a Kshatriya called Vipula and his mother, Vipula. Varuna and Subhaddha were his chief disciples, Sambhava was his personal attendant, Bhadda and Subhadda his chief female disciples, and his awakening tree was the ironwood tree. His body was eighty cubits tall, and his life span was sixty thousand years.

> After Sumana there was a leader called Revata. He 227
> had no parallel; no one was his equal and he was the
> highest conqueror.

After some time there arose a Teacher in the world called 38
Sobhita. There were three assemblies for him too: the first was of a hundred crore of monastics, his second of ninety, and his third of eighty. At that time the Bodhisatta was a Brahman called Ajita. He heard the Teacher giving a talk on the Dhamma and went for refuge. He gave a magnificent meal to the Sangha of monastics, with the Buddha at its head. He too said, "You will become a Buddha." The city of the Bhagavan was called Sudhamma, his father was a king, called Sudhamma, and his mother was called Sudhamma. The chief disciples were called Asama and Sunetto, his personal attendant was called Anoma. Nakula and Sujata were his chief female disciples, and his awakening tree was

aṭṭhapaññāsahatthubbedhaṃ sarīraṃ ahosi navutivassasahassāni āyuppamāṇan ti.

228 revatassa aparena sobhito nāma nāyako
samāhito santacitto asamo appaṭipuggalo ti.

39 tassa aparabhāge ekaṃ asaṃkheyyaṃ atikkamitvā ekasmiṃ kappe tayo buddhā nibbattiṃsu: anomadassī padumo nārado ti. anomadassissa bhagavato tayo sāvakasannipātā paṭhame aṭṭha bhikkhusatasahassāni ahesuṃ dutiye satta tatiye cha. tadā bodhisatto eko yakkhasenāpati ahosi mahiddhiko mahānubhāvo anekakoṭi. satasahassānaṃ yakkhānaṃ adhipati. so buddho uppanno ti sutvā āgantvā buddhapamukhassa saṅghassa mahādānaṃ adāsi. satthā 'pi naṃ anāgate buddho bhavissasī ti vyākāsi. anomadassissa pana bhagavato candavatī nāma nagaraṃ ahosi yasavā nāma rājā pitā yasodharā nāma mātā nisabho ca anomo ca aggasāvakā varuṇo nāma upaṭṭhāko sundarī ca sumanā ca aggasāvikā ajjunarukkho bodhi sarīraṃ aṭṭhapaññāsahatthubbedhaṃ ahosi vassasatasahassaṃ āyū ti.

229 sobhitassa aparena sambuddho dipaduttamo
anomadassī amitayaso tejasiṃ[14] duratikkamo ti.

the ironwood tree. His body was fifty-eight cubits. His life span was ninety thousand years.

> After Revata there was a leader called Sobhita. 228
> Evenly settled, tranquil in heart, unparalleled, he had no rival.

After him and after one incalculable epoch had passed, three 39
Buddhas, called Anomadassi, Paduma, and Narada appeared in the very same eon. The Bhagavan Anomadassi had three assemblies of disciples: in the first there were eight hundred thousand monastics; in the second, seven hundred thousand; and in the third, six hundred thousand. At that time the Bodhisatta was a general of the spirits, of great psychic power and splendor, commander of a hundred thousand crore of spirits.[54]

He heard that a Buddha had come into being and went and gave a magnificent feast to the Sangha, with the Buddha at its head. Yet again, the Teacher said: "You will become a Buddha." The city of the Bhagavan Anomadassi was called Candavati, his father was a king, Yasava, his mother Yasodhara. His chief disciples were called Nisabha and Anoma, his personal attendant, Varuna, and his chief female disciples were called Sundari and Sumana. His awakening tree was the arjun. His body was fifty-eight cubits tall, and his life span a hundred thousand years.

> After Sobhita there was the completely awakened 229
> Buddha Anomadassi, of infinite fame, incandescent
> and unsurpassed.

40 tassa aparabhāge padumo nāma satthā udapādi. tassā ’pi tayo sāvakasannipātā paṭhamasannipāte koṭisatasahassaṃ bhikkhū ahesuṃ dutiye tīṇi satasahassāni tatiye agāmake araññe mahāvanasaṇḍavāsīnaṃ bhikkhūnaṃ dve satasahassāni. tadā tathāgate tasmiṃ vanasaṇḍe vasante bodhisatto sīho hutvā satthāraṃ nirodhasamāpattiṃ samāpannaṃ disvā pasannacitto vanditvā padakkhiṇaṃ katvā pītisomanassajāto tikkhattuṃ sīhanādaṃ naditvā sattāhaṃ buddhārammaṇaṃ pītiṃ avijahitvā pītisukhen’ eva gocarāya apakkamitvā jīvitapariccāgaṃ katvā payirupāsamāno aṭṭhāsi. satthā sattāhaccayena nirodhā vuṭṭhito sīhaṃ oloketvā bhikkhusaṅghe pi cittaṃ pasādetvā saṅghaṃ vandissatī ti bhikkhusaṅgho āgacchatū ti cintesi. bhikkhū tāvad eva āgamiṃsu. sīho saṅghe cittaṃ pasādesi. satthā tassa manaṃ oloketvā anāgate buddho bhavissatī ti vyākāsi. padumassa pana bhagavato campakaṃ nāma nagaraṃ ahosi padumo nāma rājā pitā mātā ’pi asamā nāma sālo ca upasālo ca aggasāvakā varuṇo nām’ upaṭṭhāko rāmā ca uparāmā ca aggasāvikā soṇarukkho nāma bodhi aṭṭhapaññāsahatthubbedhaṃ sarīraṃ ahosi āyuṃ vassasatasahassan ti.

230 anomadassissa aparena sambuddho dipaduttamo
padumo nāma nāmena asamo appaṭipuggalo ti.

After him there appeared a Teacher called Paduma (Lotus). 40
He also had three assemblies: the first was of a hundred thousand crore of monastics; the second, three hundred thousand; and the third, two hundred thousand monastics, who lived in the great jungle of the forest, far from villages. At that time, when the Tathagata was living in that dense forest, the Bodhisatta was a lion. His heart was filled with faith when he saw the Teacher while he was attaining the *jhāna* of cessation.[55] He paid homage, circling him in reverence, and as joy and happiness welled up in him, he roared his lion's roar three times. He remained there, and for seven days he did not keep away from the joy and happiness of having the Buddha as the object of his mind. He sacrificed his own life and did not go after prey.

After seven days the Teacher emerged from his attainment and looked at the lion. "He will feel faith in his heart when he sees the Sangha. Let them come," he thought. Sure enough, the monastics arrived, and the lion's heart filled with faith in the Sangha. The Teacher considered his mind: "He will be a Buddha," he said. The city of the Bhagavan Paduma was called Champaka, Paduma the king was his father, and his mother was called Asama. Sala and Upasala were the chief disciples, Varuna, his personal attendant, Rama and Uparama were the chief female disciples. The awakening tree was the crimson sona. His body was fifty-eight cubits tall, and his life span was one hundred thousand years.

> After Anomadassi was the completely awakened 230
> Buddha, supreme among men. He was called Paduma,
> and he was without an equal, and without a rival.

41 tassa aparabhāge nārado nāma satthā udapādi. tassā ’pi tayo sāvakasannipātā paṭhamasannipāte koṭisatasahassabhikkhū ahesuṃ dutiye navutikoṭisatasahassāni tatiye asītikoṭisatasahassāni. tadā bodhisatto isipabbajjaṃ pabbajitvā pañcasu abhiññāsu aṭṭhasu ca samāpattīsu vasī hutvā buddhapamukhassa saṅghassa mahādānaṃ datvā lohitacandanena pūjaṃ akāsi. so ’pi taṃ anāgate buddho bhavissasī ti vyākāsi. tassa bhagavato dhaññavatī nāma nagaraṃ ahosi sumedho nāma khattiyo pitā anomā nāma mātā bhaddasālo ca jitamitto ca aggasāvakā vāseṭṭho nām’ upaṭṭhāko uttarā ca phagguṇī ca aggasāvikā mahāsoṇarukkho nāma bodhi sarīraṃ aṭṭhāsītihatthubbedhaṃ ahosi navutivassasahassāni āyū ti.

231 padumassa aparena sambuddho dipaduttamo
nārado nāma nāmena asamo appaṭipuggalo ti.

42 nāradabuddhassa aparabhāge ito satasahassakappamatthake ekasmiṃ kappe eko ’va padumuttarabuddho nāma udapādi. tassā ’pi tayo sāvakasannipātā paṭhame koṭisatasahassaṃ bhikkhū ahesuṃ dutiye vebhārapabbate navutikoṭisahassāni tatiye asītikoṭisahassāni. tadā bodhisatto jaṭilo nāma māhāraṭṭhiyo hutvā buddhapamukhassa saṅghassa cīvaradānaṃ adāsi. So pi naṃ anāgate buddho bhavissasī ti vyākāsi. padumuttarassa pana bhagavato

After that a Teacher called Narada arose. He also had three assemblies of disciples: the first of a hundred thousand crore of monastics, the second of ninety hundred thousand crore of monastics, and the third of eighty hundred thousand crore. At that time the Bodhisatta had taken the going forth, becoming a seer, with the five higher knowledges and the eight attainments. He gave a magnificent feast to the Sangha, headed by the Buddha, and made an offering of red sandalwood. Narada also foretold: "You will become a Buddha." The city of this Bhagavan was called Dhannavati, his father was a Kshatriya, Sudeva, and his mother was called Anoma. His chief disciples were Bhaddasala and Jitamitta, his personal attendant, Vasettha, and his chief female disciples were Rama and Surama. His awakening tree was the sona tree. His body was eighty-eight cubits tall and his life span a nighty thousand years. 41

> After Anomadassi there was the completely awakened 231
> one Narada, the chief of men, unparalleled and
> without a rival.

After the Buddha Narada, during an eon a hundred thousand eons before ours, there appeared only one Buddha, Padumuttara. He too had three assemblies, the first of a hundred thousand crore of monastics; the second, on the Vebhara mountain, of ninety thousand crore; and the third, eighty thousand crore. At that time the Bodhisatta was born as a matted-hair ascetic called Maharatthiya. He gave a donation of robes to the Sangha, with the Buddha at its head. Padumuttara too predicted, "You will become a Buddha." At the time of the Bhagavan Padumuttara there were no 42

kāle titthiyā n' āhesuṃ sabbe devamanussā buddham eva saraṇaṃ agamaṃsu. tassa nagaraṃ haṃsavatī nāma ahosi pitā ānando nāma khattiyo mātā sujātā nāma devalo ca sujāto ca aggasāvakā sumano nāma upaṭṭhāko amitā ca asamā ca aggasāvikā sālarukkho ca bodhi sarīraṃ aṭṭhāsītihatthubbedhaṃ ahosi sarīrappabhā samantato dvādasa yojanāni gaṇhi vassasatasahassaṃ āyuṃ

232 nāradassa aparena sambuddho dipaduttamo
padumuttaro nāma jino akkhobbho sāgarūpamo ti.

43 tassa aparabhāge tiṃsakappasahassāni atikkamitvā sumedho ca sujāto cā ti ekasmiṃ kappe dve buddhā nibbattiṃsu. sumedhassā 'pi tayo sāvakasannipātā paṭhamasannipāte sudassananagare koṭisataṃ khīṇāsavā ahesuṃ dutiye navutikoṭiyo tatiye asītikoṭiyo. tadā bodhisatto uttaro nāma māṇavo hutvā nidahitvā ṭhapitaṃ yeva asītikoṭidhanaṃ vissajjetvā buddhapamukhassa saṅghassa mahādānaṃ datvā dhammaṃ sutvā saraṇesu patiṭṭhāya nikkhamitvā pabbaji. so 'pi naṃ anāgate buddho bhavissasī ti vyākāsi.

44 sumedhassa bhagavato sudassanaṃ nāma nagaraṃ ahosi sudatto nāma rājā pitā matā 'pi sudattā nāma saraṇo ca sabbakāmo ca dve aggasāvakā sāgaro nāma upaṭṭhāko rāmā ca surāmā ca dve aggasāvikā mahānīparukkho bodhi sarīraṃ

others to take people across the water: so all the gods and humans took refuge in the Buddha alone. And his city was called Hamsavati, his father was a noble called Ananda, and his mother was called Sujata. His two chief disciples were Devala and Sujata, his personal attendant was Sumana, and his two chief female disciples were Amita and Asama. His awakening tree was a sal. His body was eighty-eight cubits in height. His bodily radiance spread around for twelve *yojanas,* and his life span was a hundred thousand years.

> After Narada there was the completely awakened 232
> one Padumuttara, a chief of men, a conqueror,
> untroubled, like the great ocean.

After him thirty thousand eons passed. And there were 43
two Buddhas in this eon, Sumedha and Sujata. Sumedha had three assemblies: the first, in the Beautiful City, had a hundred crore of arhats; the second, ninety crore of arhats; and the third, eighty crore. At that time the Bodhisatta took rebirth as a Brahman youth called Uttara.

He had laid aside eighty crore and spent some money on a magnificent feast for the Sangha, with the Buddha as its head. When he heard a talk on the Dhamma, he established himself in the precepts and renounced to take the going forth. Sumedha also foretold: "You will become a Buddha."

The city of the Bhagavan Sumedha was called Sudassana, 44
his father was a king, Sudatta; his mother, Sudatta; and his two chief disciples were Sarana and Sabbakama. Sagara was the name of his personal attendant, and his two chief female disciples were Rama and Surama. His awakening tree was

aṭṭhāsītihatthubbedhaṃ ahosi āyuṃ navutivassasahassāni.

233 padumuttarassa aparena sumedho nāma nāyako
durāsado uggatejo sabbalokuttamo munī ti.

45 tassa aparabhāge sujāto nāma satthā udapādi. tassā 'pi tayo sāvakasannipātā paṭhamasannipāte saṭṭhibhikkhusahassāni ahesuṃ dutiye paññāsaṃ tatiye cattārīsaṃ. tadā bodhisatto cakkavattirājā hutvā buddho uppanno ti sutvā upasaṃkamitvā dhammaṃ sutvā buddhapamukhassa saṅghassa saddhiṃ sattahi ratanehi catumahādīparajjaṃ datvā satthu santike pabbaji. sakalaraṭṭhavāsino raṭṭhuppādaṃ gahetvā ārāmikakiccaṃ sādhentā buddhapamukhassa saṅghassa niccaṃ mahādānaṃ adaṃsu. so 'pi naṃ satthā vyākāsi. tassa bhagavato nagaraṃ sumaṅgalaṃ nāma ahosi uggato nāma rājā pitā pabhāvatī nāma mātā sudassano ca devo ca aggasāvakā nārado nāma upaṭṭhāko nāgā ca nāgasamālā ca aggasāvikā mahāveḷurukkho bodhi so kira mandachiddo ghanakkhandho uparimahāsākhāhi morapiñjakalāpo viya virocittha. tassa bhagavato sarīraṃ paññāsahatthubbedham ahosi āyuṃ navutivassasahassānī ti.

the Indian sarsaparilla. His body was eighty cubits high, and his life span was ninety thousand years.

> After Padumuttara there was a leader called Sumedha, 233
> of great splendor, the highest Teacher for the whole
> world.

After him there was a Teacher called Sujata. Sujata had 45
three assemblies: the first had sixty thousand monastics, the second fifty thousand, and the third forty thousand. At that time the Bodhisatta was a universal monarch. Hearing that a Buddha had arisen, he approached to hear the Dhamma. He handed over the rulership of four continents, with the seven treasures of a universal monarch to the Sangha, with the Buddha at its head, and took the going forth in the presence of the Teacher. Everyone who lived in the kingdom arranged the business of the monasteries and constantly gave magnificent alms to the Sangha, with the Buddha at its head. Sujata also foretold: "You will become a Buddha." The city of that Bhagavan was called Sumangala. His father was a king, Uggata; his mother, Pabhavati; and his two chief disciples were Naga and Nagasamala. His personal attendant was called Narada, and his two chief female disciples were Rama and Surama. His awakening tree was the giant bamboo tree. They say this tree had smaller hollows and denser wood than the usual trees, and in its higher branches it was as splendid as a peacock fan. The body of this Bhagavan was fifty cubits high, and his life span was ninety thousand years.

234 tatth' eva maṇḍakappamhi sujāto nāma nāyako
sīhahanusabhakkhandho appameyyo durāsado ti.

46 tassa aparabhāge ito aṭṭhārasakappasatamatthake ekasmiṃ kappe piyadassī atthadassī dhammadassī ti tayo buddhā nibbattiṃsu. piyadassissa pi tayo sāvakasannipātā paṭhame koṭisatasahassaṃ bhikkhū ahesuṃ dutiye navutikoṭiyo tatiye asītikoṭiyo ti. tadā bodhisatto kassapo nāma māṇavo tiṇṇaṃ vedānaṃ pāraṃ gato 'va hutvā satthu dhammadesanaṃ sutvā koṭisatasahassadhanapariccāgena saṅghārāmaṃ kāretvā saraṇesu ca sīlesu ca patiṭṭhāsi. atha naṃ satthā aṭṭhārasakappasataccayena buddho bhavissasī ti vyākāsi. tassa bhagavato anomaṃ nāma nagaraṃ ahosi pitā sudinno nāma rājā mātā candā nāma pālito ca sabbadassī ca aggasāvakā sobhito nām' upaṭṭhāko sujātā ca dhammadinnā ca aggasāvikā piyaṅgurukko bodhi sarīraṃ asītihatthubbedhaṃ ahosi navutivassasahassāni āyū ti.

235 sujātassa aparena sayambhū lokanāyako
durāsado asamasamo piyadassī mahāyaso ti.

47 tassa aparabhāge atthadassī nāma satthā udapādi. tassā 'pi tayo sāvakasannipātā paṭhame aṭṭhanavutibhikkhusatasahassāni ahesuṃ dutiye aṭṭhāsītisatasahassāni tathā tatiye.

At that time, in the eon of the Cream of the Milk, 234
there was a leader called Sujata, with the jaws of a lion
and the chest of a bull, measureless and hard to match.

After him, when eighteen hundred eons had gone by, three 46
Buddhas, Piyadassi, Atthadassi, and Dhammadassi, arose. There were three assemblies of disciples for Piyadassin: the first had a hundred thousand crore of monastics, the second ninety, and the third eighty. At that time the Bodhisatta was a young Brahman called Kassapa, who had learned the three Vedas. He heard a talk by the Teacher and with an enormous donation of a hundred thousand crore, he had a monastery built.

He became established in the refuges and precepts. And Piyadassi also made a prophecy: "After eighteen hundred eons have passed, you will become a Buddha." The city of this Bhagavan was called Anoma. His father was a king, Sudinna; his mother, Canda; and his two chief disciples were Palita and Sabbadassin. His personal attendant was called Sobhita, and his two chief female disciples were Sujata and Dhammadinna. His awakening tree was the droopy leaf, the *piyaṅgu*. The body of this Bhagavan was eighty cubits high and his life span was ninety thousand years.

After Sujata there was a self-taught leader of men, 235
Piyadassi, hard to match, peerless, of great splendor.

After him a Teacher called Atthadassi arose. There were three 47
assemblies of disciples for him too: in the first there were nine million eight hundred thousand monastics; the second, eight million eight hundred thousand; and the same amount

tadā bodhisatto susīmo nāma mahiddhikatāpaso hutvā devalokato mandāravapupphachattaṃ āharitvā satthāraṃ pūjesi. so 'pi naṃ vyākāsi. tassa bhagavato sobhitaṃ nāma nagaraṃ ahosi sāgaro nāma rājā pitā sudassanā nāma mātā santo ca upasanto ca aggasāvakā abhayo nām' upaṭṭhāko dhammā ca sudhammā ca aggasāvikā campakarukkho bodhi sarīraṃ asītihatthubbedhaṃ ahosi sarīrappabhā samantato sabbakālaṃ yojanamattaṃ pharitvā aṭṭhāsi āyuṃ vassasatasahassānī ti.

236 tatth' eva maṇḍakappamhi atthadassī narāsabho
mahātamaṃ nihantvāna patto sambodhim uttaman ti.

48 tassa aparabhāge dhammadassī nāma satthā udapādi. tassā 'pi tayo sāvakasannipātā paṭhame koṭisataṃ bhikkhū ahesuṃ dutiye sattatikoṭiyo tatiye asītikoṭiyo. tadā bodhisatto sakko devarājā hutvā dibbagandhapupphehi ca dibbaturiyehi ca pūjaṃ akāsi. so 'pi naṃ vyākāsi. tassa bhagavato saraṇaṃ nāma nagaraṃ ahosi pitā saraṇo nāma rājā mātā sunandā nāma padumo ca phussadevo ca aggasāvakā sunetto nām' upaṭṭhāko khemā ca sabbanāmā ca aggasāvikā rattakuravakarukkho bodhi bimbijālo ti pi vuccati. sarīraṃ pan'

in the third. At that time the Bodhisatta was an ascetic of great psychic power, called Susima. He brought a parasol made of coral-tree flowers from a heavenly realm, took it to the Teacher, and paid homage to him. And Atthadassi also made a prophecy. The city of this Bhagavan was called Sobhita. His father was a king called Sagara, his mother Sudassana, and his two chief disciples were Santa and Upasanta. His personal attendant was called Abhaya, and his two chief female disciples were Dhamma and Sudhamma. His awakening tree was the yellow-jade orchid tree. The body of this Bhagavan was eighty cubits high: the light from his body spread all around all the time for at least a *yojana,* and his life span was a hundred thousand years.

> At that time, in the same eon of the Cream of the 236
> Milk, there was a leader named Atthadassi, a bull
> among men, who attained the highest awakening and
> dispelled the great darkness.

After him there appeared a Teacher named Dhammadassi. 48
He also had three assemblies of disciples: at the first, there were a hundred crore of monastics; at the second, seventy crore; and at the third, eighty. At that time, the Bodhisatta was born as Sakka, the king of the gods. He made offerings of heavenly perfumes and flowers, as well as divine music. Dhammadassi also made a prophecy about him. The city of that Bhagavan was called Sarana. His father was King Sarana and his mother, Sunanda. His chief disciples were Paduma and Phussadeva, his attendant, Sunetta. His two chief female disciples were Khema and Sabbanama. His awakening tree was the red amaranth, known as the *bimbijala.* His body was

assa asītihatthubbedhaṃ ahosi vassasatasahassaṃ āyū ti.

237 tatth' eva maṇḍakappamhi dhammadassī mahāyaso
tamandhakāraṃ vidhametvā atirocati sadevake ti.

49 tassa aparabhāge ito catunavutikappamatthake ekasmiṃ kappe eko 'va siddhattho nāma buddho udapādi. tassā 'pi tayo sāvakasannipātā paṭhamasannipāte koṭisatasahassaṃ bhikkhū ahesuṃ dutiye navutikoṭiyo tatiye asītikoṭiyo. tadā bodhisatto uggatejo abhiññābalasampanno maṅgalo nāma tāpaso hutvā mahājambuphalaṃ āharitvā tathāgatassa adāsi. satthā taṃ phalaṃ paribhuñjitvā catunavutikappamatthake buddho bhavissasī ti bodhisattaṃ vyākāsi. tassa bhagavato nagaraṃ vebhāraṃ nāma ahosi pitā jayaseno nāma rājā mātā suphassā nāma sambalo ca sumitto ca aggasāvakā revato nāma upaṭṭhāko sīvalī ca surāmā ca aggasāvikā kaṇikārarukkho bodhi sarīraṃ saṭṭhihatthubbedhaṃ ahosi vassasatasahassaṃ āyū ti.

238 dhammadassissa aparena siddhattho nāma nāyako
nihanitvā tamaṃ sabbaṃ suriyo 'v' abbhuggato yathā
ti.

eighty cubits tall and his life span a hundred thousand years.

In the same eon of the Cream of the Milk, Dhamma- 237
dassi, of great renown, irradiated the world with its
gods, having dispelled the impenetrable darkness.

After him, in the ninety-four eons before now, just one 49
Buddha arose in one eon, called Siddhattha. He too had three assemblies of disciples: in the first there were a hundred thousand crore of monastics; in the second, ninety crore; and in the third, eighty. At that time the Bodhisatta was an ascetic of great power called Mangala, endowed with strong higher knowledges. He brought an enormous rose apple and offered it to the Tathagata. The Teacher ate this fruit and foretold: "You will be a Buddha in ninety-four eons' time." This Bhagavan's city was called Vebhara; his father was a king called Jayasena, his mother, Suphassa. Sambala and Sumitto were his chief disciples. Revata was his personal attendant; his two chief female disciples were Khema and Sabbanama, and his awakening tree was the kanika flower tree. The body of this Bhagavan was sixty cubits in height and his life span was a hundred thousand years.

After Dhammadassi there was a leader called 238
Siddhattha,
He dissolved all darkness and arose like the sun.

50 tassa aparabhāge ito dvānavutikappamatthake tisso phusso ti ekasmiṃ kappe dve buddhā nibbattiṃsu. tissassa bhagavato tayo sāvakasannipātā paṭhamasannipāte bhikkhūnaṃ koṭisataṃ ahosi dutiye navutikoṭiyo tatiye asītikoṭiyo. tadā bodhisatto māhābhogo mahāyaso sujāto nāma khattiyo hutvā isipabbajjaṃ pabbajitvā mahiddhikabhāvaṃ patvā buddho uppanno ti sutvā dibbaṃ mandāravapadumaṃ pāricchattakapupphāni ādāya catuparisamajjhe gacchantaṃ tathāgataṃ pūjesi ākāse pupphavitānaṃ akāsi. so 'pi naṃ satthā ito dvenavutikappe buddho bhavissasī ti vyākāsi. tassa bhagavato khemaṃ nāma nagaraṃ ahosi pitā janasandho nāma khattiyo mātā padumā nāma brahmadevo ca udayo ca aggasāvakā sambhavo nāma upaṭṭhāko phussā ca sudattā ca aggasāvikā asanarukkho bodhi sarīraṃ saṭṭhihatthubbedhaṃ ahosi vassasatasahassaṃ āyū ti.

239 siddhatthassa aparena asamo appaṭipuggalo
anantasīlo amitayaso tisso lokagganāyako ti.

51 tassa aparabhāge phusso nāma satthā udapādi. tassā 'pi tayo sāvakasannipātā paṭhamasannipāte saṭṭhi bhikkhusatasahassāni dutiye paññāsa tatiye dvattiṃsa. tadā bodhis-

Tissa and Phussa

After him, ninety-two eons ago, two Buddhas called Tissa 50
and Phussa were born in one eon. The Bhagavan Tissa had three assemblies of disciples: in the first there were a hundred crore of monastics; in the second, ninety crore; and in the third, eighty. At that time the Bodhisatta was a Kshatriya, of great wealth and fame. When he had taken the going forth, he became a seer and renouncer and attained considerable psychic power. When he heard that a Buddha had arisen, he took a heavenly coral-tree flower and flowers from the coral *parichatta* tree, from the Heaven of the Thirty-Three, and paid homage, making a canopy of flowers in the sky for the Tathagata as he walked about in the midst of the four assemblies. This Teacher foretold: "You will be a Buddha in ninety-two eons' time." The city of this Bhagavan was called Khema. His father was a Kshatriya called Janasandha and his mother was called Paduma. His chief disciples were the god Brahma and Udaya. His personal attendant was Sambhava, and his two chief female disciples were Phussa and Sudatta. His awakening tree was the Indian laurel. The body of this Bhagavan was sixty cubits tall and his life span was a hundred thousand years.

> After Siddhattha there was Tissa, unequaled and without rival, 239
> Of measureless virtue and boundless splendor, a great leader of the world.

After him there was a Teacher called Phussa. He too had 51
three assemblies of disciples: in the first there were a hundred thousand monastics; in the second, fifty hundred

atto vijitāvī nāma khattiyo hutvā mahārajjaṃ pahāya satthu santike pabbajitvā tīṇi piṭakāni uggahetvā mahājanassa dhammakathaṃ kathesi sīlapāramiñ ca pūresi. so 'pi naṃ buddho tath' eva vyākāsi. tassa bhagavato kāsi nāma nagaraṃ ahosi Jayaseno nāma rājā pitā sirimā nāma mātā surakkhito ca dhammaseno ca aggasāvakā sabhiyo nāma upaṭṭhāko cālā ca upacālā aggasāvikā āmalakarukkho bodhi sarīraṃ aṭṭhapaññāsahatthubbedhaṃ ahosi navutivassasahassāni āyū ti.

240 tatth' eva maṇḍakappamhi ahū satthā anuttaro
anūpamo asamasamo phusso lokagganāyako ti.

52 tassa aparabhāge ito ekanavutikappe vipassī nāma bhagavā udapādi tassā 'pi tayo sāvakasannipātā paṭhamasannipāte aṭṭhasaṭṭhi bhikkhusatasahassaṃ ahosi dutiye ekasatasahassaṃ tatiye asītisahassāni. tadā bodhisatto mahiddhiko mahānubhāvo atulo nāma nāgarājā hutvā sattaratanakhacitaṃ sovaṇṇamayapīṭhaṃ bhagavato adāsi. so 'pi taṃ ito

thousand; and in the third, thirty-two hundred thousand. At that time the Bodhisatta was a Kshatriya called Vijitavi, who abandoned a great kingdom and took the going forth in the presence of the Teacher; he grasped the three baskets, gave a talk on Dhamma to a large amount of people, and fulfilled the perfection of virtue.

Phussa foretold he would become a Buddha. This Bhagavan's city was called Kasi. His father was a king called Jayasena and his mother was called Sirima. Surakkhita and Dhammasena were his chief disciples. Sambhiya was his personal attendant, and Cala and Upacala were his two chief female disciples. His awakening tree was the myrobalan. The body of this Bhagavan was fifty-eight cubits tall and his life span was ninety thousand years.

> And in that same Cream of the Milk eon, there was an 240
> unsurpassable Teacher, Phussa, unparalleled, without
> an equal, the highest chief of the world.

Vipassi

After him, ninety-one eons ago, there appeared a Bhagavan 52
called Vipassi. He too had three assemblies of disciples: in the first there were sixty-eight hundred thousand; in the second, one hundred thousand; and in the third, eighty thousand. At that time the Bodhisatta was a naga king called Atula, who possessed great power and glory. He donated a golden seat inlaid with seven kinds of jewels. Vipassi foretold: "In ninety-one eons' time you will become a Buddha." This Bhagavan's city was called Bandhumati. His father was a king, called Bandhuma, and his mother was called

ekanavutikappe buddho bhavissasī ti vyākāsi. tassa bhagavato bandhumatī nāma nagaraṃ ahosi bandhumā nāma rājā pitā bandhumatī nāma mātā khaṇḍo ca tisso ca aggasāvakā asoko nāma upaṭṭhāko candā ca candamittā ca aggasāvikā pāṭalirukkho bodhi sarīraṃ asītihatthubbedhaṃ ahosi sarīrappabbā sadā sattayojanāni pharitvā aṭṭhāsi asītivassasahassāni āyū ti.

241 phussassa aparena sambuddho dipaduttamo
vipassī nāma nāmena loke uppajji cakkhumā ti.

53 tassa aparabhāge ito ekatiṃsakappe sikhī ca vessabhū cā ti dve buddhā ahesuṃ. sikhissā 'pi tayo sāvakasannipātā paṭhamasannipāte bhikkhusatasahassaṃ ahosi dutiye asītisahassāni tatiye sattati. tadā bodhisatto arindamo nāma rājā hutvā buddhapamukhassa saṅghassa sacīvaraṃ mahādānaṃ pavattetvā sattaratanapatimaṇḍitaṃ hatthiratanaṃ datvā hatthipamāṇaṃ katvā kappiyabhaṇḍaṃ adāsi. so 'pi naṃ ito ekatiṃse kappe buddho bhavissasī ti vyākāsi. tassa pana bhagavato aruṇavatī nāma nagaraṃ ahosi aruṇo nāma khattiyo pitā pabhāvatī nāma mātā abhibhū ca sambhavo ca aggasāvakā khemaṃkaro nāma upaṭṭhāko makhilā ca padumā

Bandhumati. His chief disciples were Khanda and Tissa. His personal attendant was called Asoka; Canda and Candamitta were his two chief female disciples. His awakening tree was the trumpet-flower tree. The body of this Bhagavan was eighty cubits tall, and the light from his body spread for one hundred *yojanas,* all the time. His life span was ninety thousand years.

> After Phussa there was a completely awakened one, 241
> supreme among men, called Vipassi: a far-seeing one
> arose in the world.

Sikhi and Vessabhu

And after him, thirty-one eons ago, there were two Teachers 53
whose names were Sikhi and Vessabhu. Sikhi also had three assemblies of disciples: in the first there were a hundred thousand monastics; in the second, eighty thousand; and in the third, seventy. At that time the Bodhisatta was a king called Arindama. He offered a great donation of robes to the Sangha, with the Buddha at its head, and also gave a king elephant, decked with seven kinds of jewels and equipped with everything that was needed. Sikhi made his prophecy: "In thirty-one eons you will become a Buddha." The city of this Bhagavan was called Arunavati, his father was called Aruna, and his mother was called Pabhavati. His chief disciples were Abhibhu and Sambhava. His personal attendant was called Khemamkara, and his two chief female disciples were Makhila and Paduma. His awakening tree was the white mango.

ca aggasāvikā puṇḍarīkarukkho bodhi sarīraṃ sattatiṃsahatthubbedhaṃ ahosi sarīrappabhā yojanattayaṃ pharitvā aṭṭhāsi sattatiṃsavassasahassāni āyū ti.

242 vipassissa aparena sambuddho dipaduttamo
sikhīsavhayo nāma jino asamo appaṭipuggalo ti.

54 tassa aparabhāge vessabhū nāma satthā udapādi. tassā 'pi tayo sāvakasannipātā paṭhamasannipāte asītibhikkhusatasahassāni ahesuṃ dutiye sattati tatiye saṭṭhi. tadā bodhisatto sudassano nāma rājā hutvā buddhapamukhassa saṅghassa sacīvaraṃ mahādānaṃ datvā tassa santike pabbajitvā ācāraguṇasampanno buddharatane cittikārapītibahulo ahosi. so 'pi naṃ bhagavā ito ekatiṃsakappe buddho bhavissasī ti vyākāsi. tassa pana bhagavato anopamaṃ nāma nagaraṃ ahosi suppatīto nāma rājā pitā yasavatī nāma mātā soṇo ca uttaro ca aggasāvakā upasanto nāma upaṭṭhāko dāmā ca samālā ca aggasāvikā sālarukkho bodhi sarīraṃ saṭṭhihatthubbedhaṃ ahosi saṭṭhivassasahassāni āyū ti.

243 tatth' eva maṇḍakappamhi asamo appaṭipuggalo
vessabhū nāma nāmena loke uppajji so jino ti.

The body of this Bhagavan was thirty-seven cubits tall, while the radiance from his body extended for three *yojanas*. His life span was thirty-seven thousand years.

After Vipassi there was an awakened Buddha, 242
unsurpassable among men, called Sikhi, a conqueror,
without an equal and without a rival.

Vessabhu

After him a Teacher arose called Vessabhu. For him there 54
were also three assemblies of disciples: in the first were eight hundred thousand monks; in the second, seventy; and in the third, sixty. At that time, the Bodhisatta was a king by the name of Sudassana and he made a magnificent donation, with robes, to the Sangha with the Buddha at its head. He received ordination under him. As he possessed such virtuous ways, he was filled all the time with joy at the jewel of the Buddha. And Vessabhu told him, "In thirty-one eons' time, you will become a Buddha." This Bhagavan's city was called Anopama, his father was a king called Suppatita, and his mother was Yasavati. Sona and Uttara were his chief disciples, his personal attendant was Upasanta, and his chief female disciples were Dama and Samala. His awakening tree was the sal. His body was sixty cubits tall, and he lived for sixty thousand years.

In that same Cream of the Milk eon, the one called 243
Vessabhu was without equal and without a rival.
He arose, a conqueror, in the world.

55 tassa aparabhāge imasmiṃ kappe cattāro buddhā nibbattā: kakusandho koṇāgamano kassapo amhākaṃ bhagavā ti kakusandhassa bhagavato eko sannipāto tattha cattālīsaṃ bhikkhusahassāni ahesuṃ. tadā bodhisatto khemo nāma rājā hutvā buddhapamukhassa saṅghassa sapattacīvaraṃ mahādānañ c' eva añjanāni bhesajjāni c' eva datvā satthu dhammadesanaṃ sutvā pabbaji. so 'pi naṃ satthā vyākāsi. kakusandhassa pana bhagavato khemaṃ nāma nagaraṃ ahosi aggidatto nāma brāhmaṇo pitā visākhā nāma brāhmaṇī mātā vidhūro ca sañjīvo ca aggasāvakā buddhijo nāma upaṭṭhāko sāmā ca campakā ca aggasāvikā mahāsirīsarukkho bodhi sarīraṃ cattālīsahatthubbedhaṃ ahosi cattālisaṃ vassasahassāni āyū ti.

244 vessabhussa aparena sambuddho dipaduttamo
kakusandho nāma nāmena appameyyo durāsado ti.

56 tassa aparabhāge koṇāgamano nāma satthā udapādi. tassā 'pi eko sāvakasannipāto tattha tiṃsabhikkhusahassāni ahesuṃ. tadā bodhisatto pabbato nāma rājā hutvā amaccagaṇaparivuto satthu santikaṃ gantvā dhammadesanaṃ sutvā buddhapamukhaṃ bhikkhusaṅghaṃ nimantetvā mahādānaṃ pavattetvā pattuṇṇacīnapaṭṭaṃ koseyyaṃ kambalaṃ

After that, in this eon, there have been four Buddhas: Kaku- 55
sandha, Konagamana, Kassapa, and our Bhagavan. Kakusandha had just one assembly, of forty thousand monastics. At that time, the Bodhisatta was born as a king, Khema. He made great offerings, including bowls and robes, to the Sangha with the Buddha at its head. He then donated collyrium and other medicinal substances. Once he had heard the Dhamma from the Teacher, he took up the holy life. And Kakusandha also prophesied for him. The city of this Bhagavan was called Khema; his father was a king, Aggidatta, and his mother was called Visakha. Vidhura and Sanjiva were his chief disciples, Buddhija his personal attendant, and Sama and Campaka his chief female disciples. His awakening tree was the great serissa tree. His body was forty cubits high, and he lived for forty thousand years.

After Vessabhu there was a completely awakened 244
Buddha, unsurpassable among men, called
Kakusandha, immeasurable, hard to equal.

Konagamana

After him there arose a Teacher called Konagamana. He 56
too had just one assembly, in which there were thirty thousand monastics. At that time, the Bodhisatta was born as a king, Pabbata. He went with a great retinue of ministers and nobles into the presence of the Teacher and heard a talk on the Dhamma. He organized a great almsgiving to the Sangha, with the Buddha at its head, and offered washed silk, China silk, Kasi silk, woolen cloth, fine linen, and cloth woven with gold; and then he took up the holy life.

dukūlāni c' eva suvaṇṇapaṭṭakañ ca datvā satthu santike pabbaji. so 'pi naṃ vyākāsi. tassa bhagavato sobhavatī nāma nagaraṃ ahosi yaññadatto nāma brāhmaṇo pitā uttarā nāma brāhmaṇī mātā bhiyyoso ca uttaro ca aggasāvakā sotthijo nāma upaṭṭhāko samuddā ca uttarā ca aggasāvikā udumbararukkho bodhi sarīraṃ vīsatihatthubbedhaṃ ahosi tiṃsavassasahassaṃ āyū ti.

245 kakusandhassa aparena sambuddho dipaduttamo
koṇāgamano nāma jino lokajeṭṭho narāsabho ti.

57 tassa aparabhāge kassapo nāma satthā loke udapādi. tassā 'pi eko sāvakasannipāto tattha vīsatibhikkhusahassāni ahesuṃ. tadā bodhisatto jotipālo nāma māṇavo hutvā tiṇṇaṃ vedānaṃ pāragū bhūmiyañ ca antalikkhe ca pākaṭo ghaṭīkārassa kumbhakārassa mitto ahosi. so tena saddhiṃ satthāraṃ upasaṃkamitvā dhammakathaṃ sutvā pabbajitvā āraddhaviriyo tīṇi piṭakāni uggahetvā vattāvattasampattiyā buddhasāsanaṃ sobhesi. so 'pi naṃ satthā vyākāsi. tassa bhagavato jātanagaraṃ bārāṇasī nāma ahosi brahmadatto

And Konagamana also made a prophecy for him. This Bhagavan's city was called Sobhavati; his father was a Brahman, Yannadatta, and his mother was a Brahman woman called Uttara. His chief disciples were Bhiyyosa and Uttara. His personal attendant was Sotthija, and his chief female disciples, Samudda and Uttara. His awakening tree was the fig tree. His body was thirty cubits in height and his life span, thirty thousand years.

> After Kakusandha there was a completely awakened 245
> Buddha, unsurpassable among men. He was called
> Konagamana, and was a conqueror, foremost among
> men, a great hero.

Kassapa

After him a Teacher called Kassapa arose in the world. He 57
also had just one assembly, in which there were twenty thousand monastics. At that time, the Bodhisatta was born as a Brahman youth, Jotipala. He had mastered the three knowledges and was famous, on earth and in the sky. He was a friend of the potter Ghatikara. Jotipala approached the Teacher with him, and when he had heard a talk on the Dhamma, he took up the going forth. With a great heroic effort, he mastered the three baskets of the teaching, and illuminated the Buddha's order with his repeated practice of the attainments. And Kassapa also made a prophecy for him. The city of that Bhagavan's birth was called Varanasi; his father was a Brahman, Brahmadatta, and his mother was a Brahman woman called Dhanavati. Tissa and Bharadvaja were his chief disciples. His personal attendant

nāma brāhmaṇo pitā dhanavatī nāma brāhmaṇī mātā tisso ca bhāradvājo ca aggasāvakā sabbamitto nāma upaṭṭhāko anuḷā ca uruveḷā ca aggasāvikā nigrodharukkho bodhi sarīraṃ vīsatihatthubbedhaṃ ahosi vīsativassasahassāni āyū ti.

246 koṇāgamanassa aparena sambuddho dipaduttamo
kassapo nāma so jino dhammarājā pabhaṃkaro ti.

58 yasmiṃ pana kappe dīpaṃkaradasabalo udapādi tasmiṃ aññe pi tayo buddhā ahesuṃ. tesaṃ santikā bodhisattassa vyākaraṇaṃ n' atthi. tasmā te idha na dassitā aṭṭhakathāyaṃ pana tamhā kappā paṭṭhāya sabbe buddhe dassetuṃ idaṃ vuttaṃ:

247 taṇhaṃkaro medhaṃkaro atho pi saraṇaṃkaro
dīpaṃkaro ca sambuddho koṇḍañño dipaduttamo
248 maṅgalo ca sumano ca revato sobhito muni
anomadassī padumo nārado padumuttaro
249 sumedho ca sujāto ca piyadassī mahāyaso
atthadassī dhammadassī siddhattho lokanāyako
250 tisso phusso ca sambuddho vipassī sikhi vessabhū
kakusandho koṇāgamano kassapo cā 'pi nāyako
251 ete ahesuṃ sambuddhā vītarāgā samāhitā
sataraṃsī 'va uppannā mahātamavinodanā
jalitvā aggikkhandhā 'va nibbutā te sasāvakā ti.

was Sabbamitta, and his chief female disciples were Anula and Uruvela. His awakening tree was the banyan. His body was twenty cubits in height, and he lived for twenty thousand years.

> After Konagamana there was a completely awakened 246
> Buddha, the best of men, He was called Kassapa, a
> conqueror, a king in the Dhamma, and one of great
> radiance.

So, in the eon in which Dipankara, with his ten powers, 58
appeared, there were three other Buddhas. They did not give a prediction in the presence of the Bodhisatta, so they are not seen here.

But the commentary does give this statement so as to go through all the Buddhas, starting in that eon:

> Tanhankara, Medhankara, and Saranakara too, the 247
> fully awakened Kondannya, the best of men;
> Mangala, Sumana, Revata, and the wise man Sobhita, 248
> Anomadassi, Paduma, Narada, and Padumuttara,
> Sumedha, Sujata, Piyadassi of great renown, 249
> Atthadassi, Dhammadassi, and Siddhattha, leader of
> the world.
> Tissa and Phussa, and the completely awakened 250
> Vipassi, Sikhi, Vessabhu, Kakusandha, Konagamana,
> and the leader Kassapa:
> These were the completely awakened ones, without 251
> desire, and composed. They arose like the sun with
> a hundred rays, dispelling the great darkness. They
> blazed like columns of fire—and then passed into
> nibbana, with their disciples.[56]

59 tattha amhākaṃ bodhisatto dīpaṃkarādīnaṃ catuvīsatiyā buddhānaṃ santike adhikāraṃ karonto kappasatasahassādhikāni cattāri asaṃkheyyāni āgato. kassapassa pana bhagavato orabhāge ṭhapetvā imaṃ sammāsambuddhaṃ añño buddho nāma n' atthi. iti dīpaṃkarādīnaṃ catuvīsatiyā buddhānaṃ santike laddhavyākaraṇo pana bodhisatto.

yena pana tena
manussattaṃ liṅgasampatti hetu satthāradassanaṃ
pabbajjā guṇasampatti adhikāro ca chandatā
aṭṭhadhammasamodhānā abhinīhāro samijjhatī ti

60 ime aṭṭhadhamme samodhānetvā dīpaṃkarapādamūle katābhinīhārena handa buddhakare dhamme vicināmi ito c' ito ti ussāhaṃ katvā vicinanto tadā dakkhiṃ paṭhamaṃ dānapāramin ti dānapāramitādayo buddhakārakadhammā diṭṭhā ne pūrento yeva vessantarattabhāvā āgami āgacchanto 'va ye te katābhinīhārānaṃ bodhisattānaṃ ānisaṃsā saṃvaṇṇitā:

252 evaṃ sabbaṅgasampannā bodhiyā niyatā narā
saṃsaraṃ dīghaṃ addhānaṃ kappakoṭisatehi pi

Our Bodhisatta lived through four incalculable epochs and 59
a hundred thousand eons, renewing his resolution in the presence of twenty-four Buddhas, starting with Dipankara.

No Buddha appeared after the Bhagavan, Kassapa, other than this perfectly awakened one. In this way the Bodhisatta received his assurance under twenty-four Buddhas, starting with Dipankara.

For it is said: The resolve succeeds only if it is made up 60
of eight conditions: The resolution succeeds through the coming together of eight conditions: birth as a human being, the advantage of sex, a root cause, seeing a great Teacher, becoming a monk, an innate capacity for the eight attainments, the dedication of one's life, and resolve.

He had brought together these eight conditions while at the feet of Dipankara, and there he had made a resolve: "Right: I will search here and everywhere for the conditions that lead to Buddhahood." And he had seen the perfection of generosity and the other qualities needed for Buddhahood. "While searching for them I saw the first perfection, of generosity." He then fulfilled these, until he came to his birth as Vessantara.

And those rewards that come to bodhisattas who have made their resolutions are praised in this way:

In this way, possessing all the limbs of awakening, 252
these men spend long ages in samsara, for eons of
hundreds of crore.

253 avicimhi na uppajjanti tathā lokantaresu ca
nijjhāmataṇhā khuppipāsā na honti kālakañjakā
na honti khuddakā pāṇā uppajjant ā 'pi duggatiṃ
254 jāyamānā manussesu jaccandhā na bhavanti te
sotavekalyatā n' atthi na bhavanti mūgapakkhikā
255 itthibhāvaṃ na gacchanti ubhatovyañjanapaṇḍakā
na bhavanti pariyāpannā bodhiyā niyatā narā
256 muttā ānantarīkehi sabbattha suddhagocarā
micchādiṭṭhiṃ na sevanti kammakiriyadassanā
257 vasamānā 'pi saggesu asaññaṃ na uppajjare
suddhāvāsesu devesu hetu nāma na vijjati
258 nekkhammaninnā sappurisā visaṃyuttā bhavābhave
caranti lokatthacariyāyo pūrentā sabbapāramī ti

They are not born in the lowest hells, the Avici, nor in the spaces between worlds, they do not become ghosts, eaten up with hunger, thirst, and need. Although born to suffering as animals, they are not tiny creatures. 253

If born among men, they are not blind at birth, they do not have hearing difficulties, and they are not dumb. 254

They do not become women; they do not arise among those of mixed sex, nor eunuchs, these men destined for Buddhahood. 255

They are free from obstacles; they are pure wherever they go, they do not get into wrong views, and they see the workings of karma. 256

When they live in the heavens, they do not arise among beings who have no perception; there is no reason for them to be born in the heavens for those who have no more rebirths.[57] 257

Intent on renunciation, living in the world but not of it, they carry on, traveling in the world for its benefit, fulfilling all the perfections. 258

61 te ānisaṃse adhigantvā ’va āgato. pāramiyo pūrentassa c’ assa akittibrāhmaṇakāle saṃkhabrāhmaṇakāle dhanañjayarājakāle mahāsudassanakāle mahāgovindakāle nimimahārājakāle candakumārakāle visayhaseṭṭhikāle sivirājakāle vessantarakāle ti dānapāramitāya pūritattabhāvānaṃ parimāṇaṃ n’ atthi. ekantena pan’ assa sasapaṇḍitajātake

259 bhikkhāyupagataṃ[15] disvā sakattānaṃ pariccajiṃ
dānena me samo n’ atthi esā me dānapāramī ti

62 evaṃ attapariccāgaṃ karontassa dānapāramitā paramatthapāramī nāma jātā. tathā sīlavanāgarājakāle campeyyanāgarājakāle bhūridattanāgarājakāle chaddantanāgarājakāle jayaddisarājassa putta-alīnasattukumārakāle ti sīlapāramitāya pūritattabhāvānaṃ parimāṇaṃ nāma n’ atthi. ekantena pan’ assa saṃkhapālajātake

260 sūlehi vijjhayante pi koṭṭiyante pi satthihi[16]
bhojaputte na kuppāmi esā me sīlapāramī ti

Generosity

When he came, he found these rewards. And the existences 61
in which he fulfilled the perfection of generosity had no limit: at the times when he was born as the Brahman Akitti, and the Brahman Sankha, the kings Dhananjaya, Mahasudassana, and Mahagovinda, the great Nimi, the prince Canda, the merchant Visayha, the king Sivi, and as Vessantara.[58]

So, it is said of him in the birth story of the wise hare:[59]
Seeing him coming asking for alms, I offered up 259
myself,
There was no equal to me in generosity: this is my
perfection of generosity."

As he offered up himself, his perfection of generosity turned into its higher perfection.

Virtue

In the same way, the existences during which he fulfilled the 62
perfection of virtue had no limit: the times when he was born as naga kings Silava, Campeyya, Bhuridatta, and Chaddanta, and as the prince Alinasattu, son of king Jayaddisa.

"So, it is said of him in the birth story of Sankhapala:[60]
Even when they prodded me with stakes and hacked 260
me with weapons, I did not get angry with the village
lads: This is my perfection of virtue."

In this way, he offered up his life, and so found the perfection of virtue at the highest level, called a supreme perfection.

63 evaṃ attapariccāgaṃ karontassa sīlapāramitā paramatthapāramī nāma jātā. tathā somanassakumārakāle hatthipālakumārakāle ayogharapaṇḍitakāle ti mahārajjaṃ pahāya nekkhammapāramitāya pūritattabhāvānaṃ parimāṇaṃ nāma n' atthi. ekantena pana cūlasutasomajātake

261 mahārajjaṃ hatthagataṃ kheḷapiṇḍam 'va chaḍḍayiṃ
cajato na hoti laganaṃ esā me nekkhammapāramī ti

64 evaṃ nissaṅgatāya rajjaṃ chaḍḍetvā nikkhamantassa nekkhammapāramī paramatthapāramī nāma jātā. tathā vidhūrapaṇḍitakāle mahāgovindapaṇḍitakāle kuddālapaṇḍitakāle arakapaṇḍitakāle bodhiparibbājakakāle mahosadhapaṇḍitakāle ti paññāpāramiyā pūritattabhāvānaṃ parimāṇaṃ nāma n' atthi. ekantena pan' assa sattubhattajātake senakapaṇḍitakāle

Renunciation

Similarly, there was no limit to the lifetimes in which he 63
fulfilled the perfection of renunciation, such as the times he was born as the prince Somanassa, the prince Hatthipala, the wise man Ayoghara, and then abandoned his kingdom and fulfilled the perfection of renunciation.

This is clear in "The Small Story of Sutasoma Jataka":[61]

> "I rejected a great kingdom, which was under my 261
> rule, just like a glob of spittle. Giving it up, it had no
> sticking power for me: such was my perfection of
> renunciation."

In this way, throwing aside a kingdom for the sake of selflessness, his perfection of renunciation became a supreme perfection.

Wisdom

Then he fulfilled the perfection of wisdom. In the same way, 64
there is no limit to the various existences in which he fulfilled the perfection of wisdom, such as at the times of Vidhura, Mahagovinda, Kuddala, and Araka, all wise men, as well as the time of the ascetic Bodhi and the wise man Senaka.

This is surely seen in "The Barley-Meal Sack Jataka" at the time of Senaka, the wise man:[62]

262 paññāya pavicinanto 'haṃ brāhmaṇaṃ mocayiṃ
dukhā
paññāya me samo n' atthi esā me paññāpāramī ti

65 antobhastagataṃ sappaṃ dassentassa paññāpāramī paramatthapāramī nāma jātā. tathā viriyapāramitādīnam pi pūritattabhāvānaṃ parimāṇaṃ nāma n' atthi. ekantena pan' assa mahājanakajātake

263 atīradassī jalamajjhe hatā sabbe 'va mānusā
cittassa aññathā n' atthi esā me viriyapāramī ti

66 evaṃ mahāsamuddaṃ tarantassa viriyapāramī paramatthapāramī nāma jātā. khantivādajātake

264 acetanaṃ 'va koṭṭente tiṇhena pharasunā mama
kāsirāje na kuppāmi esā me khantipāramī ti

"Searching the problem with wisdom, I set the 262
Brahman free from his unhappiness. There is no
one equal to me in wisdom: this is my perfection of
wisdom."

For he pointed out that a snake had got right inside the Brahman's bag: in this way the perfection of wisdom became a supreme perfection.

Heroic Effort

In the same way, there is no limit to the various lifetimes in 65
which he fulfilled the perfection of heroic effort, as well as
the others.

"This is certainly the case in "The Great Janaka Jataka":[63]

Everyone died in the middle of the ocean, with no 263
shore in sight: But my heart did not swerve: this is my
perfection of heroic effort."

Forbearance

In "The Teacher of Forbearance Jataka":[64] 66

"I showed no anger to the King of Kasi, even 264
though he attacked me with a sharp ax, as if I were
some inanimate object. This is my perfection of
forbearance."

As he endured terrible pain, remaining steady, as if inanimate, his perfection of forbearance became a supreme perfection.

67 evaṃ acetanābhāvena viya mahādukkhaṃ adhivāsentassa khantipāramī paramatthapāramī nāma jātā. mahāsutasomajātake

265 saccavācaṃ anurakkhanto cajitvā mama jīvitaṃ
mocayiṃ ekasataṃ khattiye paramatthasaccapāramī
ti

68 evaṃ jīvitaṃ cajitvā saccam anurakkhantassa saccapāramī paramatthapāramī nāma 'jātā. mūgapakkhajātake

266 mātāpitā na me dessā na pi me dessaṃ mahāyasaṃ[17]
sabbaññutaṃ piyaṃ mayhaṃ tasmā vatam
adhiṭṭhahin ti

69 evaṃ jīvitam pi cajitvā vataṃ adhiṭṭhahantassa adhiṭṭhānapāramī paramatthapāramī nāma jātā. ekarājajātake

267 na maṃ koci uttasati na pihaṃ bhāyāmi kassaci
mettābalen' upatthaddho ramāmi pavane sadā ti

Truthfulness

In "The Great Story of Sutasoma Jataka":[65] 67

> "Guarding my truthfulness in speech and offering 265
> up my life, I freed a hundred soldiers. This is my
> perfection of truthfulness."

As he guarded his truthfulness while offering up his life, his perfection of truthfulness became a supreme perfection.

Resolve

In "The Dumb Cripple Jataka":[66] 68

> "My mother and father were not despised by me, 266
> nor was great fame. But omniscience was dear to me:
> because of that I undertook my vow."

As he risked his life, staying firm to his vow, his perfection of resolve became a supreme perfection.

Loving-Kindness

In "The Single King Jataka":[67] 69

> "No one can frighten me, and I fear no one at all. 267
> Remaining strong through the power of loving-
> kindness, I take delight in the forest."

Not even paying attention to his own life, while developing loving-kindness, his perfection of loving-kindness became a supreme perfection.

70 evaṃ jīvitam pi anavaloketvā mettāyantassa mettāpāramī paramatthapāramī nāma jātā. lomahaṃsajātake

268 susāne seyyaṃ kappemi chavaṭṭhikaṃ upadhāy' ahaṃ
gomaṇḍalā upagantvā rūpaṃ dassent' anappakan ti

71 evaṃ gāmadārakesu niṭṭhubhanādīhi c' eva mālāgandhūpahārādīhi ca sukhadukkhaṃ uppādentesu pi upekhaṃ anativattassa upekhāpāramī paramatthapāramī nāma jātā. ayam ettha saṃkhepo vitthārato pan' esa attho cariyāpiṭakato gahetabbo. evaṃ pāramiyo pūretvā vessantarattabhāve ṭhito

269 acetan ā 'yaṃ puthavī aviññāya sukhaṃdukhaṃ.
sā 'pi dānabalā mayhaṃ sattakkhattuṃ pakampathā
ti

72 evaṃ mahāpaṭhavikampanāni mahāpuññāni karitvā āyupariyosāne tato cuto tusitabhavane nibbatti. iti dīpaṃkarapādamūlato paṭṭhāya yāva ayaṃ tusitapure nibbatti ettakaṃ ṭhānaṃ dūrenidānaṃ nāmā ti veditabbaṃ.

Equanimity

In "The Hair-Standing-on-End Jataka":[68] 70

"I lay down in a charnel ground and made a pillow 268
from old bones: The cowherd's children gathered
round and teased me, in all sorts of ways."

In this way, while village children tried to upset him or make 71
him happy in all sorts of ways, by doing things like spitting at him and then offering him garlands and perfumes, he stayed in equanimity, so that the perfection of equanimity became a supreme perfection.

"This is only a short summary. Its full treatment is found in *Cariyapiṭaka* (The Basket of Conduct).[69]

When he had fulfilled the perfections in his lifetime as Vessantara, it is said:

"This insentient earth, who does not know either 269
pleasure or pain: Even she, by the power of my
generosity, trembled seven times."

In this way, after doing acts of great auspiciousness that 72
caused even the great earth to tremble, he was born at the end of that lifetime in the Tusita heaven. The story so far, from the incident at the feet of Dipankara right up to his birth in the city of Tusita, should be known as "The Far Origin."

avidūrenidāna

73 tusitapure vasante yeva pana bodhisatte buddhahalāhalaṃ nāma udapādi. lokasmiṃ hi tīṇi halāhalāni uppajjanti: kappahalāhalaṃ buddhahalāhalaṃ cakkavattihalāhalan ti. tattha vassasatasahassassa accayena kappuṭṭhānaṃ bhavissatī ti lokabyūhā nāma kāmāvacaradevā muttasirā vikiṇṇakesā rudammukhā assūni hatthehi puñjamānā rattavatthanivatthā ativiya virūpavesadhārino hutvā manussapathe vicarantā evaṃ ārocenti: mārisā ito vassasatasahassassa accayena kappuṭṭhānaṃ bhavissati ayaṃ loke vinassissati mahāsamuddo pi sussisati. ayañ ca mahāpaṭhavī sineru ca pabbatarājā uḍḍayhissanti vinassissanti yāva brahmalokā lokavināso bhavissatī ti mettaṃ mārisā bhāvetha karuṇaṃ muditaṃ upekkhaṃ mārisā bhāvetha mātaraṃ upaṭṭhahatha pitaraṃ upaṭṭhahatha kule jeṭṭhāpacāyino hothā ti. Idaṃ kappahalāhalaṃ nāma. vassasahassassa accayena pana sabbaññu-buddho loke uppajjissatī ti lokapāladevatā: ito mārisā vassasahassassa accayena buddho loke uppajjissatī ti ugghosentā āhiṇḍanti. idaṃ buddhahalāhalaṃ nāma. vassasatassa pana accayena cakkavattirājā uppajjissatī ti devatā yeva: ito mārisā vassasataccayena cakkavattiko rājā loke uppajjissatī ti ugghosentiyo āhiṇḍanti. idaṃ cakkavattihalāhalaṃ nāma. imāni tīṇi halāhalāni mahantāni honti. tesu buddhahalāhalasaddaṃ sutvā sakaladasasahassacakkavāle devatā ekato sannipatitvā asuko nāma satto

THE NEAR ORIGIN

While he was living in the city of the Tusita heaven, some- 73
thing called a hoo-ha, a "Buddha declaration," took place. For three kinds of hoo-ha declarations take place in the world: when giving an early announcement of an eon, when giving an early announcement of a Buddha, and when giving an early announcement of a universal monarch. When the sense-sphere gods called "World Array" realize that in a hundred thousand years' time there is going to be a new eon, they go round and about the world of humans, with hair loose and all over the place, with miserable faces, wiping away tears with their hands. They wear red clothes and look completely bedraggled. "Friends!" they say, "in a hundred thousand years' time there is going to be a new eon. This world will be destroyed. The great ocean will dry up. The great earth and the king of the mountains, Sineru, will burn up and collapse. The destruction of the world will extend as far as the meditative heavens. So, friends: develop loving-kindness, compassion, joy in joy and equanimity! Friends: look after your father and mother and honor the elders in your family." This is the early announcement of an eon.

And when there is going to be an omniscient Buddha in a hundred thousand years' time, the gods who protect the world roam around and announce: "Friends, in a hundred thousand years' time there will be a Buddha in the world!" This is the early announcement of a Buddha.

And when there is going to be a universal monarch in a hundred years' time, gods roam around and proclaim: "In

buddho bhavissatī ti ñatvā taṃ upasaṃkamitvā āyācanti āyācamānā ca pubbanimittesu uppannesu āyācanti. tadā pana sabbā 'pi tā ekekacakkavāle cātummahārāja-sakka-suyāma-santusitapparanimmitavasavatti-mahābrahmehi saddhiṃ ekacakkavāle sannipatitvā tusitabhavane bodhisattassa santikaṃ gantvā mārisā tumhehi dasapāramiyo pūrentehi na sakkasampattiṃ na māra-brahma-cakkavattisampattiṃ patthentehi pūritā lokanittharaṇatthāya pana sabbaññutaṃ patthentehi pūritā so vo dāni kālo mārisa buddhattāya samayo mārisa buddhattāyā ti yāciṃsu. atha mahāsatto devatānaṃ paṭiññaṃ adatvā 'va kāladīpadesakulajanettiāyuparicchedavasena pañcamahāvilokanan nāma vilokesi.

74 tattha kālo nu kho ti akālo nu kho ti paṭhamaṃ kālaṃ vilokesi. tattha vassasatasahassato uddhaṃ vaḍḍhitaāyukālo kālo nāma na hoti kasmā? tadā hi sattānaṃ jātijarāmaraṇāni na paññāyanti buddhānañ ca dhammadesanā tilakkhaṇamuttā nāma n' atthi tesaṃ aniccaṃ dukkhama nattā ti kathentānaṃ kin nām' etaṃ kathentī ti n' eva sotabbaṃ na

a hundred years there is going to be a universal monarch!" Then there is the early announcement of a universal monarch.

These three early announcements are great.

When the gods of the ten thousand world systems hear an early announcement about a Buddha, they meet all together and work out that "such-and-such a being is going to be a Buddha." Then they approach him and make a request; they do this when the four signs appear. This time, all of them, together with the Four Great Kings, the gods of the Tavatimsa, Yama, Tusita, the heaven of great power, and the Great Brahmas of each world system, met together in one world system, and went to the Bodhisatta in the Tusita realm.[1] They made their request: "Friend: when you were fulfilling the ten perfections, you did not do this to become a Sakka or a Mara, a Brahma, or a universal monarch. Rather, you have fulfilled them, friend, for Buddhahood. Now, friend, it is the moment for your Buddhahood."

And then the Great Being, before giving his consent, had a look and considered the five great things to look for: time, area, region, family, and the mother and her life span.

First of all, he considered: "Is it the right time, or is it 74
not?" Here, if the usual span of life is more than a hundred thousand years, it is not the right time. Why? Because in such an era, the birth, decay, and death of beings are hardly noticed. Dhamma teachings by Buddhas are never without these three signs: of impermanence, unsatisfactoriness, and nonself. So when they are spoken about, people will not consider it worth paying attention to, and will not feel faith, but will say, "What are they on about?" As there is

saddhātabbaṃ maññanti tato abhisamayo na hoti tasmiṃ asati aniyyānikaṃ sāsanaṃ hoti tasmā so akālo. vassasatato ūnaūyukālo pi kālo na hoti kasmā? tadā sattā ussannakilesā honti ussannakilesānañ ca dinno ovādo ovādaṭṭhāne na tiṭṭhati udake daṇḍarāji viya khippaṃ vigacchati tasmā so 'pi akālo. vassasatasahassato pana paṭṭhāya heṭṭhā vassasatato paṭṭhāya uddhaṃ āyukālo kālo nāma tadā ca vassasatakālo atha mahāsatto nibbattitabbakālo ti passi. tato dīpaṃ vilokento saparivāre cattāro dīpe oloketvā tīsu dīpesu buddhā na nibbattan ti jambudīpe yeva nibbattantī ti dīpaṃ passi. tato jambudīpo nāma mahādasayojanasahassaparimāṇaṃ katarasmiṃ nu kho padese buddhā nibbattantī ti okāsaṃ vilokento majjhimadesaṃ passi. majjhimadeso nāma puratthimadisāya kajaṅgalan nāma nigamo tassa aparena mahāsālo tato paraṃ paccantimā janapadā orato majjhe pubbadakkhiṇāya disāya salalavatī nāma nadī tato paraṃ paccantimā janapadā orato majjhe dakkhiṇāya disāya setakaṇṇikan nāma nigamo tato paraṃ paccantimā janapadā orato majjhe pacchimāya disāya thūṇan nāma brāhmaṇagāmo tato paraṃ paccantimā janapadā orato majjhe uttarāya disāya usīraddhajo nāma pabbato tato paraṃ paccantimā janapadā orato majjhe ti evaṃ vinaye vutto padeso. so āyāmato tīṇi yojanasatāni vitthārato aḍḍhatiyāni parikkhepato navayojanasatānī ti. etasmiṃ padese buddhā paccekabuddhā aggasāvakā mahāsāvakā asīti mahāsāvakā cakkavattirājā aññe ca mahesakkhā khattiyabrāhmaṇagahapatimahāsālā uppajjanti. idaṃ c' ettha kapilavatthukaṃ nāma nagaraṃ

no good opportunity, that time of teaching will not lead to realization. So, it is not the right time.

When the life span is less than a hundred years, it is also not the right time. Why? Beings then are overflowing with defilements. Teaching given to those overflowing with defilements does not endure as a teaching. Rather, like a line drawn in water with a stick, it quickly disappears. So, that too is not the time.

But when the life span is under a hundred thousand years and more than a hundred years, that is a good time. At that time, life expectancy stood at a hundred years. So the Great Being saw it was the right time for him to be born.

Next, considering the continents, he looked at the four continents and their surrounding islands, and he realized: "Buddhas are not born on three of the continents: they are born only in the land of the rose-apple tree, Jambudipa." In this way, he saw the continent. Then he considered the area: "Jambudipa is very large—ten thousand *yojanas* in extent. Which is the region where Buddhas are born?" And he saw the Middle Region. The Middle Region is the area described in the *Vinaya:* "To the east is the town of Kajangala, and beyond it is Mahasala, and on the near side are the frontier territories. In the middle of the southeastern district is the river Salalavati. The Middle Region extends up to the frontier territories, beyond that. It extends too to the south, to the town of Setakannika, and the frontier territories beyond that. And to the west is the Brahman village of Thuna: the Middle Region extends to the frontier regions, farther than that."[2] It is 300 *yojanas* long, 250 *yojanas* wide, and 900 *yojanas* in circumference. It is within this area that

tattha mayā nibbattitabban ti niṭṭhaṃ agamāsi. tato kulaṃ vilokento buddhā nāma vessakule vā suddakule vā na nibbattanti lokasammate pana khattiyakule vā brāhmaṇakule vā ti dvīsu yeva kulesu nibbattanti idāni ca khattiyakulaṃ lokasammataṃ tattha nibbattissāmi suddhodano nāma rājā me pitā bhavissatī ti kulaṃ passi. tato mātaraṃ vilokento buddhamātā nāma lolā surādhuttā na hoti kappasatasahassaṃ pana pūritapāramī jātito paṭṭhāya akhaṇḍapañcasīlā yeva hoti ayañ ca mahāmāyā nāma devī edisā ayañ ca me mātā bhavissatī ti kittakaṃ pan' assā āyun ti dasannaṃ māsānaṃ upari satta divasāni passi. iti imaṃ pañcamahāvilokanaṃ viloketvā kālo me mārisa buddhabhāvāyā ti devatānaṃ saṅgahaṃ karonto paṭiññaṃ datvā gacchatha tumhe ti tā devatā uyyojetvā tusitadevatāhi parivuto tusitapure nandanavanaṃ pāvisi. sabbadevalokesu hi nandanavanaṃ atthi yeva. tatra naṃ devatā ito cuto sugatiṃ gacchā ti pubbe katakusalakammokāsaṃ sārayamānā vicaranti.

Buddhas and *paccekabuddhas,* chief disciples and other leading disciples, the eighty great disciples, universal monarchs, and other powerful Kshatriya and Brahman householders with great halls are born.[3] And he concluded: "The city of Kapilavatthu is situated right here and I should be born there."

He then reflected on the family. "Buddhas are not born in a Vaishya or a Sudra family but come from a Kshatriya or a Brahman family—whichever people think is superior at the time. Kshatriya families are considered higher at the moment, so I will be born in one. The king, Suddhodana, will be my father." And he saw his family.

Then he thought about the mother. "The mother of a Buddha is not lascivious, nor is she addicted to drink. She has fulfilled the perfections for a hundred thousand eons, and her keeping of the five precepts has had no chink since birth. This queen, Great Maya, is just like that. She will be my mother. So what is her span of life? And he saw that it was ten months and seven days.[4]

When he had considered the five necessary factors, he paid his respects to the gods and gave his consent: "Friends: it is time for me to become a Buddha." And he said goodbye to the gods: "Now you may go." Then he went into the Garden of Delight in the city of the Tusita, with a retinue of Tusita gods. Now, there is a Garden of Delight in each of the heavens. In this, gods wander around reminding each other of the times in the past when they have done good things: "From here, you will go to a happy rebirth!"

75 so evaṃ devatāhi kusalaṃ sārayamānāhi parivuto tattha vicaranto cavitvā mahāmāyāya deviyā kucchismiṃ paṭisandhiṃ gaṇhi. tass' āvibhāvatthaṃ ayaṃ anupubbikathā: tadā kira kapilavatthunagare āsāḷhinakkhattaṃ ghuṭṭhaṃ ahosi. mahājano nakkhattaṃ kīḷati. mahāmāyā devī pure puṇṇamāya sattamadivasato paṭṭhāya vigatasurāpānaṃ mālāgandhavibhūtisampannaṃ nakkhattakīḷaṃ anubhavamānā sattamadivase pāto 'va uṭṭhāya gandhodakena nahāyitvā cattāri satasahassāni vissajjetvā mahādānaṃ datvā sabbālaṃkāravibhūsitā varabhojanaṃ bhuñjitvā uposathaṅgāni adhiṭṭhāya alaṃkatapaṭiyattaṃ sirigabbhaṃ pavisitvā sirisayane nipannā niddaṃ okkamamānā imaṃ supinaṃ addasa: cattāro kira naṃ mahārājāno sayanen' eva saddhiṃ ukkhipitvā himavantaṃ netvā saṭṭhiyojanike manosilātale sattayojanikassa mahāsālarukkhassa heṭṭhā ṭhapetvā ekamantaṃ aṭṭhaṃsu. atha nesaṃ deviyo āgantvā deviṃ anotattadahaṃ netvā manussamalaharaṇatthaṃ nahāpetvā dibbavatthaṃ nivāsāpetvā gandhehi vilimpāpetvā dibbapupphāni pilandhāpetvā-tato avidūre rajatapabbato tassa anto kanakavimānaṃ atthi-tattha pācīnasīsakaṃ dibbasayanaṃ paññāpetvā nipajjāpesuṃ. atha bodhisatto setavaravāraṇo hutvā-tato avidūre eko suvaṇṇapabbatotattha caritvā tato

He too was surrounded by gods who reminded him of the 75
good he had done, and as he wandered around, he passed away, and took conception in the womb of the great Queen Maya.

Here is an explanation of the events that took place, right from the beginning. The story goes that the festival of Asalha was announced in the city of Kapilavatthu.[5] People were having fun for this holiday.

From the seventh day before the full moon the great queen took part in the festival, which involved no strong drink but was filled with garlands and perfumes. On the seventh day she got up early, bathed in scented water, dressed in beautifully decorated clothes, and offered a great feast and donations, worth four hundred thousand. She ate some fine food and made the resolve to keep the *uposatha* day.[6] Then she went into her royal chamber and lay down on her regal couch. Falling asleep, she had the following dream. The story goes that then the Four Great Kings lifted her from her bed and took her to the Himalayas and laid her beneath a great sal tree, seven *yojanas* in height, that grew on a plateau of red arsenic, sixty *yojanas* in length. Then their queens led her to Lake Anotatta and washed her to get rid of the stains of humans and dressed her in heavenly garments. They anointed her with divine perfumes and decorated her with divine flowers. Not far from there, there was a silver mountain, and inside that there was a golden chamber. Inside that, they prepared a heavenly couch with its head to the east and asked her to rest there.

Now the Bodhisatta, in the form of a noble white elephant, was roaming around on the golden mountain, quite near

oruyha rajatapabbataṃ abhirūhitvā uttaradisato āgamma rajatadāmavaṇṇāya soṇḍāya setapadumaṃ gahetvā koñcanādaṃ naditvā kanakavimānaṃ pavisitvā mātusayanaṃ tikkhattuṃ padakkhiṇaṃ katvā dakkhiṇapassaṃ tāḷetvā kucchiṃ paviṭṭhasadiso ahosi. evaṃ uttarasāḷhanakkhattena paṭisandhiṃ gaṇhi. punadivase pabuddhā devī taṃ supinaṃ rañño ārocesi. rājā catusaṭṭhimatte brāhmaṇapāmokkhe pakkosāpetvā haritupattāya lājādīhi katamaṅgalasakkārāya bhūmiyā mahārahāni āsanāni paññāpetvā tattha nisinnānaṃ brāhmaṇānaṃ sappimadhusakkarābhisaṃkhatassa varapāyāsassa suvaṇṇarajatapātiyo pūretvā suvaṇṇarajatapātīhi yeva paṭikujjetvā adāsi aññehi ca ahatavatthakapilagāvidānādīhi te santappesi. atha tesaṃ sabbakāmehi santappitānaṃ supinaṃ ārocāpetvā kiṃ bhavissatī ti pucchi. brāhmaṇā āhaṃsu: mā cintayi mahārāja deviyā te kucchimhi gabbho patiṭṭhito so ca kho purisagabbho na itthigabbho putto te bhavissati so sace agāraṃ ajjhāvasissati rājā bhavissati cakkavattī sace agārā nikkhamma pabbajissati buddho bhavissati loke vivattacchaddo ti.

76 bodhisattassa pana mātukucchimhi paṭisandhigahaṇakkhaṇe ekappahāren' eva sakaladasasahassī lokadhātu saṃkampi sampakampi sampavedhi. dvattiṃsa pubbanimittāni pātur ahiṃsu: dasasu cakkavāiasahassesu appamāṇo

there. He came down from that and climbed the silver mountain. He came from the northern direction, carrying a white lotus in his trunk, with its sheen of a silver chain; and then he trumpeted. He entered the golden chamber and walked in reverence around her three times. As he tapped her right side, it was as if he entered her womb. In this way, he took conception, at the last part of the Asalha constellation.

The next day, the queen woke up and told the king about her dream. The king summoned sixty-four leading Brahmans and had expensive seats prepared on ground made ready for the auspicious occasion. It was covered with green leaves and rice grain and other things.[7] He offered them gold and silver bowls covered with gold and silver lids and filled with delicate milk-rice, mixed with ghee and sweet honey. He offered them this food and gave other gifts such as untreated natural cloth and tawny cows. Then he told the Brahmans, whose every desire had now been satisfied, about the dream. He asked them, "What is going to happen?" The Brahmans said: "Do not worry, great king. A child has been conceived in the queen's womb."

"It is a male child, not a female: there will be a son. If he leads the life of a householder, he will become a universal monarch. But if he renounces his home and takes the going forth, he will become a Buddha who will draw aside the covering over the world."

At the moment the Bodhisatta took conception in his 76
mother's womb, the entire ten-thousand-world system trembled, quaked, and shook, all at the same time. Thirty-two auspicious signs appeared. A limitless radiance shone out, so that the entire ten-thousand-world system was filled

obhāso phari tassa taṃ siriṃ daṭṭhukāmā viya andhā cakkhūni paṭilabhiṃsu badhirā saddaṃ suṇiṃsu mūgā samālapiṃsu khujjā ujugattā ahesum paṅgalā padasā gamanaṃ paṭilabhiṃsu bandhanagatā sabbasattā andubandhanādīhi mucciṃsu sabbanarakesu aggi nibbāyi pittivisaye khuppipāsā vūpasami tiracchānānaṃ bhayaṃ n' āhosi sabbasattānaṃ rogo vūpasami sabbasattā piyaṃvadā ahesuṃ madhurenākārena assā hasiṃsu vāraṇā gajjiṃsu sabbaturiyāni sakasakaninnādaṃ muñciṃsu aghaṭṭitāni yeva manussānaṃ hatthupagādīni ābharaṇāni viraviṃsu sabbadisā vippasannā ahesum sattānaṃ sukhaṃ uppādayamāno mudu sītalo vāto vāyi akālamegho vassi paṭhavito pi udakaṃ ubbhijjitvā vissandi pakkhino ākāsagamanaṃ vijahiṃsu nadiyo assandamānā aṭṭhaṃsu mahāsamudde madhuraṃ udakaṃ ahosi sabbatthakam eva pañcavaṇṇehi padumehi sañchannatalo ahosi thalajajalajādīni sabbapupphāni pupphiṃsu rukkhānaṃ khandhesu khandhapadumāni sākhāsu sākhāpadumāni latāsu latāpadumāni pupphiṃsu thale silātalāni bhinditvā uparūpari satta satta hutvā daṇḍapadumāni nāma nikkhamiṃsu ākāse olambakapadumāni nāma nibbattiṃsu samantato pupphavassaṃ vassiṃsu ākāse dibbaturiyāni vajjiṃsu sakaladasasahassī lokadhātu vaṭṭetvā vissaṭṭhamālāguḷaṃ viya uppīḷetvā baddhamālākalāpo viya alaṃkatapaṭiyattaṃ mālāsanaṃ viya ca ekamālāmālinī vipphurantavālavījanī pupphadhūpagandhaparivāsitā

with light. The blind, as if wishing to see this glory, regained their sight. The deaf regained their hearing. Those impaired in speech were able to chat, and those with bent backs stood upright. Those who were physically handicapped could walk on their feet. All kinds of beings in chains were released. The fires in all the hells were quenched. In the realm of hungry ghosts, hunger and thirst were allayed. There was no fear in the animal kingdom. Disease in all beings was dispersed. All creatures spoke kindly to one another. Horses neighed and elephants trumpeted with a sweet sound. All kinds of instruments spontaneously played out their music. Bracelets and other ornaments for human beings jangled without striking each other. All the directions became clear and quiet. A soft cool breeze blew, refreshing everyone. Rain fell, out of season. Water gushed from the earth and overflowed. The birds rested from their journey through the sky. Rivers were stilled, and the water of the great ocean became fresh. The surface of the land everywhere was covered with five kinds of lotuses. All kinds of flowers blossomed on land and on water, and the flowers that grow on creepers bloomed. Lotuses on stalks burst out together in sevens, breaking through the dry ground. Hanging cascades of lotuses appeared in midair. Showers of flowers rained down everywhere. In the sky, heavenly instruments played. The entire ten-thousand-world system revolved, rising up and around just like a cluster of flowers released into the air, or like bunched strings of waving flowers, or a shrine table brimming with flowers. Garlands upon garlands, as if scattered by a yak-tail whisk: flowers, incense, and perfumes of luminous beauty were everywhere.

paramasobhaggappattā ahosi. evaṃ gahitapaṭisandhikassa bodhisattassa paṭisandhito paṭṭhāya bodhisattassa c' eva bodhisattamātuyā ca upaddavanivāraṇatthaṃ khaggahatthā cattāro devaputtā ārakkhaṃ gaṇhiṃsu. bodhisattamātu purisesu rāgacittaṃ n' uppajji lābhaggayasaggappattā ca ahosi sukhinī akilantakāyā bodhisattañ ca antokucchigataṃ vippasanne maṇiratane āvutapaṇḍusuttaṃ viya passati. yasmā ca bodhisattena vasitakucchi nāma cetiyagabbhasadisā na sakkā hoti aññena āvasituṃ vā paribhuñjituṃ vā tasmā bodhisattamātā sattāhajāte bodhisatte kālaṃ katvā tusitapure nibbattati. yathā ca aññā itthiyo dasamāse appatvā 'pi atikkamitvā 'pi nisinnā 'pi nipannā 'pi vijāyanti na evaṃ bodhisattamātā sā pana bodhisattaṃ dasamāse kucchinā pariharitvā ṭhitā 'va vijāyati ayaṃ bodhisattamātu dhammatā. mahāmāyā 'pi devī pattena telaṃ viya dasamāse kucchiyā bodhisattaṃ pariharitvā paripuṇṇagabbhā ñātigharaṃ gantukāmā suddhodanamahārājassa ārocesi: icchām' ahaṃ deva kulasantakaṃ devadahanagaraṃ gantun ti. rājā sādhū ti sampaṭicchitvā kapilavatthuto yāva devadahanagarā maggaṃ samaṃ kāretvā kadalipuṇṇaghaṭadhajapaṭākādīhi alaṃkārāpetvā deviṃ sovaṇṇasivikāya nisīdāpetvā amaccasahassena ukkhipāpetvā mahantena parivārena pesesi.

77 dvinnaṃ pana nagarānaṃ antare ubhayanagaravāsīnam pi lumbinivanaṃ nāma maṅgalasālavanaṃ atthi. tasmiṃ samaye mūlato paṭṭhāya yāva aggasākhā sabbaṃ eka-

From the time of his conception, which happened in this way, four gods with swords in their hands stood guard over the mother and the Bodhisatta, right from that moment, to keep danger away. No feelings of desire toward men arose in the Bodhisatta's mother. She was happy, as she attained the height of heavenly bliss, and her body was not tired out. And she could see the Bodhisatta lying in her womb, like a yellow thread strung inside a clear precious crystal. The womb where the Bodhisatta lives is like a special chamber in a shrine. No other being can occupy it or take nourishment there. Because of this, the mother of a Bodhisatta dies seven days after his birth and is reborn in the city of the Tusita heaven. Unlike other women, who give birth sitting or lying down, not quite reaching ten months, she looks after the Bodhisatta in her womb for ten months and gives birth standing up. This is the way with the mother of a Bodhisatta. When Queen Mahamaya was in an advanced stage of her pregnancy and had cared for the Bodhisatta for ten months, like a vessel of oil, she wished to go to her family home. She informed King Suddhodana: "Your majesty, I want to go to my family's home, the kingdom of Devedaha." The king replied: "Yes, of course." And he had the road from Kapilavatthu to the city of Devedaha evened out, and had it decorated with plantain trees, jars filled with water, and streamers and bunting and things like that. Then he sat the queen down in a golden palanquin, and asked a thousand ministers to carry it, with a great retinue in tow.

Now between the two cities there is an area of woodland, 77
with auspicious sal trees, called Lumbini Grove, which belonged to the people from both towns. At that time the

phāliphullaṃ ahosi sākhantarehi c' eva pupphantarehi ca pañcavaṇṇabhamaragaṇā nānappakārā ca sakuṇasaṅghā madhurassarena vikūjantā vicaranti. sakalaṃ lumbinivanaṃ cittalatāvanasadisaṃ mahānubhāvassa rañño susajjitaāpānamaṇḍalaṃ viya ahosi. deviyā taṃ disvā sālavanakīḷaṃ kīḷitukāmatā udapādi. amaccā deviṃ gahetvā sālavanaṃ pavisiṃsu. sā maṅgalasālamūlaṃ gantvā sālasākhāyaṃ gaṇhitukāmā ahosi. sālasākhā suseditavettaggaṃ viya onamitvā deviyā hatthapathaṃ upagañchi. sā hatthaṃ pasāretvā sākhaṃ aggahesi. tāvad eva c' assā kammajavātā caliṃsu. Ath' assā sāṇim parikkhipitvā mahājano paṭikkami. sālasākhaṃ gahetvā tiṭṭhamānāya eva c' assā gabbhavuṭṭhānaṃ ahosi. taṃ khaṇaṃ yeva cattāro pi suddhacittā mahābrahmāno suvaṇṇajālaṃ ādāya sampattā tena suvaṇṇajālena bodhisattaṃ sampaṭicchitvā mātu purato ṭhapetvā attamanā devi hohi mahesakkho te putto uppanno ti āhaṃsu. yathā pana aññe sattā mātukucchito nikkhamantā paṭikkūlena asucinā makkhitā nikkhamanti na evaṃ bodhisatto.

78 bodhisatto pana dhammāsanato otaranto dhammakathiko viya nisseṇito otaranto puriso viya ca dve ca hatthe dve ca pāde pasāretvā ṭhitako mātukucchisambhavena kenaci asucinā amakkhito suddho visado kāsikavatthe

trees were one mass of blossoming flowers, from the roots right up to the topmost branches. In among the branches and flowers, five varieties of bees, in swarms, and different kinds of birds, in flocks, roamed around, buzzing and warbling with mellifluous sounds. The entire Lumbini Grove was like the Many-Colored Creeper Forest, or like the richly decorated circle of a feasting hall for a powerful king. The queen saw a garden in the sal woods and wanted to relax and enjoy herself there. The ministers bearing the queen entered the sal woods. She went up to the roots of one auspicious sal tree and wished to take hold of one of the branches. The branch bent down like a fresh moist bamboo sapling and came near within reach of her hand. She stretched out her hand and grasped hold of the branch.

At that moment, the urgent movements of labor shook her; people made a screen around her and drew aside. Standing, and grasping the branch of the tree, she gave birth. At that moment the four great Brahmas, pure of heart, arrived, bringing a golden net. They received the Bodhisatta in the golden net, and placed him in front of his mother, saying, "Be happy, your highness. A great son has been born to you." Whereas other living beings when they leave their mother's womb discharge impure matter, the Bodhisatta does not.

He left his mother's womb like someone giving a talk 78
on the Dhamma, descending from a special seat, or a man getting down from a ladder. He was erect, stretched out both hands and both feet, and was unstained by any impurities from being in his mother's womb, unsmeared and pure, shining like a pure jewel placed on fine Benares cloth. But even though that was the case, two showers of water poured down

nikkhittamaṇiratanaṃ viya jotanto mātukucchito nikkhami. evaṃ sante pi bodhisattassa ca bodhisattamātuyā ca sakkāratthaṃ ākāsato dve udakadhārā nikkhamitvā bodhisattassa ca mātu c' assa sarīre utuṃ gāhāpesuṃ. atha naṃ suvaṇṇajālena paṭiggahetvā ṭhitānaṃ brahmānaṃ hatthato cattāro mahārājāno maṅgalasammatāya sukhasamphassāya ajinappaveṇiyā gaṇhiṃsu tesaṃ hatthato manussā dukūlacumbaṭakena manussānaṃ hatthato muñcitvā[1] paṭhaviyaṃ patiṭṭhāya puratthimadisaṃ olokesi. anekāni cakkavāḷasahassāni ekaṅgaṇāni ahesum. tattha devamanussā gandhamālādīhi pūjayamānā mahāpurisa idha tumhehi sadiso añño n' atthi kut' ettha uttaritaro ti āhaṃsu. evaṃ catasso disā ca catasso anudisā ca heṭṭhā uparī ti dasa pi disā anuviloketvā attano sadisaṃ adisvā ayaṃ uttarā disā ti sattapadavītihārena agamāsi mahābrahmunā setacchattaṃ dhāriyamāno suyāmena vālavījaniṃ aññehi ca devatāhi sesarājakakudhabhaṇḍahatthāhi anugammamāno tato sattamapade ṭhito aggo 'ham asmi lokassā ti ādikaṃ āsabhiṃ vācaṃ nicchārento sīhanādaṃ nadi. bodhisatto hi tīsu attabhāvesu mātukucchito nikkhantamatto eva vācaṃ nicchāresi mahosadhattabhāve vessantarattabhāve imasmiṃ attabhāve ti. mahosadhattabhāve kir' assa mātukucchito nikkhamantass' eva sakko devarājā āgantvā candanasāraṃ hatthe ṭhapetvā gato. so taṃ muṭṭhiyaṃ katvā 'va nikkhanto. atha naṃ mātā tāta kiṃ gahetvā āgato 'sī ti pucchi. osadhaṃ ammā ti. iti osadhaṃ gahetvā āgatattā osadhadārako t' ev'

from the sky and refreshed the Bodhisatta and his mother.

And then the Four Great Kings received him on a cloth of antelope skins, soft to the touch, as are used on royal state occasions. From their hands, human beings received him on a roll of fine muslin. Released from their hands, he stood on the ground, and looked toward the east. Thousands of world systems became open to him, like one vast open space. Gods and men paid homage to him with perfumes and garlands, and said: "Great Being: there is no one equal to you here; where is there one greater?" So he searched the four directions, the four intermediate points, and he searched above and below: he explored ten directions, and not seeing anyone equal to himself, he took seven strides. "This is the best direction," he announced. Great Brahma held a white parasol over him, followed by Suyama, holding a fan, and other gods, with other royal symbols in their hands. The Bodhisatta stopped at the seventh step, and with the roar of a lion shouted the cry of victory, starting with: "I am the chief of the world."

Now in three existences, the Bodhisatta spoke words on leaving his mother's womb: in his life as Mahosadha, in his life as Vessantara, and in this life.[8] The story goes that as he was leaving his mother's womb in the Mahosadha rebirth, the divine king Sakka came and placed some fine sandalwood in his hands, and then went away. He emerged from the womb holding it in his fist. His mother asked him, "What is that you are holding, dear one?" He said, "It is medicine, mother." Because he arrived carrying medicine, they gave him the name "Medicine Boy." Taking the medicine, they kept it in a jar. It became a medicine whereby all the sickness

assa nāmaṃ akaṃsu. taṃ osadhaṃ gahetvā cāṭiyaṃ pakkhipiṃsu. āgatāgatānaṃ andhabadhirādīnaṃ tad eva sabbarogavūpasamāya bhesajjaṃ ahosi. tato mahantaṃ idaṃ osadhaṃ mahantaṃ idaṃ osadhan ti uppannavacanaṃ upādāya mahosadho t' ev' assa nāmaṃ jātaṃ. vessantarattabhāve pana mātukucchito nikkhamanto dakkhiṇahatthaṃ pasāretvā 'va atthi nu kho amma kiñci gehasmiṃ dānaṃ dassāmī ti vadanto nikkhami. ath' assa mātā sadhane kule nibbatto 'si tātā ti puttassa hatthaṃ attano hatthatale katvā sahassatthavikaṃ ṭhapāpesi.

79 imasmiṃ pana attabhāve imaṃ sīhanādaṃ nadī ti. evaṃ bodhisatto tīsu attabhāvesu mātukucchito nikkhantamatto 'va vācaṃ nicchāresi. yathā ca paṭisandhikkhaṇe jātikkhaṇe pi 'ssa dvattiṃsa pubbanimittāni pātur ahiṃsu. yasmiṃ pana samaye amhākaṃ bodhisatto lumbinivane jāto tasmiṃ yeva samaye rāhulamātā devī channo amacco kāḷudāyi amacco kanthako assarājā mahābodhi rukkho cattāro nidhikumbhiyo ca jātā tattha ekā gāvutappamāṇā ekā addhayojanappamāṇā ekā tigāvutappamāṇa ekā yojanappamāṇā ahosī ti ime satta sahajātā nāma. ubhayanagaravāsino bodhisattaṃ gahetvā kapilavatthunagaram eva agamaṃsu. taṃ divasaṃ yeva ca kapilavatthunagare suddhodanamahārājassa putto jāto ayaṃ kumāro bodhitale nisīditvā buddho bhavissatī ti tāvatiṃsabhavane haṭṭhatuṭṭhā devasaṅghā celukkhepādīni pavattentā kīḷiṃsu.

of those who could not see or hear, and of those who came with other afflictions, was healed. And the saying came to be, "This is a powerful medicine; this is a powerful medicine!" and his name became Mahosadha.

In the Vessantara birth, after he had left his mother's womb, he held out his right hand and said, "Dear mother, is there anything in the house? I will give a gift." And his mother replied, "You are reborn, my dear, in a wealthy family." Taking his hand in hers, she placed in it a pouch containing a thousand.

And in this birth, he roared the lion's roar. So, in three 79
births he spoke with words as after leaving his mother's womb. And just as at the moment of conception the thirty-two auspicious signs were manifest, so it was at his birth. And at the very moment that the Bodhisatta was born in Lumbini Grove, his queen Rahulamata was born, as was Channa, his minister, Kaludayi the minister, the noble elephant, the royal horse Kanthaka, and the Great Bodhi Tree. Four great jars of treasure came into being.[9] One of these was two miles, one four, one six, and one eight miles in size; these seven phenomena are known as the things that "arise together."

People from both towns took the Bodhisatta and went to Kapilavatthu. And on that day the inhabitants of the Heaven of the Thirty-Three Gods were amazed and delighted; they danced around waving their cloaks and things: "A son has been born to King Suddhodana in Kapilavatthu! One day, this boy will sit under a Bodhi Tree and will become a Buddha!"

Now at that time there was an ascetic called Kala Devala, a private adviser to King Suddhodana, who had achieved the

tasmiṃ samaye suddhodanamahārājassa kulūpako aṭṭhasamāpattilābhī kāḷadevalo nāma tāpaso bhattakiccaṃ katvā divāvihāratthāya tāvatiṃsabhavanaṃ gantvā tattha divāvihāraṃ nisinno tā devatā disvā kiṃkāraṇā tumhe evaṃ tuṭṭhamānasā kīḷatha mayhaṃ p' etaṃ kāraṇaṃ kathethā ti pucchi. devatā āhaṃsu: mārisa suddhodanarañño putto jāto so bodhitale nisīditvā buddho hutvā dhammacakkaṃ pavattessati tassa anantaṃ buddhalīḷhaṃ daṭṭhuṃ dhammañ ca sotuṃ lacchāmā ti iminā kāraṇena tuṭṭh' amhā ti. tāpaso tāsaṃ vacanaṃ sutvā khippaṃ devalokato oruyha rājanivesanaṃ pavisitvā paññattāsane nisinno putto kira te mahārāja jāto passissāmi nan ti āha. rājā alaṃkatapaṭiyattaṃ kumāraṃ ānāpetvā tāpasaṃ vandāpetuṃ abhihari. bodhisattassa pādā parivattitvā tāpasassa jaṭāsu patiṭṭhahiṃsu. bodhisattassa hi ten' attabhāvena vanditabbayuttako añño nāma n' atthi sace hi ajānantā bodhisattassa sīsaṃ tāpasassa pādamūle ṭhapeyyuṃ sattadhā assa muddhaṃ phaleyya. tāpaso na me attānaṃ nāsetuṃ yuttan ti uṭṭhāyāsanā bodhisattassa añjalim paggahesi. rājā taṃ acchariyaṃ disvā attano puttaṃ vandi. tāpaso atīte cattālīsa kappe anāgate cattālīsā ti asīti kappe anussarati. bodhisattassa lakkhaṇasampattiṃ disvā bhavissati nu kho buddho udāhu no ti āvajjitvā upadhārento nissaṃsayaṃ buddho bhavissatī ti ñatvā acchariyapuriso ayan ti sitaṃ akāsi.

eight stages of meditative attainment. He had just eaten his midday meal and had visited the Heaven of the Thirty-Three gods to rest during the heat of the day. While he was sitting there, he saw the gods and asked: "Why are you all so happy, dancing around? Do tell me the reason for this."

The gods said, "Sir, King Suddhodana has had a son. One day he will sit under the Bodhi Tree and become a Buddha. And he will set in motion the wheel of the Dhamma. We are going to get a chance to hear his teaching and to see the infinite grace of a Buddha. That is the reason we are happy."

The ascetic heard these words and quickly came down from the heavenly realm. He entered the royal palace and sat down on a specially prepared seat. He said: "Great king, they say a son has been born to you. I will look at him." The king had the child brought in, dressed in beautiful clothes, and carried him to pay homage to the ascetic. The Bodhisatta's feet turned around and alighted on the matted locks of the ascetic. For in that birth no one can receive homage from a Bodhisatta. If they, through ignorance, had planted the Bodhisatta's head at the ascetic's feet, the man's head would have split into seven. The ascetic thought, "It would not be right to bring about my own destruction." So, he rose from his seat and made a gesture of respect with his palms cupped together. The king saw this miracle and paid homage to his son. The ascetic could bring to mind events in eighty eons—forty in the past and forty in the future. He looked at the characteristic marks of the Bodhisatta: "Will he become a Buddha, or will he not?" As he inspected him, he realized: "Without a doubt, he will become a Buddha: this is a wonderful being." And he smiled.

80 tato ahaṃ imaṃ buddhabhūtaṃ daṭṭhuṃ labhissāmi nu kho ti upadhārento na labhissāmi antarā yeva kālaṃ katvā buddhasatena pi buddhasahassena pi gantvā bodhetum asakkuneyyo arūpabhave nibbattissāmī ti disvā evarūpaṃ nāma acchariyapurisaṃ buddhabhūtaṃ daṭṭhuṃ na labhissāmī ti mahatī vata me jāni bhavissatī ti parodi. manussā disvā amhākaṃ ayyo idān' eva hasitvā puna rodituṃ upaṭṭhito kin nu kho bhante amhākaṃ ayyaputtassa koci antarāyo bhavissatī ti pucchiṃsu. n' atth' etassa antarāyo nissaṃsayena buddho bhavissatī ti. atha kasmā paroditthā ti. evarūpaṃ purisaṃ buddhabhūtaṃ daṭṭhuṃ na labhissāmi mahatī vata me jāni bhavissatī ti attānaṃ anusocanto rodāmī ti āha.

81 tato kin nu kho me ñātakesu koci etaṃ buddhabhūtaṃ daṭṭhuṃ labhissati na labhissatī ti upadhārento bhāgineyyaṃ nālakadārakaṃ addasa. so bhaginiyā gehaṃ gantvā kahaṃ te putto nālako ti. gehe ayya. pakkosāhi nan ti. attano santikaṃ āgataṃ āha: tāta suddhodanamahārājassa kule putto jāto buddhaṃkuro esa pañcatiṃsa vassāni atikkamitvā buddho bhavissatī ti tvaṃ etaṃ daṭṭhuṃ labhissasī ti ajj' eva pabbajāhī ti. sattāsītikoṭidhane kule nibbatto dārako na maṃ mātulo anatthe niyojessatī ti cintetvā tāvad eva antarāpaṇato

Then he thought: "Will I get a chance to see him when he 80
does become a Buddha?" He saw: "I will not. I will die before that time, and will take up rebirth in a formless heaven, where it would be impossible to find awakening. In this realm, I will not be the lucky one able to see this Buddha, even for a hundred or perhaps a thousand existences!" And he wept.

People saw him and asked: "Our honorable sir laughs and then cries. Sir, what disaster is going to happen to our teacher's little boy?"

"There will be no disaster," he replied. "Without a doubt, he will become a Buddha."

—"But why are you crying?"

—"Because I will not get a chance to see such a great man when he does become a Buddha, even if I live for a thousand existences. I cry because I am weeping for myself."

So, then he asked: "Will there be an opportunity for any 81
of my relatives to see him as a Buddha?" He saw there would be a chance for his nephew Nalaka. So he went to his sister's house and said to her: "Where is your son Nalaka?" "In the house, sir." "Call him," he said.

And when he had arrived, he said: "Dear one, a son has been born today to the great king Suddhodana, the seedling of a Buddha. When he has reached the age of thirty-five, he will become a Buddha. You will get the chance to see him then: so today, take the going forth!"

The young man was born into a rich family, with eighty-seven crore. But he thought: "My uncle does not encourage

kāsāvāni c' eva mattikāpattañ ca āharāpetvā kesamassum ohāretvā kāsāyāni vatthāni acchādetvā yo loke uttamapuggalo taṃ uddissa mayhaṃ pabbajjā ti bodhisattābhimukhaṃ añjalim paggayha pañcapatiṭṭhitena vanditvā pattaṃ thavikāya pakkhipitvā aṃsakūṭe olambetvā himavantaṃ pavisitvā samaṇadhammaṃ akāsi. so paramābhisambodhiṃ pattaṃ tathāgataṃ upasaṃkamitvā nālakapaṭipadaṃ kathāpetvā puna himavantaṃ pavisitvā arahattaṃ patvā ukkaṭṭhapaṭipadaṃ paṭipanno satt' eva māse āyuṃ pāletvā ekaṃ suvaṇṇapabbataṃ nissāya ṭhitako 'va anupādisesāya nibbānadhātuyā parinibbāyi. bodhisattam pi kho pañcamadivase sīsaṃ nahāpetvā nāmagahaṇaṃ gaṇhissāmā ti rājabhavanaṃ catujātikagandhehi vilimpitvā lājapañcamakāni pupphāni vikiritvā asambhinnapāyāsaṃ pacāpetvā tiṇṇaṃ vedānaṃ pārage aṭṭhasataṃ brāhmaṇe nimantetvā rājabhavane nisīdāpetvā subhojanaṃ bhojetvā mahāsakkāraṃ katvā kin nu kho bhavissatī ti lakkhaṇāni paṭiggahāpesuṃ.

things without good reason." So, he had yellow robes and an earthenware bowl brought from a store inside immediately. Then he shaved off his hair and beard, and put on the robes, saying: "Whoever is the highest in the world, that's the one my renunciation is for!" Paying homage in the direction of the Bodhisatta, he stretched out with the five parts of the body touching the ground in prostration, pressing his palms together to pay respects. He placed his bowl in his bag, hung it over his shoulders, and went into the Himalayan regions, fulfilling the duties of a mendicant. And when the Buddha did reach his final awakening, he approached him and asked him to teach "The Way of Progress for Nalaka."[10] On his return to the Himalayan regions, Nalaka attained arhatship. He pursued his noble path and lived for seven months more. Then, while staying on the Golden Mountain, he attained the basis of complete release and finally entered into nibbana.

On the fifth day they had the Bodhisatta's head washed and said, "Let us have a naming ceremony." They sprinkled the royal palace with four kinds of perfumes, and scattered five kinds of flowers, with rice grain as the fifth. They had thick milk-rice prepared and invited 108 Brahmans who had mastered the three Vedas. They seated them in the royal apartments and fed them with the choicest food. After according them the highest honor, they asked them to read his marks. "What will he be?" they asked.

tesu

rāmo dhajo lakkhaṇo cā 'pi mantī
koṇḍañño ca bhojo suyāmo sudatto
ete tadā aṭṭha ahesuṃ brāhmaṇā
chaḷaṅgavā mantaṃ vyākariṃsū ti

82 ime aṭṭh' eva brāhmaṇā lakkhaṇapaṭiggāhakā ahesuṃ. paṭisandhigahaṇadivase supino pi eteh' eva paṭiggahīto. tesu satta janā dve aṅguliyo ukkhipitvā dvedhā vyākariṃsu: imehi lakkhaṇehi samannāgato agāraṃ ajjhāvasamāno rājā hoti cakkavattī pabbajamāno buddho ti sabbaṃ cakkavattirañño siribhavaṃ ācikkhiṃsu. tesaṃ pana sabbadaharo goṭṭato koṇḍañño nāma māṇavo bodhisattassa lakkhaṇavaranipphattiṃ oloketvā etassa agāramajjhe ṭhānakāraṇaṃ n' atthi ekanten' eva vivattacchaddo buddho bhavissatī ti ekam eva aṅguliṃ ukkhipitvā ekaṃsavyākaraṇaṃ vyākāsi. ayaṃ hi katādhikāro pacchimabhavikasatto paññāya itare satta jane abhibhavitvā imehi lakkhaṇehi samannāgatassa agāramajjhe ṭhānaṃ nāma n' atthi asaṃsayaṃ buddho bhavissatī ti ekam eva gatiṃ addasa tasmā ekaṃ aṅguliṃ ukkhipitvā evaṃ vyākāsi. atha te brāhmaṇā attano

Among them were:
There were eight Brahmans there, Rama, Dhaja, 270
Lakkhana, and Manti, Kondannya, Bhojo, Suyama,
and Sudatta, skilled in reading the six traditional
bodies of lore. They explained their art.

These were the eight Brahmans who were adept in reading 82
the marks; they had interpreted the dream on the day of conception, too. Seven of them raised two fingers as they explained two possible courses:

"If someone with these marks stays in the householders' life, he will be a universal monarch; if he takes the going forth, he will be a Buddha."

And they expounded all the great glory of a universal monarch. But the youngest of them all, a young man with the family name Kondannya, examined the great perfection of the marks on the Bodhisatta, and spoke. "There is no reason for this one to stay in the household life. For he will become a Buddha, drawing away the covering from the world." And he raised only one finger as he made this unequivocal prediction. This man, who was now in his last existence, having made previous vows in earlier lives, surpassed the other

gharāni gantvā putte āmantayiṃsu: tātā amhe mahallakā suddhodanamahārājassa puttaṃ sabbaññutaṃ pattaṃ mayaṃ sambhaveyyāma vā no vā tumhe tasmiṃ kumāre sabbaññutaṃ patte tassa sāsane pabbajeyyāthā ti. te satta pi janā yāvatāyukaṃ ṭhatvā yathākammaṃ gatā. koṇḍañño māṇavo 'va arogo ahosi. so mahāsatte buddhim anvāya mahābhinikkhamanaṃ abhinikkhamitvā anukkamena uruvelaṃ gantvā ramaṇīyo vata ayaṃ bhūmibhāgo alaṃ vat' edaṃ kulaputtassa padhānatthikassa padhānāyā ti cittaṃ uppādetvā tattha vāsaṃ upagato. mahāpuriso pabbajito ti sutvā tesaṃ brāhmaṇānaṃ putte upasaṃkamitvā evam āha: siddhatthakumāro kira pabbajito so nissaṃsayaṃ buddho bhavissati sace tumhākaṃ pitaro arogā assuṃ ajja nikkhamitvā pabbajeyyuṃ sace tumhe pi iccheyyātha etha ahan taṃ purisaṃ anuppabbajissāmīti. te sabbe ekacchandā bhavituṃ nāsakkhiṃsu. tayo janā na pabbajiṃsu.

seven in wisdom. He saw only one path open: "There are no grounds for the one possessing these marks to stay in the midst of the household life. Without a doubt he will become a Buddha." He saw only one course of action, and as he made his prediction, he raised only one finger.

So those Brahmans went home, and spoke to their sons: "Dear ones, we are old. We might or might not live to see the son of the great king Suddhodana attain omniscience. But when he does obtain omniscience, you should take the going forth and follow his Dhamma." And when all seven had fulfilled their life span, they died and were reborn according to their actions.

Now the young man Kondannya was healthy. He left behind everything for the sake of wisdom and made the great renunciation. He arrived at Uruvela and thought: "This is a delightful piece of land. It is just the thing for a man of good family to make the great struggle, with all his effort." And he went to live there. When he heard that the Great Being had indeed taken the going forth, Kondannya then approached those sons of the Brahmans. "They are saying that Siddhattha has taken the going forth. He will, without any doubt, become a Buddha. If your fathers had been in good health, they would have left their homes and taken the going forth themselves. So, if you would like it, come too: I am going to follow him and take the going forth." But they could not all be of the same mind.

83 koṇḍaññabrāhmaṇaṃ jeṭṭhakaṃ katvā itare cattāro pabbajiṃsu. te pañca pi janā pañcavaggiyatherā nāma jātā. tadā pana rājā kiṃ disvā mayhaṃ putto pabbajissatī ti pucchi. cattāri pubbanimittānī ti. kataraṃ katarañ cā ti. jarājiṇṇaṃ vyādhitaṃ mataṃ pabbajitan ti. rājā ito paṭṭhāya evarūpānaṃ mama puttassa santikaṃ upasaṃkamituṃ mā adattha mayhaṃ puttassa buddhabhāvena kammaṃ n' atthi ahaṃ mama puttaṃ dvisahassadīpaparivārānaṃ catunnaṃ mahādīpānaṃ issariyādhipaccaṃ rajjaṃ kārentaṃ chattiṃsayojanaparimaṇḍalāya parisāya parivutaṃ gaganatale vicaramānaṃ passitukāmo ti evañ ca pana vatvā imesaṃ catuppakārānaṃ purisānaṃ kumārassa cakkhupathe āgamanaṃ nivāraṇatthaṃ catusu disāsu gāvute gāvute ārakkhaṃ ṭhapesi. taṃ divasañ ca pana maṅgalaṭṭhāne sannipatitesu asītiyā ñātikulasahassesu ekeko ekamekaṃ puttaṃ paṭijāni: ayaṃ buddho vā hotu rājā vā mayaṃ ekamekaṃ puttaṃ dassāma sace pi buddho bhavissati khattiyasamaṇeh' eva purakkhataparivārito vicarissati sace pi rājā bhavissati khattiyakumāreh' eva purakkhataparivārito vicarissatī ti. rājā bodhisattassa uttamarūpasampannā vigatasabbadosā dhātiyo paccupaṭṭhāpesi. bodhisatto anantena parivārena mahantena sirisobhaggena vaḍḍhati.

Three did not take the going forth. The other four made 83
Kondannya their leader and did renounce. These five were called "the company of five elders." Now at that time, the king asked, "What will my son see so that he takes the going forth?"

—"Four signs."

The king said, "What are they?"

—"A person worn out with old age, a sick person, a dead person, and an ascetic."

The king thought, "From now on, let no such thing come near my son. My son has no need to become a Buddha. I'd like to see my son exercising rule and mastery over the four great continents and the two thousand islands that surround them, ruling the skies, attended by a retinue as large as thirty-six *yojanas*." When he had decided this, he placed guards at intervals of a *gāvuta*, in each of the four directions, to prevent these four kinds of persons coming anywhere near the sight of his son.[11]

On that day too, eighty thousand men from the same clan met together in the festive area, and each dedicated a son. They said, "Whether the child becomes a Buddha or a king, we each give a son. If he becomes a Buddha, he will live attended to and honored by Kshatriya caste monastics. And if he becomes a king, he will be attended to and honored by Kshatriya caste ministers." And the king appointed for the Bodhisatta nurses of great beauty and free from any fault. He grew up surrounded by great glory, with an innumerable following around him.

84 ath' ekadivasaṃ rañño vappamaṅgalaṃ nāma ahosi. taṃ divasaṃ sakalanagaraṃ devavimānaṃ viya alaṃkaronti. sabbe dāsakammakarādayo ahatavatthanivatthā gandhamālādipatimaṇḍitā rājakule sannipatanti. rañño kammante naṅgalasahassaṃ yojīyati. tasmiṃ pana divase ekena ūnaṃ aṭṭhasataṃ saddhiṃ balivaddarasmiyottehi rajataparikkhatāni honti. rañño ālambananaṅgale pana rattasuvaṇṇaparikkhataṃ hoti. balivaddānaṃ siṅgarasmipatodā 'pi suvaṇṇaparikkhatā 'va honti. rājā mahāparivārena nikkhamanto puttaṃ gahetvā agamāsi. kammantaṭṭhāne eko jamburukkho bahalapalāso sandacchāyo ahosi. tassa heṭṭhā kumārassa sayanaṃ paññāpetvā upari suvaṇṇatārakhacitaṃ vitānaṃ bandhāpetvā sāṇipākārena parikkhipāpetvā ārakkhaṃ ṭhapetvā rājā sabbālaṃkāraṃ alaṃkaritvā amaccaparivuto naṅgalakaranaṭṭhānaṃ agamāsi. tattha rājā suvaṇṇanaṅgalaṃ gaṇhāti amaccā ekaūnaṭṭhasataṃ rajatanaṅgalāni kassakā sesanaṅgalāni te tāni gahetvā ito c'

Now one day the king called what is known as the Plowing Festival. On that day they decorate the entire town like a heavenly palace. All the workers and servants, in fresh new clothes, crowned with sweetly smelling garlands, assemble in the royal area. For the king's job, a thousand plows are yoked. For this event, eight hundred were decorated with silver, with reins and crossbars, bar one. And the one for the king was decorated with tawny gold, as were the horns, the reins, and the goads for the oxen. 84

The king left his palace with a great entourage and took his son too as he went to the place. There was a rose-apple tree there with dense foliage, providing deep shade. The king had the child's couch prepared under it. Over the couch, a canopy was set up, scattered with golden stars, and a hemp curtain was knotted around this. Leaving guards there, the king, in his sumptuous outfit, went off to wield the plow, with a large retinue in tow. There, the king took up the golden plow, and the ministers took up the 799 silver plows, and the plowmen the remaining plows. They took up the plows and worked them, backward and forward. The king plowed from one side to another, and then back again, and in that spot the splendor was glorious.

The nurses looking after the Bodhisatta left the tent and cried, "Let's have a look at the king's success!" When the Bodhisatta saw that no one was around, he dashed up onto the couch and sat cross-legged. Watching the inbreath and the outbreath closely, he attained the first *jhāna*. The nurses were roaming around with food and drink and were a bit delayed. The shadows of the other trees moved away; but the

ito ca kasanti. rājā orato vā pāraṃ gacchati pārato vā oraṃ āgacchati etasmiṃ ṭhāne mahāsampattiṃ anubhosi. bodhisattaṃ parivāretvā nisinnā dhātiyo rañño sampattiṃ passissāmā ti antosāṇito bahi nikkhantā. bodhisatto ito c' ito ca olokento kañci adivā vegena uṭṭhāya pallaṃkaṃ ābhujitvā ānāpāne pariggahetvā paṭhamajjhānaṃ nibbattesi. dhātiyo khajjabhojjantare vicaramānā thokaṃ cirāyiṃsu. sesarukkhānaṃ chāyā ativattā tassa pana rukkhassa parimaṇḍalā hutvā aṭṭhāsi.

dhātiyo ayyaputto ekako ti vegena sāṇiṃ ukkhipitvā anto pavisamānā bodhisattaṃ sayane pallaṃkena nisinnaṃ tañ ca pāṭihāriyaṃ disvā gantvā rañño ārocesuṃ: deva kumāro evaṃ nisinno aññesaṃ rukkhānaṃ chāyā ativattā jamburukkhassa chāyā parimaṇḍalā ṭhitā ti. rājā vegen' āgantvā pāṭihāriyaṃ disvā idaṃ te tāta dutiyaṃ vandanan ti puttaṃ vandi.

85 Atha anukkamena bodhisatto soḷasavassapadesiko jāto. rājā bodhisattassa tiṇṇaṃ utūnaṃ anucchavike tayo pāsāde kāresi ekaṃ navabhūmakaṃ ekaṃ sattabhūmakaṃ ekaṃ pañcabhūmakaṃ cattālīsasahassā ca nāṭakiyo upaṭṭhāpesi. bodhisatto devo viya accharāsaṅghaparivuto alaṃkatanāṭakaparivuto nippurisehi turiyehi paricāriyamāno mahāsampattiṃ anubhavanto utuvārena utuvārena tesu tesu pāsādesu viharati. rāhulamātā pan' assa devī aggamahesī ahosi. tass' evaṃ mahāsampattiṃ anubhavantassa ekadivasaṃ ñātisaṅghassa abbhantare ayaṃ kathā udapādi: siddhattho kīḷāpasuto 'va vicarati na kiñci sippaṃ sikkhati saṅgāme

one made by the rose-apple tree remained stable, spreading around in a circle. The attendants then remembered: "The boy is alone!" and hurriedly went back and lifted the curtain. They saw then the Bodhisatta sitting on the couch and saw the wonder. They went up to the king: "Your highness, your son remains seated, and while the shadows of the other trees have moved on, the shadow on him remains, spread out in a circle."

The king rushed back to witness the miracle, and paid homage to him: "This, my dear one, is my second homage to you."

In due course, the Bodhisatta reached the age of sixteen. 85
The king had three palaces built, suited to the three seasons: one was nine stories high, one seven, and one was five. He provided forty thousand dancing women. He was surrounded by forty thousand dancing girls. The Bodhisatta was like a god, with a circle of heavenly nymphs, being entertained by music made by an all-female orchestra. He lived in these three palaces in turn with the seasons, enjoying the greatest luxuries. Rahulamata, his queen, was chief consort.

While he was enjoying this great abundance, one day murmurings started among some of his relatives: "Siddhattha spends so much time having fun he has not learned how to do anything. What will he do if war breaks out?"

The king sent for his son and spoke to him: "Dear one, your family is saying that you are spending too much time having fun and have not learned how to do anything. What do you think you should do about this?"

"Dear sir, your highness, it is not necessary for me to have any training. Have the drum beaten in the city for my

paccupaṭṭhite kiṃ karissatī ti. rājā bodhisattaṃ pakkosāpetvā tāta tava ñātakā siddhattho kiñci sippaṃ asikkhitvā kīḷāpasuto 'va vicaratī ti vadanti ettha kiṃ pattakāle maññasī ti. deva mama sippaṃ sikkhanakiccaṃ n' atthi nagare mama sippaṃ dassanatthaṃ bheriñ carāpetha ito sattamadivase ñātakānaṃ sippaṃ dassessāmī ti. rājā tathā akāsi. bodhisatto akkhaṇavedhivālavedhidhanuggahe sannipātāpetvā mahājanassa majjhe aññehi ca dhanuggahehi asādhāraṇaṃ ñātakānaṃ dvādasavidhaṃ sippaṃ dassesi. taṃ sarabhaṅgajātake āgatanayena veditabbaṃ. tadāssa ñātisaṅgho nikkaṃkho ahosi.

86 ath' ekadivasaṃ bodhisatto uyyānabhūmiṃ gantukāmo sārathiṃ āmantetvā rathaṃ yojehī ti āha. so sādhū ti paṭisuṇitvā mahārahaṃ uttamarathaṃ sabbālaṃkārena alaṃkaritvā kumudapattavaṇṇe cattāro maṅgalasindhave yojetvā bodhisattassa paṭivedesi. bodhisatto devavimānasadisaṃ rathaṃ abhirūhitvā uyyānābhimukho agamāsi. devatā siddhatthakumārassa abhisambujjhanakālo āsanno pubbanimittaṃ dassessāmā ti ekaṃ devaputtaṃ jārājajjaraṃ khaṇḍadantaṃ palitakesaṃ vaṃkaṃ obhaggasarīraṃ daṇḍahatthaṃ pavedhamānaṃ katvā dassesuṃ. taṃ bodhisatto c' eva sārathi ca passanti. tato bodhisatto sārathiṃ samma ko nām' esa puriso kesāpi 'ssa na yathā aññesan ti mahāpadāne āgatanayena pucchitvā tassa vacanaṃ

display of the arts. On the seventh day I'll show my relatives my training!" The king did this. The Bodhisatta had some archers assembled who could hit their targets during a flash of lightning or split a horse's hair. And in the middle of the assembly, he displayed his skills to his family, in twelve ways not shared in common with other archers. This should be understood as given in "The Sarabhanga Jataka." Then his family members had no more doubts.

Now one day, the Bodhisatta wanted to go to a pleasure 86
park, and said to his carriage driver: "Get the carriage yoked." He agreed and said, "Certainly." He decked a magnificent carriage, of priceless value, with all kinds of ornaments and yoked four white Sindh state horses, whose color was like the white lotus. He had this announced to the Bodhisatta. The Bodhisatta got up into a carriage that was like a pavilion for the gods and set off for the pleasure park. The gods said to each other: "The time for Prince Siddhattha's awakening is drawing near. Let us show him the signs." They manifested one of the gods as an old man overcome with decay, with broken teeth, and white hair. His body was crooked and broken, trembling, with a stick in his hand. The Bodhisatta, and the carriage driver too, saw him. Then the Bodhisatta asked the carriage driver, as is described in the "The Great Discourse on the Harvest of Deeds," "Sir, what kind of person is this man? His hair is not like other people's."[12] When he had heard the answer to this question, he exclaimed: "Shame on birth: for where there is birth, old age is seen too!" With his heart filled with urgency, he turned back and went up into the palace.

sutvā dhi-r-atthu vata bho jātiyā yatra hi nāma jātassa jarā paññāyissatī ti saṃviggahadayo tato 'va paṭinivattivā pāsādam eva abhirūhi. rājā kiṃkāraṇā mama putto khippaṃ paṭinivattī ti pucchi. jiṇṇaṃ purisaṃ disvā devā ti jiṇṇaṃ purisaṃ disvā pabbajissatī ti āhaṃsu. tasmā maṃ nāsetha sīghaṃ puttassa nāṭakāni sajjetha sampattiṃ anubhavanto pabbajjāya satiṃ na karissatī ti vatvā ārakkhaṃ vaḍḍhetvā sabbadisāsu addhayojane addhayojane ṭhapesi. pun' ekadivasaṃ bodhisatto tath' eva uyyānaṃ gacchanto devatāhi nimmitaṃ vyādhitaṃ purisaṃ disvā purimanayen' eva pucchitvā saṃviggahadayo nivattitvā pāsādaṃ abhirūhi. rājā 'pi pucchitvā heṭṭhāvuttanayen' eva saṃvidahitvā puna vaḍḍhetvā samantato tigāvutappamāṇe padese ārakkhaṃ ṭhapesi. aparaṃ pana ekadivasaṃ bodhisatto tath' eva uyyānaṃ gacchanto devatāhi nimmitaṃ kālakataṃ disvā purimanayen' eva pucchitvā saṃviggahadayo puna nivattitvā pāsādaṃ abhirūhi. rājā 'pi pucchitvā heṭṭhāvuttanayen' eva saṃvidahitvā puna vaḍḍhetvā samantato yojanappamāṇe padese ārakkhaṃ ṭhapesi. aparaṃ pana ekadivasaṃ uyyānaṃ gacchanto tath' eva devatāhi nimmitaṃ sunivatthaṃ supārutaṃ pabbajitaṃ disvā ko nām' eso sammā ti sārathiṃ pucchi. sārathi kiñcā 'pi buddhuppādassa abhāvā pabbajitaṃ vā pabbajitaguṇe vā na jānāti devānubhāvena pana pabbajito

The king asked, "Why has my son turned back in such a hurry?"

He said, "He has seen an old man, your highness."

—"They say that once he has seen an old man, he will take the going forth."

—"You destroy me with this. Arrange for dramatic shows for him. While he is enjoying happiness, he will not have a mind for renunciation." And he increased the guards, placing them at half a *yojana* apart, in all the directions around.

Then one day, the Bodhisatta went to the pleasure park and saw a sick man, made manifest by the gods. He asked the same question as before, and again, turned back and entered into the palace with a heart filled with urgency. The king asked the same question too and gave the same orders as before. He increased the guard and placed them for an area that extended to three *gāvutas*.

And on another day, the Bodhisatta went to the pleasure park and saw a dead man, made manifest by the gods. He made the same inquiry as he had done before, and then again turned back and entered into the palace with a heart filled with urgency. The king also inquired again and gave the same orders as before. And he increased the guards, placing them all around for the extent of a *yojana*.

On yet another day the Bodhisatta went to the pleasure park. He saw a renouncer, carefully dressed, and properly fitted out, and asked his carriage driver, "What kind of man is this?" Now at that time there was no Buddha at all in the world, and the carriage driver did not understand what a renouncer was, nor his distinguishing features. Despite this, through divine inspiration, he said, "This is a renouncer."

nām' esa devā ti vatvā pabbajjāya guṇe vaṇṇesi. bodhisatto pabbajjāya ruciṃ uppādetvā taṃ divasaṃ uyyānaṃ agamāsi.

87 dīghabhāṇakā panāhu: cattāri nimittāni ekadivasen eva disvā agamāsī ti. tattha divasabhāgaṃ kīḷitvā maṅgalapokkharaṇiyaṃ nahāyitvā atthaṃgate suriye maṅgalasilāpaṭṭe nisīdi attānaṃ alaṃkārāpetukāmo. ath' assa paricārakapurisā nānāvaṇṇāni dussāni nānāppakārā ābharaṇavikatiyo mālāgandhavilepanāni ca ādāya samantā parivāretvā aṭṭhaṃsu. tasmiṃ khaṇe sakkassa nisinnāsanaṃ uṇhaṃ ahosi. so ko nu kho maṃ imamhā ṭhānā cāvetukāmo ti upadhārento bodhisattassa alaṃkaraṇakālaṃ disvā vissakammaṃ āmantesi: samma vissakamma siddhatthakumāro ajja aḍḍharattasamaye mahābhinikkhamanaṃ nikkhamissati ayam assa pacchimo alaṃkāro uyyānaṃ gantvā mahāpurisaṃ dibbālaṃkārehi alaṃkarohī ti. so sādhū ti paṭisuṇitvā devatānubhāvena taṃ khaṇaṃ yeva upasaṃkamitvā tass' eva kappakasadiso hutvā kappakassa hatthato veṭhanadussaṃ gahetvā bodhisattassa sīsaṃ veṭhesi. bodhisatto hatthasamphassen' eva nāyaṃ manusso devaputto eko ti aññāsi. veṭhanen' eva veṭhitamatte sīsamoliyaṃ maṇiratanākārena dussasahassaṃ abbhuggañchi puna veṭhentassa dussasahassan ti dasakkhattuṃ veṭhentassa dasadussasahassāni abbhuggacchiṃsu. sīsaṃ khuddakaṃ dussāni bahūni kathaṃ abbhuggatānī ti na cintetabbaṃ tesu hi sabbamahantaṃ sāmalatāpupphappamāṇaṃ avasesāni kutumbakapupphappamāṇāni ahesuṃ. bodhisattassa sīsaṃ kiñjakkhagavacchitaṃ viya kuyyakapupphaṃ ahosi. ath' assa sabbālaṃkārapatimaṇḍitassa sabbatālāvacaresu sakāni sakāni ca paṭibhānāni dassayantesu brāhmaṇesu jaya-nandā-ti-ādi-vacanehi sūtamāghatandhakādīsu nānappakārehi

He extolled the virtues of renouncing the world. And that day the Bodhisatta started to hold a light for renunciation.

The reciters of "The Long Discourses of the Buddha" say, 87
however, that he saw all four signs on the same day, and then went on to the pleasure park.[13] There, during the day, he relaxed and bathed in its beautiful lake, and at sunset he sat on the auspicious royal slab, wanting to be robed. And his attendants brought all kinds of garments of different colors, and various garlands, perfumes, and ointments, and stood all around him. At that moment, the throne of Sakka became hot.

He thought, "Who is it who now wants me to come down from here?" He saw that the time for the dressing of the Bodhisatta had come. He spoke to Vissakamma:[14] "Dear Vissakamma, today, at midnight, the young man Siddhattha is going to make the great renunciation. This is the last time he will be dressed in glory. Go to the pleasure park and dress the Great Being with heavenly robes and accessories." He agreed saying, "Very well."

And through his divine power, at that very moment, he approached him, looking like a court attendant. And taking from his court attendant's hand the material for the turban, he arranged it around the Bodhisatta's head. At the touch of his hand, the Bodhisatta knew: "This is no human being, it is a son of the gods." While the turban was being wound around, a thousand folds sprung up, forming the appearance of a jeweled crest; and while it was being wound again, once more a thousand folds sprung up; when it had been wound ten times, ten thousand folds appeared. It is beyond the power of imagination to conceive how so many folds

maṅgalavacanathutighosehi sambhavantesu sabbālaṃkārapatimaṇḍitaṃ rathavaraṃ abhirūhi. tasmiṃ samaye rāhulamātā puttaṃ vijātā ti sutvā suddhodanamahārājā puttassa me tuṭṭhiṃ nivedethā ti sāsanam pahiṇi. bodhisatto taṃ sutvā rāhulo jāto bandhanaṃ jātan ti āha. rājā kiṃ me putto avacā ti pucchitvā taṃ vacanaṃ sutvā ito paṭṭhāya me nattu rāhulakumāro yeva nāmaṃ hotū ti. bodhisatto pi kho rathavaraṃ āruyha mahantena yasena atimanoramena sirisobhaggena nagaraṃ pāvisi. tasmiṃ samaye kisāgotamī nāma khattiyakaññā uparipāsādavaratalagatā nagaraṃ padakkhiṇaṃ kurumānassa bodhisattassa rūpasiriṃ disvā pītisomanassajātā imaṃ udānaṃ udānesi:

271 nibbutā nūna sā mātā
nibbuto nūna so pitā
nibbutā nūna sā nāri
yass' āyaṃ īdiso patī ti.

could spring up on such a small head! For the largest of them were like the white flower of the black creeper, while the rest were like whorls of white-nettle blossoms. The head of the Bodhisatta became like a spatika flower, with a lattice of interwoven filaments.

While he was arrayed in all his rich glory, the musicians showed off their particular excellences, the Brahmans honored him with songs of victory and delight, and bards and Magadhans sang songs of rejoicing, all together, with various kinds of whoops of joy. He ascended into his carriage.

Now at that time, great king Suddhodana heard that Rahulamata, the queen, had given birth to a son. He ordered a message to be sent: “Speak of my joy to my son!” The Bodhisatta heard this, and said, “Rahula has been born; a bond has come into being.”[15]

The king asked, “What did my son say?” and heard this comment. He said, “From now on, let my grandson be known by the name Rahula.” And now the Bodhisatta, riding in his beautifully adorned carriage, entered the town with great splendor and overwhelming magnificence.

At that time, a noble girl called Kisagotami had gone to the flat roof on the upper story of her palace, and she saw the beautiful appearance of the Bodhisatta as he paraded around the city. Filled with delight and happiness, she burst out into a song of joy:

“Peaceful indeed is the mother, 271
Peaceful indeed is the father,
Peaceful indeed is the woman,
Who has a husband just like him.”

88 bodhisatto taṃ sutvā cintesi: ayam evaṃ āha evarūpaṃ attabhāvaṃ passantiyā mātuhadayaṃ nibbāyati pituhadayaṃ nibbāyati pajāpatihadayaṃ nibbāyatī ti kasmiṃ nu kho nibbute hadayaṃ nibbutaṃ nāma hotī ti. ath' assa kilesesu virattamānasassa etad ahosi: rāgaggimhi nibbute nibbutaṃ nāma hoti dosaggimhi mohaggimhi nibbute nibbutaṃ nāma hoti mānadiṭṭhiādisu sabbakilesadarathesu nibbutesu nibbutaṃ nāma hoti ayaṃ me sussavaṇaṃ sāvesi ahaṃ hi nibbānaṃ gavesanto carāmi ajj' eva mayā gharāvāsaṃ chaḍḍetvā nikkhamma pabbajitvā nibbānaṃ gavesituṃ vaṭṭati ayaṃ imissā ācariyabhāgo hotū ti kaṇṭhato omuñcitvā kisāgotamiyā satasahassagghaṇakaṃ muttāhāraṃ pesesi. sā siddhatthakumāro mayi paṭibaddhacitto hutvā paṇṇākāraṃ pesesī ti somanassajātā ahosi.

89 bodhisatto pi mahantena sirisobhaggena attano pāsādaṃ abhirūhitvā sirisayane nipajji. tāvad eva naṃ sabbālaṃkārapatimaṇḍitā naccagītādisu susikkhitā devakaññā viya rūpappattā itthiyo nānāturiyāni gahetvā samparivārayitvā abhiramāpentiyo naccagītavāditāni payojayiṃsu. bodhisatto kilesesu virattacittatāya naccādisu anabhirato muhuttaṃ niddaṃ okkami. tā 'pi itthiyo yass' atthāya mayaṃ naccādīni payojayema so niddaṃ upagato idāni kimatthaṃ kilamāmā

The Bodhisatta heard this and mused. "She says that a mother's heart is made peaceful, a father's heart is made peaceful, and a wife's heart is made peaceful, just by seeing the physical form. But what should be made peaceful in the heart before peace comes?" As his mind was free from defilements, he reflected: "Only when the fire of desire is made peaceful, and the fire of hatred is made peaceful, and there is peace from conceit and views, with all the defilements, is one really peaceful. This was a very apt statement for me. I do search for the peaceful: nibbana. It is right that today I give up the householder's life and take the going forth; and I will search for the peace of nibbana. This should go to her as a fee for a teacher." And he took off a string of pearls, worth a hundred thousand, and sent it to Kisagotami, saying, "Let this go to her as the fee for the teacher." And she was delighted and thought: "Prince Siddhattha has fallen in love with me and sent me a present!" 88

The Bodhisatta returned to his own palace in great splendor, and when he had gone upstairs, he rested on a magnificent couch. Immediately, beautiful women, adorned and richly decked out came up to him, carrying musical instruments. With all their songs and dances they were like heavenly nymphs, and they surrounded him, trying to get him to enjoy joining in and enticing him with songs and dances and all the rest. 89

The Bodhisatta's mind was free from defilements, so he took no delight in the entertainments and went to sleep. At that the women murmured: "Why should we try to get him going with dances and the like? He has just gone to sleep. Why should we bother?" Lamps filled with scented oil were

ti gahitagahitāni turiyāni ajjhottharitvā nipajjiṃsu. gandhatelapadīpā jhāyanti. bodhisatto pabujjhitvā sayanapiṭṭhe pallaṃkena nisinno addasa tā itthiyo turiyabhaṇḍāni avattharitvā niddāyantiyo ekaccā paggharitakheḷā lālākilinnagattā ekaccā dante khādantiyo ekaccā kākacchantiyo ekaccā vippalapantiyo ekaccā vivaṭamukhā ekaccā apagatavatthā pākaṭabhībhacchasambādhaṭṭhānā. so tāsaṃ taṃ vippakāraṃ disvā bhiyyoso mattāya kāmesu viratto ahosi. tassa alaṃkatapaṭiyattaṃ sakkabhavanasadisam pi taṃ mahātalaṃ vippaviddhanānākuṇapabharitaṃ āmakasusānaṃ viya upaṭṭhāsi tayo bhavā ādittagehasadisā viya khāyiṃsu upaddutaṃ vata bho upassaṭṭhaṃ vata bho ti udānaṃ pavatti ativiya pabbajjāya cittaṃ nami.

90 so ajj' eva mayā mahābhinikkhamanaṃ nikkhamituṃ vaṭṭatī ti sayanā vuṭṭhāya dvārasamīpaṃ gantvā ko etthā ti āha. ummāre sīsaṃ katvā nipanno channo ahaṃ ayyaputta channo ti āha. ahaṃ ajja mahābhinikkhamanaṃ nikkhamitukāmo ekaṃ me assaṃ kappehī ti. so sādhu devā 'ti assabhaṇḍakaṃ gahetvā assasālaṃ gantvā gandhatelapadīpesu jalantesu sumanapaṭṭavitānassa heṭṭhā ramaṇīye bhūmi-bhāge ṭhitaṃ kanthakaṃ assarājānaṃ disvā ajja mayā imam eva kappetuṃ vaṭṭatī ti kanthakaṃ kappesi. so kappiyamāno 'va aññāsi: ayaṃ kappanā atigāḷhā aññesu divasesu uyyānakīḷādigamane kappanā viya na hoti mayhaṃ ayyaputto ajja mahābhinikkhamanaṃ nikkhamitukāmo bhavissatī

burning. The Bodhisatta woke up and, sitting cross-legged on his couch, he looked at the women, with their musical instruments abandoned. They were asleep: some were dribbling saliva out of their mouths, some had bodies wet with perspiration, some were grinding their teeth, some were chatting away in their sleep, some were groaning, some had their mouths wide open, and some had their clothes in disarray, clearly exposing parts of the body that should be hidden through self-respect. He saw this disorder and became even more free from sense-desires. The large courtyard of the palace, beautifully decorated and resembling the realm of King Sakka, seemed to him like a charnel ground, filled with corpses scattered around. The three realms of existence just seemed to him like houses on fire. He gave out a spontaneous cry: “Oh, this is so burdensome! This is so depressing!” And his heart inclined toward renunciation.

He got up from his bed. “Right. Today is the day I leave 90
for the great renunciation.” He went to the door and called: “Who is there?” Channa, his driver, who was resting with his head against the door, said: “Your highness, it is me, Channa.” “I wish to set out on my great renunciation today. Prepare a horse for me.” “Certainly,” said Channa. Taking the livery for a horse, he went to the stable. Scented oil lamps were burning there, so he could see the state horse, Kanthaka, standing on a delightful spot beneath a silken canopy scattered with jasmine flowers. “This is the one I should get ready for today.” And he got him ready.

Even while he was being prepared, the horse realized: “This is very heavy-duty equipment. On other days, for relaxing outings to the pleasure park, the livery is not like

ti tato tuṭṭhamānaso mahāhasitaṃ hasi. so saddo sakalanagaraṃ pattharitvā gaccheyya. devatā pana taṃ saddaṃ nirumhitvā na kassaci sotuṃ adaṃsu. bodhisatto pi kho channaṃ pesetvā 'va puttaṃ tāva passissāmī ti cintetvā nisinnapallaṃkato vuṭṭhāya rāhulamātāya vasanaṭṭhānaṃ gantvā gabbhadvāraṃ vivari. Tasmiṃ khaṇe antogabbhe gandhatelappadīpo jhāyati. rāhulamātā sumanamallikādīnaṃ pupphānaṃ ammaṇamattena abhippakiṇṇasayane puttassa matthake hatthaṃ ṭhapetvā niddāyati. bodhisatto ummāre pādaṃ ṭhapetvā ṭhitako 'va oloketvā sac' āhaṃ deviyā hatthaṃ apanetvā mama puttaṃ gaṇhissāmi devī pabujjhissatī ti evaṃ me gamanantarāyo bhavissatī ti buddho hutvā 'va āgantvā passissāmī ti pāsādatato otari. yaṃ pana jātakaṭṭhakathāya tadā sattāhajāto rāhulakumāro hotī ti vuttaṃ taṃ sesaṭṭhakathāsu n' atthi. tasmā idam eva

this. Today my master wants to make the great renunciation." Very happy in heart, he neighed his delight. The sound would have gone and filled the entire town, but the gods muffled the noise so no one could hear it. The Bodhisatta dismissed Channa. He thought, "I am going to see my son." He rose from his seated position and went up to the apartment of Rahulamata and opened the door of the bedroom. A lamp filled with scented oil burned inside the room. Rahulamata was sleeping on a bed strewn with a measure of jasmine flowers and Arabian jasmine, resting her hand upon her son. The Bodhisatta had his foot in the entrance way and had a look: "If I move her hand and take hold of my son the queen will wake. And she will pose an obstacle to my going. I will see him when I become a Buddha." And he stepped down from the upper part of the palace.

The statement made in the Jataka commentary that the prince was seven days old at the time is not found in other commentaries: because of this, this account alone should be accepted.

In this way, the Bodhisatta came down from the upper story of the palace. He approached his horse and said: "Dear Kanthaka, today you are going to take me across in one night and through your help I will take the world with its gods across too." And he leaped upon Kanthaka's back. Kanthaka was eighteen cubits in length, starting from his neck, and was of comparable height. He was strong and rapid, and completely white, like a washed conch shell. If he neighed or pawed the ground, the sound would carry through the entire town, so the gods, through their power, muffled the sound of his snorts so no one could hear it, and put their hands under

gahetabbaṃ. evaṃ bodhisatto pāsādatalā otaritvā assasamīpaṃ gantvā evam āha: tāta kanthaka tvaṃ ajja ekarattiṃ maṃ tāraya ahaṃ taṃ nissāya buddho hutvā sadevakaṃ lokaṃ tāressāmī ti tato ullaṃghitvā kanthakassa piṭṭhiṃ abhirūhi. kanthako gīvato paṭṭhāya āyāmena aṭṭhārasahattho hoti tadanucchavikena ubbedhena samannāgato thāmajavasampanno sabbaseto dhotasaṃkhasadiso. so sace haseyya vā pādasaddaṃ kareyya vā saddo sakalanagaraṃ avatthareyya tasmā devatā attano ānubhāvena tassa yathā na koci suṇāti evaṃ hasitaṃsaddaṃ sannirumbhitvā akkamaṇākkamaṇapadavāre hatthatalāni upanāmesuṃ. bodhisatto assavarassa piṭṭhivaramajjhagato channaṃ assassa vāladhiṃ gāhāpetvā aḍḍharattasamaye mahādvārasamīpaṃ patto. tadā pana rājā evaṃ bodhisatto yāya kāyaci velāya nagaradvāraṃ vivaritvā nikkhamituṃ na sakkhissatī ti dvīsu dvārakavāṭesu ekekaṃ purisasahassena vivaritabbaṃ kārāpesi. bodhisatto thāmabalasampanno hatthigaṇanāya koṭisahassahatthīnaṃ balaṃ dhāreti purisagaṇanāya dasapurisakoṭisahassassa. so cintesi: sace dvāraṃ na avāpurīyati ajja Kanthakassa piṭṭhe nisinno 'va vāladhiṃ gahetvā ṭhitena channena saddhiṃ yeva kanthakaṃ ūrūhi nippīḷetvā aṭṭhārasahatthubbedhaṃ pākāraṃ uppatitvā atikkamissāmī ti. channo cintesi: sace dvāraṃ na vivarīyati ahaṃ ayyaputtaṃ khandhe nisīdāpetvā kanthakaṃ dakkhiṇahatthena kucchiyaṃ parikkhipanto upakacchantare katvā pākāraṃ uppatitvā atikkamissāmī ti. kanthako pi cintesi: sace dvāraṃ na vivarīyati ahaṃ attano sāmikaṃ piṭṭhiyaṃ yathānisinnam eva channena vāladhiṃ gahetvā ṭhitena saddhiṃ yeva ukkhipitvā pākāraṃ uppatitvā atikkamissāmī ti. sace dvāraṃ na avāpurīyittha yathācintitam eva

his hooves at each step. The Bodhisatta mounted the back of the stately horse, and he got Channa to grab onto his tail. At midnight they reached the main gate of the city.

Now at one time the king had had an idea: "If at any time the Bodhisatta wants to open the gates to the town, he will not be able to." So he fixed the doors on the gateways so that a thousand men were needed to open each door. The Bodhisatta was endowed with great physical stamina and power: worked out in terms of elephant power, he had the strength of a thousand crore of elephants; worked out in manpower, he had the strength of ten thousand crore of men.

The Bodhisatta thought about it: "If the door does not open of its own accord, I will now, while sitting on Kanthaka's back, and with Channa clinging onto the tail, press Kanthaka hard with my thighs and just leap over the ramparts, all eighteen cubits high, and get on my way."

Channa thought about it: "If the door does not open of its own accord, I will leap over the rampart, putting my master on my shoulder and keeping Kanthaka under my arms, taking him firmly round his flanks, and so get on my way."

Kanthaka thought about it: "If the door does not open of its own accord, I will jump upward, with my master still astride my back, with Channa clutching on to my tail too, and I'll clear the rampart and get on my way."

tīsu janesu aññataro sampādeyya. dvāre adhivatthā devatā pana dvāraṃ vivari.

91 tasmiṃ yeva khaṇe māro bodhisattaṃ nivattessāmī ti āgantvā ākāse ṭhito āha: mārisa mā nikkhami ito te sattame divase cakkaratanaṃ pātubhavissati dvisahassaparittadīpaparivārānaṃ catunnaṃ mahādīpānaṃ rajjaṃ kāressasi nivatta mārisā ti āha. ko si tvan ti. ahaṃ vasavat tī ti māra jānām' ahaṃ mayhaṃ cakkaratanapātubhāvaṃ anatthiko 'haṃ rajjena dasasahassilokadhātuṃ unnādetvā buddho bhavissāmī ti āha. māro ito dāni te paṭṭhāya kāmavitakkaṃ vā vyāpādavitakkaṃ vā vihiṃsāvitakkaṃ vā cintitakāle jānissāmī ti otārāpekho chāyā viya anapagacchanto anubandhi. bodhisatto pi hatthagataṃ cakkavattirajjaṃ kheḷapiṇḍaṃ viya anapekho chaḍḍetvā mahantena sakkārena nagarā nikkhamitvā āsāḷhipuṇṇamāya uttarāsāḷhanakkhatte vattamāne nikkhamitvā ca puna nagaraṃ apaloketukāmo jāto evañ ca pan' assa citte uppannamatte yeva mahāpurisa na tayā nivattitvā olokanakammaṃ katan ti vadamānā viya mahāpaṭhavī kulālacakkaṃ viya chijjitvā parivatti. bodhisatto nagarābhimukho ṭhatvā nagaraṃ

Had the door not opened of its own accord, one of the three would have achieved their intention.

But the god who lived in the gateway opened it for them.

Mara

At that moment, Mara arrived, thinking, "I will get the 91
Bodhisatta to turn back." He stood in the sky and said: "Do not renounce, sir! For in seven days the wheel treasure will appear. You will rule a kingdom of the four great continents and their two thousand surrounding islands. Turn back, sir!"

—"Who are you?"

—"I am the Powerful One."

"Mara, I know very well about the appearance of the wheel treasure, but I have no use for a kingdom. I will become a Buddha, making the ten thousand world systems resound!"

Mara warned: "From now on, when any thought of desire, or thought of hatred, or thought of malevolence arises in your mind: I will know." And he followed him closely, constantly on the watch for any lapse, just like a shadow that never leaves.

The Bodhisatta renounced the kingdom that had been given to him like a glob of spittle, without any hankering for it. He set out from the city with great honor on the full moon day of Asalha, as the constellation of Asalha was on the wane But he did wish to look back at the city once more.[16] As this thought arose in his mind, the great earth revolved, like a potter's wheel breaking off its bearings, as if to say: "Great Being, there is no need to turn back to look, for you to do your work." The Bodhisatta stood in front of the city, and did look

oloketvā tasmiṃ puthavippadese kanthakanivattanacetiyaṭṭhānaṃ dassetvā gantabbamaggābhimukhaṃ kanthakaṃ katvā pāyāsi mahantena sakkārena uḷārena sirisobhaggena.
92 tadā kir' assa devatā purato saṭṭhiṃ ukkāsahassāni dhārayiṃsu pacchato saṭṭhiṃ dakkhiṇapassato saṭṭhiṃ vāmapassato saṭṭhiṃ. aparā devatā cakkavāḷamukhavaṭṭiyaṃ aparimāṇā ukkā dhārayiṃsu aparā devatā ca nāgasupaṇṇādayo ca dibbehi gandhehi mālehi cuṇṇehi dhūpehi pūjayamānā gacchanti pāricchattakapupphehi c' eva ghanameghavuṭṭhikāle dhārāhi viya nabhaṃ nirantaraṃ ahosi. dibbāni saṅgītāni pavattanti samantato aṭṭhaturiyāni saṭṭhituriyānī ti aṭṭhasaṭṭhituriyasatasahassāni pavajjayiṃsu samuddakucchiyaṃ meghatthanitakālo viya yugandharakucchiyaṃ sāgaranigghosakālo viya vattati. iminā sirisobhaggena gacchanto bodhisatto ekaratten' eva tīṇi rajjāni atikkamma tiṃsayojanamatthake anomānāmanadītīraṃ pāpuṇi. kiṃ pana asso tato paraṃ gantuṃ na sakkotī ti. no na sakkoti so hi ekacakkavāḷagabbhaṃ nābhiyā ṭhitacakkassa nemivaṭṭiṃ maddanto viya antantena caritvā pure pātarāsam eva āgantvā attano sampāditaṃ bhattaṃ bhuñjituṃ samattho. tadā pana devatānāgasupaṇṇādīhi ākāse ṭhatvā ossaṭṭhehi gandhamālādīhi yāva ūruppadesā sañchannaṃ sarīraṃ ākaḍḍhitvā gandhamālājaṭaṃ chindantassa atipapañco ahosi tasmā tiṃsayojanamattam eva agamāsi. atha bodhisatto nadītīre ṭhatvā channaṃ pucchi:

at it, and indicated the place for a shrine commemorating the spot where he had left with Kanthaka.

Then he led Kanthaka to the opening of the route they were going to follow, and he left with great honor and magnificent nobility.

The story goes that at that time the gods carried sixty 92
thousand torches in front, and sixty thousand torches to the rear, and to the right and the left too. Some gods, encircling round the ranges of the ends of the world, carried boundless numbers of torches too. Nagas, garudas, and many other supernatural beings came along, paying homage with divine perfumes, garlands, powdered sandalwood, and incense. The sky was filled with coral *parichatta* flowers from Sakka's heaven, as if rain clouds were pouring rain, making an endless cloud. Heavenly songs filled the air, and sixty million eight hundred thousand musical instruments played everywhere, like thunder roaring in the middle of the seas, or like the great ocean surging up from the heart of the mountain Yugandhara.

Proceeding with such dramatic magnificence, the Bodhisatta crossed three kingdoms in one night and arrived at the banks of the river Anoma, the Not Insignificant River, having traveled a distance of thirty *yojanas*. And how was his horse not able to go further? It was not that he lacked power: he was capable of traveling from one end of the circle of the world to another, as if he were stepping over the circumference of a wheel that had been placed on its side. He could do that in a morning and still be able to come back and eat food that had been prepared for him. But this time he was greatly impeded, having to drag himself and cut his way through the

kin nāma ayaṃ nadī ti. anomā nāma devā ti. amhākam pi pabbajjā anomā nāma bhavissa tī ti paṇhiyā ghaṭṭento assassa saññaṃ adāsi. asso uppatitvā aṭṭhausabhavitthārāya nadiyā pārimatīre aṭṭhāsi. bodhisatto assapiṭṭhito oruyha rajatapaṭṭasadise vālukāpuline ṭhatvā channaṃ āmantesi: samma channa tvaṃ mayhaṃ ābharaṇāni c' eva kanthakañ ca ādāya gaccha ahaṃ pabbajissāmī ti. aham pi deva pabbajissāmī ti. bodhisatto na labbhā tayā pabbajituṃ gaccha tvan ti tikkhattuṃ paṭibāhitvā ābharaṇāni c' eva kanthakañ ca paṭicchāpetvā cintesi: ime mayhaṃ kesā samaṇasāruppā na hontī ti añño bodhisattassa kese chindituṃ yuttarūpo n' atthi tato sayam eva khaggena chindissāmī ti dakkhiṇahatthena asiṃ gaṇhitvā vāmahatthena moliyā saddhiṃ cūḷaṃ gahetvā chindi. kesā dvaṅgulamattā hutvā dakkhiṇato āvattamānā sīsaṃ allīyiṃsu tesaṃ yāvajīvaṃ tad eva pamāṇaṃ ahosi massuñ ca tadanurūpaṃ ahosi. puna kesamassuohāraṇakiccaṃ nāma n' āhosi.

vast masses of garlands and flowers showering down from all the nagas, garudas, and other supernatural beings hovering in the sky. Even his thighs were hidden. Because of this, he managed only thirty *yojanas*.

The Bodhisatta, stopping by the side of the river, asked Channa, his driver: "What is this river called?"

Channa replied, "The Anoma, your highness."

—"Ah; my renunciation will also be not insignificant either." And he signaled to his horse by pressing him with his heel. The horse leaped up over the river, which was eight *usabhas* in width, and stood firm on the far bank.

The Bodhisatta alighted from his horse and stood on the bank, a sandy dune that was like a sheet of silver. He spoke to Channa. "Dear Channa, go now, and take my ornaments and Kanthaka back with you. I am going to take the going forth."

—"But your highness, I will take the going forth too."

The Bodhisatta said, "It is not permitted for you to take the going forth. Just go."

He refused Channa's request three times and entrusted him with the ornaments and with Kanthaka too. Then he thought: "This hair is not right for an ascetic. But it is not suitable for anyone else to cut the hair of a Bodhisatta. I'll cut it myself with my sword." He picked up his sword with his right hand and holding his topknot in a turban in his left hand, he chopped it off. The hairs that were left on his head were two finger-widths long and curled around to the right. They stayed that length for the remainder of his life, and his beard was just the same: he never needed a haircut or a shave again.

93 bodhisatto saha molinā cūḷaṃ gahetvā sac' āhaṃ buddho bhavissāmi ākāse tiṭṭhatu no ce bhūmiyaṃ patatū 'ti antalikkhe khipi taṃ cūḷāmaṇiveṭhanaṃ yojanappamāṇaṃ ṭhānaṃ gantvā ākāse aṭṭhāsi. sakko devarājā dibbacakkhunā oloketvā yojaniyaratanacaṃgoṭakena sampaṭicchitvā tāvatiṃsabhavane cūḷāmaṇicetiyan nāma patiṭṭhāpesi:

272 chetvāna moliṃ varagandhavāsitaṃ
vehāsayaṃ ukkhipi aggapuggalo
sahassanetto sirasā paṭiggahī
suvaṇṇacaṃgoṭavarena vāsavo ti.

94 puna bodhisatto cintesi: imāni kāsikavatthāni mayhaṃ na samaṇasāruppānī ti. ath' assa kassapabuddhakāle purāṇasahāyako ghaṭīkāro mahābrahmā ekaṃ buddhantaraṃ jaraṃ appattena mittabhāvena cintesi: ajja me sahāyako mahābhinikkhamanaṃ nikkhanto samaṇaparikkhāram assa gahetvā gacchissāmī ti.

273 ticīvarañ ca patto ca
vāsi sūciñ ca bandhanaṃ
parissāvanena aṭṭh' ete
yuttayogassa bhikkhuno ti

The Bodhisatta took hold of the jeweled turban and spoke. 93
"If I am to become a Buddha, may it remain in the air, and may it not fall to the ground." He flung it into the air, and the turban, woven with jewels, rose to the height of a *yojana*, and then just stayed there. Sakka, the king of the gods, saw this with his divine eye, and receiving it into a jeweled box a *yojana* high, he took it up to the Heaven of the Thirty-Three Gods, and placed it there; it was called the Shrine of Jewels.

> The highest of men cut off his turban, instilled with the 272
> choicest perfumes, and threw it up to the heavens. The thousand-eyed one, Sakka, received it with respect, and kept it in a golden casket.

And then the Bodhisatta thought: "These clothes of the 94
finest cloth are not suitable for an ascetic." Now, Great Brahma Ghatikara had been his dear friend at the time of the Buddha Kassapa. Out of his love, which had not become old in the time that had passed, he had this thought: "Today my dear friend is making the great renunciation. I will go to him, taking the clothes of an ascetic."

> Three robes, a bowl, a razor, a needle, a belt, and a 273
> water strainer: These eight items are just the right thing for a monk devoted to spiritual practice.

95 ime aṭṭha samaṇaparikkhāre āharitvā adāsi. bodhisatto arahaddhajaṃ nivāsetvā uttamapabbajjāvesaṃ gaṇhitvā channa mama vacanena mātāpitunnaṃ ārogyaṃ vadehī ti uyyojesi. channo bodhisattaṃ vanditvā padakkhiṇaṃ katvā pakkāmi. kanthako pana channena saddhiṃ mantayamānassa bodhisattassa vacanaṃ suṇanto ṭhatvā n' atth' idāni mayhaṃ puna sāmino dassanan ti cakkhupathaṃ vijahanto sokaṃ adhivāsetuṃ asakkonto hadayena phalitena kālaṃ katvā tāvatiṃsabhavane kanthako nāma devaputto hutvā nibbatti. channassa paṭhamaṃ eko 'va soko ahosi kanthakassa pana kālakiriyāya dutiyena sokena pīḷito rodanto paridevanto nagaraṃ agamāsi. bodhisatto pi pabbajitvā -- tasmiṃ yeva padese anūpiyaṃ nāma ambavanaṃ atthi tattha sattāhaṃ pabbajjāsukhena vītināmetvā ekadivasen' eva tiṃsayojanamaggaṃ padasā gantvā rājagahaṃ pāvisi pavisitvā sapadānaṃ piṇḍāya cari. sakalanagaraṃ bodhisattassa rūpadassanena dhanapālakena paviṭṭha-rājagahaṃ viya asurindena paviṭṭha-devanagaraṃ viya ca saṃkhobhaṃ agamāsi. rājapurisā gantvā deva evarūpo nāma satto nagare piṇḍāya carati devo vā manusso vā nāgo vā supaṇṇo vā ko nām' eso ti na jānāmā ti ārocesuṃ. rājā pāsādatale ṭhatvā mahāpurisaṃ disvā acchariyabbhuto jāto purise āṇāpesi: gacchatha bhaṇe vīmaṃsatha sace amanusso bhavissati nagarā nikkhamitvā antaradhāyissati sace devatā

And he brought these eight requisites for an ascetic and gave 95
them to him. The Bodhisatta put on the banner of the worthy ones, and now wearing the clothes of an ascetic, he sent Channa on his way: "Dear Channa, tell my parents for me that I am well." Channa paid his respects to the Bodhisatta, walked around him reverentially, and started on his way.

But Kanthaka stood nearby and heard the words of the Bodhisatta as he was in conversation with Channa and thought: "From this time forward I will never see my master again." He could not bear the grief, and slipping away from their line of vision, he died, with his heart broken. And Kanthaka was reborn as a son of the gods, in the Heaven of the Thirty-Three Gods. Up till then, Channa's grief had been single, but at Kanthaka's death it was a double grief. And so, weeping and crying, he made his way back to the city.

The Bodhisatta had become an ascetic. He spent a week in a mango grove called Anupiya, in that very region, just enjoying the happiness of having taken the going forth. One day he went along a road of three *yojanas* and went into Rajagaha, and once there he went on a house-by-house alms round. As he arrived, the whole city was thrown into excitement at the sight of the Bodhisatta, as if it were the entry of Dhanapalaka to Rajagaha, or the entry of the chief of the Asuras in the city of the gods. The king's men approached the king and informed him: "Your highness, there is such a person who is going on an alms round in the city! We do not know if he is a god, or a man, or a naga, or a garuda, or what he is." The king stood on the roof of the palace and watched the Great Being and was filled with amazement and wonder. He ordered his men, "Go and find out. If he is not a human

bhavissati ākāsena gacchissati sace nāgo bhavissati paṭhaviyaṃ nimujjitvā gamissati sace manusso bhavissati yathāladdhaṃ bhikkhaṃ paribhuñjissatī ti. mahāpuriso pi kho missakabhattaṃ saṃharitvā alaṃ me ettakaṃ yāpanāyā ti ñatvā paviṭṭhadvāren' eva nagarā nikkhamitvā paṇḍavapabbatachāyāya puratthābhimukho nisīditvā āhāraṃ paribhuñjituṃ āraddho. ath' assa antāni parivattitvā mukhena nikkhamanākārappattāni ahesuṃ. tato tena attabhāvena evarūpassa āhārassa cakkhunā 'pi adiṭṭhapubbatāya tena paṭikkūlāhārena aṭṭiyamāno evaṃ attanā 'va attānaṃ ovadi: siddhattha tvaṃ sulabhānnapānakule tivassikagandhasālibhojanaṃ nānaggarasehi bhuñjanaṭṭhāne nibbattivā 'pi ekaṃ paṃsukūlikaṃ disvā kadā nu kho aham pi evarūpo hutvā piṇḍāya caritvā bhuñjissāmi bhavissati nu kho me so kālo ti cintetvā nikkhanto idāni kiṃ nām' etaṃ karosī ti. evaṃ attanā 'va attānaṃ ovaditvā nibbikāro hutvā āhāraṃ paribhuñji. rājapurisā taṃ pavattiṃ disvā gantvā rañño ārocesuṃ. rājā dūtavacanaṃ sutvā vegena nagarā nikkhamitvā bodhisattassa santikaṃ gantvā iriyāpathasmiṃ yeva pasīditvā bodhisattassa sabbaṃ issariyaṃ niyyādesi. bodhisatto mayhaṃ mahārāja vatthukāmehi vā kilesakāmehi vā attho n' atthi ahaṃ paramābhisambodhiṃ patthayanto nikkhanto ti. rājā anekappakāraṃ yācanto pi tassa cittaṃ alabhitvā addhā tvaṃ buddho bhavissasi buddhabhūtena pana te paṭhamaṃ mama vijitaṃ āgantabban ti.

being, he will disappear when he leaves the city: if he is a god, he will go up into the sky; if he is a naga he will go and dive into the earth. But if he is human, he will just eat the food that he has been given."

The Great Being collected a meal of various foods and realized: "That is quite enough for me." He left the city by the gate that he entered through, and in the shadow of the mountain Pandava he sat down facing the east and began to eat his food. But then his stomach started to turn, and it was as if the food was going to be vomited up through his mouth. He was disgusted with the revolting food, which was like nothing he had set eyes on before. He gave himself a telling off: "Siddhattha, you have come from a family where there is food and drink in abundance and have eaten only perfumed rice from the third season, with various delicacies. You saw an ascetic dressed in rag robes and wondered whether or not you could eat the food you obtained on an alms round. What are you doing about that now?"

He spoke to himself in this way, overcame his repugnance, and just ate the food. The king's men saw what happened and reported back to the king. The king heard the messengers' account, and in haste left the city and went up to the Bodhisatta. He became so inspired at the bearing of the Bodhisatta that he offered him a prosperous living. The Bodhisatta replied, "Your highness, I do not have any need for possessions or for sensory pleasures. I have renounced, so as to find the highest awakening." The king framed his request in all sorts of ways, but he could not change his mind. He said, "Certainly you are going to become a Buddha. And when Buddhahood has taken place, come to my region first."

96 ayam ettha saṃkhepo vitthāro pana pabbajjaṃ kittayissāmi yathā pabbaji cakkhumā ti imaṃ pabbajjāsuttaṃ saddhiṃ aṭṭhakathāya oloketvā veditabbo. bodhisatto pi rañño paṭiññaṃ datvā anupubbena cārikaṃ caramāno āḷārañ ca kālāmaṃ uddakañ ca rāmaputtaṃ upasaṃkamitvā samāpattiyo nibbattetvā nāyaṃ maggo bodhiyā ti tam pi samāpattibhāvanaṃ analaṃkaritvā sadevakassa lokassa attano thāmaviriyasandassanatthaṃ mahāpadhānaṃ padahitukāmo uruvelaṃ gantvā ramaṇīyo vat' āyaṃ bhūmibhāgo ti tatth' eva vāsaṃ upagantvā mahāpadhānaṃ padahi. te pi koṇḍaññapamukhā pañca pabbajitā gāmanigamarājadhānīsu bhikkhāya carantā tattha bodhisattaṃ sampāpuniṃsu. atha naṃ chabbassāni mahāpadhānaṃ padahantaṃ idāni buddho bhavissati idāni buddho bhavissatī ti pariveṇasammajjanādikāya vattapaṭivattāya upaṭṭhahamānā santikāvacarā c' assa ahesuṃ. bodhisatto pi kho koṭippattaṃ dukkarakārikaṃ karissāmī ti ekatilataṇḍulādīhi pi vītināmesi sabbaso pi āhārūpacchedaṃ akāsi devatā 'pi lomakūpehi ojaṃ upasaṃharamānā paṭikkhipi. ath' assa tāya nirāhāratāya paramakasimānappattakāyassa suvaṇṇavaṇṇo

This is the story in brief, but a longer account is given, and 96
can be looked up and followed in "The Discourse on Going Forth," along with its commentary, starting with the lines, "I shall praise the renunciation, and how the wise one took the going forth..."[17]

The Bodhisatta gave the king his word, and went traveling, stage by stage, until he came upon Alara Kalama and Uddaka Ramaputta.[18] He then found meditative attainment but realized, "This is not the path to awakening."

He was dissatisfied with the cultivation of those attainments and wanted to find the great challenge, which would show to gods and men stamina and a real application of effort. So he went to Uruvela and thought: "This is a delightful spot." And he went to stay there and conducted his truly heroic struggle. The five ascetics, with Kondannya at their head, were on the move, wandering through villages, market towns, and royal cities for alms. They met up with the Bodhisatta. For six years they based themselves near him as he embarked on his great struggle. They thought, "Now he will become a Buddha, now he will become a Buddha," and they swept the sleeping areas, and attended him.

Then the Bodhisatta thought: "I will practice extreme mortification." He survived on one sesame seed or one grain of rice each day, and such things. Sometimes he went completely without food. He stopped the gods from infusing nutritive essence into his skin. Then his body, which had been golden in complexion, turned dark from the terrible emaciation it experienced as a result of that fasting. The thirty-two marks of the Great Being were obscured.

kāyo kāḷavaṇṇo ahosi dvattiṃsa mahāpurisalakkhaṇāni paṭicchannāni ahesuṃ. app-ekadā appāṇakaṃ jhānaṃ jhāyanto mahāvedanāhi abhitunno visaññībhūto caṅkamanakoṭiyaṃ patati. atha naṃ ekaccā devatā kālakato samaṇo gotamo ti vadanti ekaccā vihāro 'v' eso arahatan ti āhaṃsu. tattha yāsaṃ kālakato ti ahosi tā gantvā suddhodanamahārājassa ārocesum: tumhākaṃ putto kālakato ti. mama putto buddho hutvā kālakato ahutvā ti. buddho bhavituṃ n' āsakkhi padhānabhūmiyaṃ yeva patitvā kālakato ti.

97 idaṃ sutvā rājā n' āhaṃ saddahāmi mama puttassa bodhiṃ appatvā kālakiriyā nāma n' atthī ti paṭikkhipati. kasmā pana rājā na saddahatī ti kāḷadevalatāpasassa vandāpanadivase jamburukkhamūle ca pāṭihāriyānaṃ diṭṭhattā. puna bodhisatte saññaṃ paṭilabhitvā uṭṭhite tā devatā āgantvā ārogo te mahārāja putto ti ārocenti. rājā jānām' ahaṃ puttassa amaraṇabhāvan ti vadeti. mahāsattassa chabbassāni dukkarakāriyaṃ karontassa ākāse gaṇṭhikaraṇakālo viya ahosi. so ayaṃ dukkarakārikā nāma bodhāya maggo na hotī ti oḷārikaṃ āhāraṃ āhāretuṃ gāmanigamesu piṇḍāya caritvā āhāraṃ āhari. ath' assa dvattiṃsa mahāpurisalakkhaṇāni pākatikāni ahesuṃ kāyo suvaṇṇavaṇṇo ahosi. pañcavaggiyā bhikkhū ayaṃ chabbassāni dukkarakārikaṃ karonto pi sabbaññutaṃ paṭivijjhituṃ n' āsakkhi idāni gāmādisu piṇḍāya caritvā

One day, while practicing a *jhāna* that involved suppressing the breath, he passed out from the agonizing pains, and collapsed at the edge of the area for walking meditation.

At that point some of the gods said, "The ascetic Gotama has died." Though some said, "This is just an abiding for those who have attained." Those present thought he was dead and went to King Suddhodana and informed him: "King Suddhodana, your son is dead."

The king responded: "Did he die after he had become a Buddha?"

—"He was not able to become a Buddha. He collapsed at the place where he was practicing his exertions, and then died."

When he heard this, the king said: "Then I do not believe 97
it. My son will die only after he has attained awakening." Now, why did the king not believe it? Because he had seen the miracle of Kaladeva and the miracle at the foot of the rose-apple tree. Then the Bodhisatta regained his faculties and got up. The same gods went back to the king and told him, "Your son is well, your highness." The king replied, "I knew my son could not have died."

While the Great Being had been practicing his austerities for six years, it was as if it was a time when a tangle of knots had been made in the sky. He decided: "Practicing these mortifications is not the path to awakening." He went wandering for alms from village to town, in order to eat solid food, and survived on that. At this, the thirty-two marks of the Great Being reappeared, and his body became golden again. The five monks thought: "Even though he has been

oḷārikaṃ āhāraṃ āhariyamāno kiṃ sakkhissati bāhuliko esa padhānavibbhanto sīsaṃ nahāyitukāmassa ussāvabinduta-kkaṇaṃ viya amhākaṃ etassa santikā visesatakkaṇaṃ kiṃ no iminā ti mahāpurisaṃ pahāya attano attano pattacīva-raṃ gahetvā aṭṭhārasayojanamaggaṃ gantvā isipatanaṃ pavisiṃsu.

98 tena kho pana samayena uruvelāyaṃ senāninigame senā-nikuṭimbikassa gehe nibbattā sujātā nāma dārikā vaya-ppattā ekasmiṃ nigrodharukkhe patthanaṃ akāsi: sace samajātikaṃ kulagharaṃ gantvā paṭhamagabbhe puttaṃ labhissāmi anusaṃvaccharaṃ te satasahassapariccāgena balikammaṃ karissāmī ti. tassā sā patthanā samijjhi. sā mahāsattassa dukkarakārikaṃ karontassa chaṭṭhe vasse paripuṇṇe visākhapuṇṇamāya balikammaṃ kātukāmā hutvā puretaraṃ dhenusahassaṃ laṭṭhimadhukavane carāpetvā tāsaṃ khīraṃ pañca dhenusatāni pāyetvā tāsaṃ khīraṃ aḍḍhatiyānī ti evaṃ yāva soḷasannaṃ dhenūnaṃ khīraṃ aṭṭha dhenuyo pivanti tāva khīrassa bahalatañ ca madhuratañ ca ojavantatañ ca. patthayamānā khīrapari-vattanaṃ nāma akāsi. sā visākhapuṇṇamadivase pāto 'va balikammaṃ karissāmī ti rattiyā paccūsasamayaṃ paccuṭṭ-hāya tā aṭṭha dhenuyo duhāpesi. vacchakā dhenūnaṃ thanamūlaṃ n' āgamaṃsu. thanamūle pana navabhājanesu upanītamattesu attano dhammatāya khīradhārā pavattiṃsu. taṃ acchariyaṃ disvā sujātā sahatthen' eva khīraṃ gahetvā navabhājane pakkhipitvā sahatthen' eva aggiṃ katvā paci-tuṃ ārabhi. tasmiṃ pāyāse paccamāne mahantamahantā bubbulā uṭṭhahitvā dakkhiṇāvattā hutvā sañcaranti ekaphu-sitam pi bahi na patati uddhanato appamattako pi dhūmo na uṭṭhahati. tasmiṃ samaye cattāro lokapālā āgantvā uddhane

practicing mortifications for six years, he has not been able to penetrate through to awakening.

"And how can he do it now, while he is going traveling for alms in the towns and suchlike, and he is eating solid food? He has shirked the great effort and is being indulgent. Any thought for distinction while we are near him is like a man trying to wash his head from a drop or two of dew. What use is he to us?" They took up their bowls and their robes and went away. They traveled a distance of eighteen *yojanas* and entered Isipatana.

Now at that time there was a young woman called Sujata, 98
born in the family of the householder Senani, in the village of Senani in Uruvela. When she had come of age, she made a wish at a banyan tree. "If I marry someone from a family of equal rank to mine and manage to have a son as my first child, I'll make an offering every year to you, of a hundred thousand." And her prayer was successful. She wanted to make her offering on the full-moon day in May, Vesakha—in the sixth year since the Bodhisatta had started on his austerities. She had first of all sent a thousand cows out to graze on a field of sugarcane. She had then got five hundred cows to drink their milk, and then two hundred and fifty to drink theirs. Going on like this she had brought the number down to the last sixteen, whose milk she got eight cows to drink. And she made the milk "do the rounds" like this to make it thick and sweet and rich with nourishment.

As she had decided she would make her offering early in the morning on the May full-moon day, she got up at dawn and milked the eight cows. The calves did not go near their mothers' udders—for at the moment new churns were placed

ārakkhaṃ gaṇhiṃsu. mahābrahmā chattaṃ dhāresi. sakko alātāni samānento aggiṃ jālesi. devatā dvisahassadīpaparivāresu catusu mahādīpesu devānañ ca manussānañ ca upakappanaojaṃ attano devānubhāvena daṇḍakabaddhaṃ makhupaṭalaṃ pīḷetvā madhuṃ gaṇhamānā viya saṃharitvā tattha pakkhipiṃsu. aññesu hi kālesu devatā kabaḷe kabaḷe ojaṃ pakkhipanti sambodhidivase ca pana parinibbānadivase ca ukkhaliyaṃ yeva pakkhipanti. sujātā ekadivasen' eva tattha attano pākaṭāni anekāni acchariyāni disvā puṇṇadāsiṃ āmantesi: amma puṇṇe ajja amhākaṃ devatā ativiya pasannā mayā ettake kāle evarūpaṃ acchariyaṃ nāma na diṭṭhapubbaṃ vegena gantvā devaṭṭhānaṃ paṭijaggāhī ti. sā sādhu ayye ti tassā vacanaṃ sampaṭicchitvā turitaturitā rukkhamūlaṃ agamāsi.

99 bodhisatto pi kho tasmiṃ rattibhāge pañca mahāsupine disvā parigaṇhanto nissaṃsayen' āhaṃ buddho ajja bhavissāmī ti katasanniṭṭhāno tassā rattiyā accayena katasarīrapaṭijaggano bhikkhācārakālaṃ āgamayamāno pāto 'va āgantvā tasmiṃ rukkhamūle nisīdi attano pabhāya sakalarukkhaṃ

under their udders, streams of milk poured into them, quite of their own accord. Seeing this wonder, Sujata took the milk with her own hands and poured it into new pans. With her own hands, she laid the fire and started to boil the milk. And while the milk-rice was simmering, great big bubbles started to form on the surface and swirled around, circling to the right. Not a drop fell outside the pan. Not even a whiff of smoke arose from the open stove: for on this occasion, the four Great Protectors of the world had arrived, and had set up a guard over the stove. Great Brahma was there, holding a parasol, and King Sakka had arranged the sticks together and lit the fire. Just as a man crushing a honeycomb formed on a stick would extract the honey, the gods had gathered up a life-essence that would nourish gods and men throughout the four continents and their two thousand surrounding islands; they infused it into the milk-rice. At other times, gods infuse such essence drop by drop, but on the day of the awakening and on the day of the entrance into nibbana, they infuse it into the very cooking pot itself. Sujata saw the wonders that were shown to her on one and the same day, and said to Punna (Full Moon), her servant girl, "Dear Punna, our god is really happy today. I have seen such miracles today that I've never seen before. Do hurry and offer it at the place where the god stays." Punna replied, "Yes, lady." And she followed her command and hastened to the foot of the tree.

Meanwhile, the Bodhisatta had dreamed five powerful 99
dreams in the night, and had realized: "Without a doubt, today is the day I will become a Buddha." With the passing of night, he had washed, seen to his bodily needs and, early in the morning, had sat at the foot of the tree. He was now filling

obhāsayamāno. atha kho sā puṇṇā āgantvā addasa bodhisattaṃ rukkhamūle pācīnalokadhātuṃ olokayamānaṃ nisinnaṃ sarīrato c' assa nikkhantāhi pabhāhi sakalarukkhaṃ suvaṇṇavaṇṇaṃ disvā tassā etad ahosi: ajja amhākaṃ devatā rukkhato oruyha sahatthen' eva balikammaṃ paṭicchituṃ nisinnā maññe ti ubbegapattā hutvā vegena gantvā sujātāya etam atthaṃ ārocesi.

100 sujātā tassā vacanaṃ sutvā tuṭṭhamānasā hutvā ajja dāni paṭṭhāya mama jeṭṭhadhītuṭṭhāne tiṭṭhāhī ti dhītu anucchavikaṃ sabbālaṃkāraṃ adāsi. yasmā pana buddhabhāvaṃ pāpuṇanadivase satasahassagghanikaṃ suvaṇṇapātiṃ laddhuṃ vaṭṭati tasmā sā suvaṇṇapātiyaṃ pāyāsaṃ pakkhipissāmī ti cittaṃ uppādetvā satasahassagghanikaṃ suvaṇṇapātiṃ nīharāpetvā tattha pāyāsaṃ pakkhipitukāmā pakkabhājanaṃ āvajjesi. sabbo pāyāso padumapattā udakaṃ viya vinivaṭṭitvā pātiyaṃ patiṭṭhāsi ekapātipūramatto 'va ahosi. sā taṃ pātiṃ aññāya suvaṇṇapātiyā paṭikujjetvā vasanena veṭhetvā sabbālaṃkārehi attabhāvaṃ alaṃkaritvā taṃ pātiṃ attano sīse ṭhapetvā mahantena ānubhāvena nigrodhamūlaṃ gantvā bodhisattaṃ oloketvā balavasomanassajātā rukkhadevatā ti saññāya diṭṭhaṭṭhānato paṭṭhāya onatonatā gantvā sīsato thālaṃ otāretvā vivaritvā suvaṇṇabhiṃkārena gandhapupphavāsitaṃ udakaṃ gahetvā bodhisattaṃ upagantvā aṭṭhāsi. ghaṭīkāramahābrahmunā

the whole tree with his radiance as he waited for the time to set out and go for alms. The servant girl Punna arrived and saw the Bodhisatta sitting at the roots of the tree, gazing out to the east. And she saw that the whole tree was golden, filled with the rays of light emanating from his body. When she saw this, she thought: "Today our god in the tree has come down, and is sitting there, I think, to receive the offering with his own hands." Filled with excitement, she rushed back and told Sujata about it.

When she heard this, Sujata was overcome with joy. She 100
said to Punna, "From now on, you are going to have the position of my eldest daughter." And she gave her all the ornaments that were suitable for her daughter. Now it is right that for the day of the coming to be of a Buddha he should receive a golden bowl worth a hundred thousand. So, this wish arose up in her: "I will serve the milk-rice in a golden bowl." She had a golden bowl worth a hundred thousand brought to her and wanting to put the milk-rice inside it, she tilted the pan in which the rice had been cooked. All the perfectly cooked milk-rice rolled into the bowl like water from a lotus leaf. The bowl was filled to the brim with it. She covered the bowl with another golden dish and wrapped it in a cloth. Making herself beautiful with adornments, she put the bowl on her head, and walked with great grace to the roots of the banyan tree. Powerful happiness arose in her when she saw the Bodhisatta; she thought he must be the god of the tree. Keeping her head bowed, she approached from the place where she saw him. Taking the bowl from her head, she uncovered it, and bringing in a golden jar of fresh water, scented with flower petals, she came near to

dinnamattikāpatto ettakaṃ addhānaṃ bodhisattaṃ avijahitvā tasmiṃ khaṇe adassanaṃ gato. bodhisatto pattaṃ apassanto dakkhiṇahatthaṃ pasāretvā udakaṃ sampaṭicchi. sujātā sah' eva pātiyā pāyāsaṃ mahāpurisassa hatthe ṭhapesi. mahāpuriso sujātaṃ olokesi. sā ākāraṃ sallakkhetvā ayya mayā tumhākaṃ pariccattaṃ gaṇhitvā yathāruciṃ gacchathā ti vanditvā yathā mayhaṃ manoratho nipphanno evaṃ tumhākaṃ pi nippajjatū ti vatvā satasahassagghanikāya suvaṇṇapātiyā purāṇapaṇṇaṃ viya anapekkhā hutvā pakkāmi.

101 bodhisatto pi kho nisinnaṭṭhānā uṭṭhāya rukkhaṃ padakkhiṇaṃ katvā pātiṃ ādāya nerañjarāya tīraṃ gantvā anekesam bodhisattasahassānaṃ abhisambujjhanadivase otaritvā nahānaṭṭhānaṃ suppatiṭṭhitatitthaṃ nāma atthi tassa tīre pātiṃ ṭhapetvā otaritvā nahātvā anekabuddhasatasahassānaṃ nivāsanaṃ arahaddhajaṃ nivāsetvā puratthābhimukho nisīditvā ekaṭṭhitālapakkappamāṇe ekūnapaññāsa piṇḍe katvā sabbaṃ appodakaṃ madhupāyāsaṃ paribhuñji. so eva hi 'ssa buddhabhūtassa sattasattāhaṃ bodhimaṇḍe vasa-

the Bodhisatta and stood beside him. At that moment, the earthenware bowl given to him by Great Brahma, Ghatikara, which had never left him before that, disappeared. Not seeing the pot, the Bodhisatta extended out his hand and accepted the water. Sujata placed the bowl of milk-rice into the hands of the Great Being. The Great Being looked at Sujata. She pointed to the food and spoke. "Sir, please accept this offering to you from me, and may you go wherever you please." And then she gave him homage: "Just as my heart's desire came to me, may yours come to you too." And she went away, feeling as little regard for the golden bowl worth a hundred thousand as for a withered leaf.

The Bodhisatta then rose from his seated position and 101
walked a reverential circle around the tree. Carrying the bowl, he went to the banks of the Neranja River and, as other thousands of bodhisattas have done on the day of their awakening, he went down into it. There is a ford there, a bathing place, Suppatittha. Leaving the bowl on the bank, he bathed there and put on the robes of an awakened one, as hundreds of thousands of earlier bodhisattas have done before him. He sat down, facing the east, and divided the milk-rice into forty-nine balls, the size of a single-seed palmyra fruit. This was all the food he had in the forty-nine days that he spent at the tree of awakening, after he had become a Buddha. During that time, he ate no other food, and did not bathe, wash his face, or expel waste matter from his body. He spent his time in the bliss of *jhāna,* the bliss of the path, and the bliss of the fruits of the path. When he had eaten the milk-rice, he picked up the golden bowl: "If I am going to attain Buddhahood today, may this bowl go upstream. If I cannot,

ntassa ekūnapaññāsa divasāni āhāro ahosi ettakaṃ kālaṃ n' eva añño āhāro atthi na nahānaṃ na mukhadhovanaṃ na sarīravalañjo jhānasukhena maggasukhena phalasukhen' eva vītināmesi. taṃ pana pāyasaṃ bhuñjitvā suvaṇṇapātiṃ gahetvā sac' āhaṃ ajja buddho bhavituṃ sakkhissāmi ayaṃ pāti paṭisotaṃ gacchatu no ce sakkhissāmi anusotaṃ gacchatū ti vatvā pakkhipi. sā sotaṃ chindamānā nadīmajjhaṃ gantvā majjhamajjhaṭṭhānen' eva javasampanno asso viya asītihatthamattaṭṭhānaṃ paṭisotaṃ gantvā ekasmiṃ āvatte nimujjitvā kālanāgarājabhavanaṃ gantvā tiṇṇaṃ buddhānaṃ paribhogapātiyo kili kilī ti rāvaṃ kārayamānā paharitvā tāsaṃ sabbaheṭṭhimā hutvā aṭṭhāsi kālo nāgarājā taṃ saddaṃ sutvā hiyyo eko buddho nibbatti puna ajja eko nibbatto ti anekehi padasatehi thutiyo vadamāno aṭṭhāsi. tassa pana mahāpaṭhaviyā ekayojanatigāvutappamāṇaṃ nabhaṃ pūretvā ārohanakālo ajja vā hiyyo vā ti sadiso ahosi. bodhisatto pi nadītīramhi supupphitasālavane divāvihāraṃ katvā sāyaṇhasamaye pupphānaṃ vaṇṭato muñcanakāle devatāhi alaṃkatena aṭṭhūsabhavitthārena maggena sīho 'va vijambhamāno bodhirukkhābhimukho pāyāsi. nāgayakkhasupaṇṇādayo dibbehi gandhapupphādīhi pūjayiṃsu dibbasaṃgītāni pavattayiṃsu dasasahassīlokadhātu ekagandhā ekamālā ekasādhukārā ahosi. tasmiṃ samaye sotthiyo nāma tiṇahārako tiṇaṃ ādāya paṭipathe āgacchanto mahāpurisassa ākāraṃ ñatvā aṭṭha tiṇamuṭṭhiyo adāsi. bodhisatto tiṇaṃ gahetvā bodhimaṇḍaṃ āruyha dakkhiṇadisābhāge uttarābhimukho aṭṭhāsi.

let it go with the current of the stream." And he threw it. Cutting its way through the stream right to the middle of the river and staying there, it went against the stream of the current for eighty cubits, with the rapidity of a fast horse. Then it sunk in a whirlpool and dropped down to the home of the naga king Kala, where it struck against the bowls used by the three previous Buddhas, and made a clanging noise: "Clink, clink." And then it sank right to the bottom of them. Kala, the naga king, heard that sound, and started to sing songs of praise, in hundreds of verses, saying, "A Buddha was born yesterday. Today there will be another one." For to him all the time during which the earth emerged and filled the sky to an extent of a *yojana* and three *gāvutas* was just like yesterday and today.

The Bodhisatta spent his midday rest by the banks of the river in the blossoming sal grove. Then, in the evening, just at the time the flowers droop in their stems, he shook off his sleepiness like a lion and made his way toward the Bodhi Tree, along a path that was eight *usabhas* wide and decorated by the gods. Nagas, *yakkhas,* and garudas honored him with celestial perfumes, flowers, and suchlike, playing heavenly music to him. The ten thousand world systems were also filled with perfumes and garlands, as well as whoops of joy.

At that time a grass-seller called Sotthiya was coming in the opposite direction, carrying a bundle of grasses. Recognizing the caliber of the Great Being, he offered him eight handfuls of grass. The Bodhisatta accepted the grass and went up to the circle under the Bodhi Tree; he stood on the southern side, facing the north.

102 tasmiṃ khaṇe dakkhiṇacakkavālaṃ osīditvā heṭṭhā avīcisampattaṃ viya ahosi uttaracakkavālaṃ ullaṃghitvā upari bhavaggappattaṃ viya ahosi. bodhisatto idaṃ sambodhiṃ pāpuṇanaṭṭhānaṃ na bhavissati maññe ti padakkhiṇaṃ karonto pacchimadisābhāgaṃ gantvā puratthābhimukho aṭṭhāsi. tato pacchimacakkavālaṃ osīditvā heṭṭhā avīcisampattaṃ viya ahosi puratthimacakkavāḷaṃ ullaṃghitvā bhavaggappattaṃ viya ahosi ṭhitaṭhitaṭṭhāne kir' assa nemivaṭṭapariyante akkante nābhiyā patiṭṭhitamahāsakaṭacakkaṃ viya mahāpaṭhavī onatunnatā ahosi. bodhisatto idam pi sambodhiṃ pāpuṇanaṭṭhānaṃ na bhavissati maññe ti padakkhiṇaṃ karonto uttaradisābhāgaṃ gantvā dakkhiṇābhimukho aṭṭhāsi. tato uttaracakkavāḷaṃ osīditvā heṭṭhā avīcisampattaṃ viya ahosi dakkhiṇacakkavāḷaṃ ullaṃghitvā bhavaggappattaṃ viya ahosi. bodhisatto idam pi sambodhipāpuṇanaṭṭhānaṃ na bhavissati maññe ti padakkhiṇaṃ karonto puratthimadisābhāgaṃ gantvā pacchimābhimukho aṭṭhāsi. puratthimadisābhāge pana sabbabuddhānaṃ pallaṃkaṭṭhānaṃ taṃ n' eva chambhati na kampati. mahāsatto idaṃ sabbabuddhānaṃ avijahitācalaṭṭhānaṃ kilesapañjaraviddhaṃsanaṭṭhānan ti ñatvā tāni tiṇāni agge gahetvā cālesi. tāvad eva cuddasahattho pallaṃko ahosi. tāni pi kho tiṇāni tathārūpena saṇṭhānena saṇṭhahiṃsu yathārūpaṃ sukusalo pi cittakāro vā potthakāro vā ālikhitum pi samattho n' atthi. bodhisatto bodhikhandhaṃ piṭṭhito katvā puratthimābhimukho daḷhamānaso hutvā kāyaṃ taco ca nahāru ca aṭṭhi ca avasussatu upasussatu sarīre maṃsalohitaṃ na tv-eva sammāsambodhiṃ appatvā imaṃ pallaṃkaṃ bhindissāmī ti asanisatasannipātenā 'pi abhejjarūpaṃ aparājitapallaṃkaṃ ābhujitvā

At that moment the southern rim of the circle made by the horizon sank, as if dipping down to the Avici hell below. The northern rim of the horizon rose up and appeared to have reached the highest heaven above. 102

The Bodhisatta reflected: "I think this will not be the place to attain awakening."

Circling to the right, he went and stood on the western side, facing the east. Then the western rim of the circle made by the horizon sank, as if dipping down to the Avici hell below; the eastern rim rose and seemed to reach the highest heaven. Wherever he stood, the great earth seemed to bow down, so that it looked like the way a great cartwheel flips up on one side if someone stands on the other edge.

The Bodhisatta reflected: "I think this will not be the place to attain awakening."

Circling to the right, he went and stood on the northern side, facing to the south. There, the northern rim of the horizon sank, as if dipping down to the Avici hell below. The southern rim of the horizon rose and appeared to reach the highest heavens above.

The Bodhisatta reflected: "I think this will not be the place to attain awakening."

Circling to the right, he went and stood on the eastern side, facing the tree in the west. The seat where all Buddhas sit cross-legged is on the eastern side. It does not shake or tremble.[19] The Great Being realized: "This is the place for all Buddhas. It is stable and does not shake. It is the place for the destruction of the enclosure of the defilements." And he took the tips of the grasses and shook them. At that moment, a place for sitting cross-legged, fourteen cubits

nisīdi. tasmiṃ samaye māro devaputto siddhatthakumāro mayhaṃ vasaṃ atikkamitukāmo na dāni 'ssa atikkamituṃ dassāmī ti mārabalassa santikaṃ gantvā etam atthaṃ ārocetvā māraghosanaṃ nāma ghosāpetvā mārabalaṃ ādāya nikkhami. sā mārasenā mārassa purato dvādasa yojanāni hoti dakkhiṇato ca vāmato ca dvādasa yojanāni pacchato yāva cakkavāḷapariyantaṃ katvā ṭhitvā uddhaṃ navayojanubbedhā yassā unnadantiyā unnādasaddo yojanasahassato paṭṭhāya paṭhavīudrīyanasaddo viya sūyati.

103 atha māro devaputto diyaḍḍhayojanasatikaṃ girimekhalaṃ nāma hatthiṃ abhirūhitvā bāhusahassaṃ māpetvā nānāvudhāni aggahesi. avasesāya pi māraparisāya dve jānā ekasadisakaṃ āvudhaṃ na gaṇhiṃsu nānappakāravaṇṇā nānāppakāramukhā hutvā mahāsattaṃ ajjhottharamānā āgamiṃsu. dasasahassacakkavāḷe devatā pana mahāsattassa thutiyo vadamānā aṭṭhaṃsu. sakko devarājā vijayuttarasaṃkhaṃ dhamamāno aṭṭhāsi so kira saṃkho vīsaṃhatthasatiko hoti sakiṃ vātaṃ gāhāpetvā dhamanto cattāro māse saddaṃ karitvā nissaddo hoti. mahākālanāgarājā atirekapadasatena vaṇṇaṃ vadanto aṭṭhāsi.

long, appeared.[20] For those blades of grass arranged themselves in such a shape that even a brilliant painter or potter or writer could not evoke it.

The Bodhisatta then put his back to the Bodhi Tree. Facing the east, he made his resolve strong. “Let only my skin, sinews, and bones remain, and let the flesh and blood in my body dry up. I will not give up this cross-legged position.” And he bent his legs into an unswerving cross-legged position from which he could not be moved, even by thunderbolts.

At that time, Mara, the deity, thought: “Prince Siddhat- 103
tha wishes to go beyond my dominion. I will not give him a chance to do this now.” And he went to inform Mara’s army, and getting them to shout the Mara chant, he urged them forward and led the forces of Mara. Mara’s army was 12 *yojanas* long in front, and 12 *yojanas* to the right and to the left; behind him it extended right up to the edges of the universe, and upward to a height of 9 *yojanas*. A great roar resounded and was heard 1,000 *yojanas* away, like the rumble of a great quaking of the earth. Then Mara the deity mounted on an elephant called Girimekhala, who was 150 *yojanas* in height. He created many thousands of arms and seized all kinds of weapons for them. And no two of the rest of his army had exactly the same weapon; rather they assumed manifold colors, forms, and appearances, and all went hoping to overwhelm the Great Being.

The gods of the ten thousand world systems, however, stood around the Great Being, singing songs of praise for him. Sakka, the king of the gods, stood blowing his conch-shell trumpet, Vijayuttara. And they say that this shell was

mahābrahmā setacchattaṃ dhārayamāno aṭṭhāsi. mārabale pana bodhimaṇḍaṃ upasaṃkamante upasaṃkamante tesaṃ eko pi ṭhātuṃ nāsakkhi sammukhasammukhaṭṭhānen' eva palāyiṃsu. kālo nāgarājā paṭhaviyaṃ nimujjitvā pañcayojanasatikaṃ mañjerikanāgabhavanaṃ gantvā ubhohi hatthehi mukhaṃ pidahitvā nipanno. sakko vijayuttarasaṃkhaṃ piṭṭhiyaṃ katvā cakkavāḷamukhavaṭṭiyaṃ aṭṭhāsi. mahābrahmā setacchattaṃ cakkavāḷakoṭiyam ṭhapetvā brahmalokam eva agamāsi. ekadevatā 'pi ṭhātuṃ samattho n' āhosi. mahāpuriso ekako 'va nisīdi. māro pi attano parisaṃ āha: tātā suddhodanaputtena siddhatthena sadiso añño puriso nāma n' atthi mayaṃ sammukhā yuddhaṃ dātuṃ na sakkhissāma pacchābhāgena dassāmā ti. mahāpuriso pi tīṇi passāni oloketvā sabbadevatānaṃ palātattā suññā ti[3] addasa. puna uttarapassena mārabalaṃ ajjhottaramānaṃ[4] disvā ayam ettako jano maṃ ekakaṃ sandhāya mahantaṃ vāyāmaṃ parakkamaṃ karoti imasmiṃ ṭhāne mayhaṃ mātāpitā vā bhātā vā añño vā koci ñātako n' atthi imā pana dasa pāramiyo 'va mayhaṃ dīgharattaṃ puṭṭhaparijanasadisā tasmā pāramiyo 'va phalakaṃ katvā pāramisatthen' eva paharitvā ayaṃ balakāyo mayā viddhaṃsetuṃ

two thousand cubits long. It blows by getting the wind to enter it of its own accord and, sounded once, it takes four months before the sound fades away. Mahakala, the Great Black One, king of the nagas, stood singing praises in many hundreds of verses. Great Brahma stood holding up his white parasol. But when the great army of Mara approached the circle of the Bodhi Tree, and had got near, not even one of them was able to stay. They fled in whatever direction they were facing at the time. The black naga king dived into the earth, and went to his naga kingdom, Manjeri, of five hundred *yojanas.* He lay down flat, covering his face with his hands. Sakka stood at the ridge of the circle of the horizon, with Vijayuttara, the conch shell, on his back. Great Brahma left his white parasol on the outermost peak at the edge of the world and went back to his Brahma world. Not one of the deities was able to stand firm.

The Great Being sat on his own. Mara said to his assembly: "My friends: there is no other man equal to Siddhattha, the son of Suddhodana. We cannot give him a battle face to face. We will attack him from behind." The Great Being looked around on three sides and saw that with all the gods running away, all was "empty." Then he saw the army of Mara flooding through on the northern side and reflected on the ten perfections: "Such a great army is surging with immense force, and making war on me, a man on his own. There is no father here, no mother, no brother, and no relative at all in this spot. But the ten perfections have been like faithful retainers I have kept for a long time. Because of this, it is necessary for me to make the perfections not just a powerful body to effect destruction, but my shield too."

vaṭṭatī ti dasa pāramiyo āvajjamāno nisīdi. atha māro devaputto eten' eva siddhatthaṃ palāpessāmī ti vātamaṇḍalaṃ samuṭṭhāpesi. taṃ khaṇaṃ yeva puratthimādibhedā vātā samuṭṭhahitvā aḍḍhayojanadviyojanatiyojanappamāṇāni pabbatakūṭāni padāletvā vanagaccharukkhādīni ummūletvā samantā gāmanigame cuṇṇavicuṇṇaṃ kātuṃ samatthā 'pi mahāpurisassa puññatejena vihatānubhāvā bodhisattaṃ patvā cīvarakaṇṇamattam pi cāletuṃ nāsakkhiṃsu.

104 tato udakena naṃ ajjhottharitvā māressāmī ti mahāvassaṃ samuṭṭhāpesi tassānubhāvena uparūpari satapaṭalasahassapaṭalādibhedā valāhakā uṭṭhahitvā vassiṃsu vuṭṭhidhārāvegena paṭhavi chiddā ahosi vanarukkhādīnaṃ uparibhāgena mahāogho āgantvā mahāsattassa cīvare ussāvabinduṭṭhānamattam pi temetuṃ n' āsakkhi. tato pāsāṇavassaṃ samuṭṭhāpesi mahantāni mahantāni pabbatakūṭāni dhūpayantāni pajjalantāni ākāsen' āgantvā bodhisattaṃ patvā dibbamālāguḷabhāvaṃ āpajjiṃsu. tato paharaṇavassaṃ samuṭṭhāpesi ekatodhārāubhatodhārāasisattikhurappādayo dhūpayantā pajjalantā ākāsen' āgantvā bodhisattaṃ patvā dibbapupphāni ahesuṃ. tato aṅgārakavassaṃ samuṭṭhāpesi kiṃsukavaṇṇā aṅgārā ākāsen' āgantvā bodhisattassa pādamūle dibbapupphāni hutvā vikiriṃsu. tato kukkuḷavassaṃ samuṭṭhāpesi accuṇho aggivaṇṇo kukkuḷo ākāsen' āgantvā bodhisattassa pādamūle candanacuṇṇaṃ hutvā nipati. tato vālukavassaṃ samuṭṭhāpesi atisukhumavālukā dhūpayantā pajjalantā ākāsen' āgantvā bodhisattassa pādamūle dibbapupphāni hutvā nipatiṃsu. tato kalalavassaṃ samuṭṭhāpesi taṃ kalalaṃ dhūpayantaṃ pajjalantaṃ ākāsen' āgantvā bodhisattassa pādamūle dibbavilepanaṃ hutvā nipati. tato iminā bhiṃsetvā siddhatthaṃ palāpessāmī ti andhakāraṃ samu-

Then the god Mara decided: "I will drive away Siddhattha," and raised a whirling of winds. At that moment, hurricanes of winds arose from the east, and the other directions, which could have shattered mountain peaks of the height of up to half a *yojana,* two *yojanas,* or even three *yojanas,* or could have uprooted the shrubs and trees of the forest, or reduced villages and towns everywhere around to powder. But through the power and auspiciousness of the Great Being, they lost their force, and on reaching the Bodhisatta they could not even shake the hem of his robe.

Then Mara thought: "I will destroy him by flooding him 104
out with water." And he caused torrential rains. By his great power, dark thunderclouds gathered in their hundreds of thousands, heaps upon heaps, and gushed down rain. Through the violence of their downpour the earth was saturated through, and a great flood, engulfing forests, trees, and suchlike, made its way toward the Great Being. But it could not even moisten a patch on his robe the size of a dew drop.

Next Mara raised an avalanche of rocks. Mountain peak on mountain peak came thundering through the air, smoking, and blazing with flames; but reaching the Bodhisatta, they became clusters of divine flowers and garlands.

Then he raised a storm of weapons, and swords, daggers, arrows, and other weapons, single-edged and double-edged, came hurtling through the air, but reaching the feet of the Bodhisatta, they become heavenly flowers.

Then he raised a storm of burning charcoal. But although the embers came through the sky the color of red flame-of-the-forest flowers, they showered down at the feet of the Bodhisatta as heavenly blossoms.

ṭṭhāpesi taṃ caturaṅgasamannāgataṃ mahātamaṃ hutvā bodhisattaṃ patvā suriyappabhāvihataṃ viya andhakāraṃ antaradhāyi. evaṃ māro imāhi navahi vātavassapāsāṇapaharaṇaṅgārakukkuḷavālikakalalandhakāravuṭṭhīhi bodhisattaṃ palāpetuṃ asakkonto kiṃ bhaṇe tiṭṭhatha imaṃ kumāraṃ gaṇhatha hanatha palāpethā ti parisaṃ āṇāpetvā sayam pi girimekhalassa hatthino khandhe nisinno cakkāvudhaṃ ādāya bodhisattaṃ upasaṃkamitvā siddhattha uṭṭhahatha etasmā pallaṃkā n' āyaṃ tuyhaṃ pāpuṇāti mayhaṃ eso pāpuṇātī ti āha. mahāsatto tassa vacanaṃ sutvā avoca: māra n' eva tayā dasa pāramiyo pūritā na upapāramiyo na paramatthapāramiyo na pi pañcamahāpariccāgā pariccattā na ñānatthacariyā na lokatthacariyā na buddhicariyā pūritā n' āyaṃ pallaṃko tuyhaṃ pāpuṇati mayh' ev' eso pāpuṇātī ti.

Next, he raised a storm of ashes: red-hot ashes, glowing like flames, came through the sky, but at the feet of the Bodhisatta, they fell like sandalwood powder.

Next, he raised a sandstorm: minuscule fine grains of sand came smoking and smoldering through the sky, but at the feet of the Bodhisatta, they became divine flowers.

Then he raised a storm of mud: the mud was smoking and smoldering as it flew through the air, but at the feet of the Bodhisatta, it fell as heavenly ointments.

Then Mara thought, "Right, with this I'll really terrify Siddhattha and drive him away!"

And he raised a great darkness, that had the four attributes.[21] But when it reached the Bodhisatta it just disappeared, as if dispersed by the radiance of the sun.

In these nine ways—with winds, rain, rocks, charcoal, weapons, ashes, sand, mud, and darkness—Mara could not terrify the Bodhisatta.

He gave an order to his army: "Why men, do you just stand there? Seize hold of this prince, or kill him, or terrify him away!" He came near to the Bodhisatta, sitting on his elephant, Girimekhala, and taking up the wheel-weapon that was on the side of the elephant, he shouted: "Siddhattha! Get up from that seat. It does not belong to you. It belongs to me." When he heard these words the Great Being replied: "Mara, you have not fulfilled the ten perfections, or the higher perfections, or the highest perfections. You have not made the five great acts of generosity. You have not fulfilled the way of life that has wisdom, nor the way of life for the benefit of the world, nor the way of life leading to awakening.

105 māro kuddho kodhavegaṃ asahanto mahāpurisassa cakkāvudhaṃ vissajjesi tan tassa dasa pāramiyo āvajjentassa uparibhāge mālāvitānaṃ hutvā aṭṭhāsi. taṃ kira khuradhāraṃ cakkāvudhaṃ aññadā tena kuddhena vissaṭṭhaṃ ekaghanapāsāṇe thambhe vaṃsakaḷīre viya chindantaṃ gacchati. idāni pana tasmiṃ mālāvitānaṃ hutvā ṭhite avasesā māraparisā idāni pallaṃkato vuṭṭhāya palāyissatī ti mahantamahantāni selakūṭāni vissajjesuṃ tāni pi mahāpurisassa dasa pāramiyo āvajjentassa mālāguḷabhāvaṃ āpajjitvā bhūmiyaṃ patiṃsu. devatā cakkavāḷamukhavaṭṭiyaṃ ṭhitā gīvaṃ pasāretvā sīsaṃ ukkhipitvā naṭṭho vata bho siddhatthakumārassa rūpaggappatto attabhāvo kin nu kho karissatī ti olokenti. tato mahāpuriso pāritapāramīnaṃ bodhisattānaṃ abhisambujjhanadivase pattapallaṃkaṃ mayhaṃ pāpuṇātī ti vatvā ṭhitaṃ māraṃ āha: māra tuyhaṃ dānassa dinnabhave ko sakkhī ti āha. māro ime ettakā sakkhino ti mārabalābhimukhaṃ hatthaṃ pasāresi. tasmiṃ khaṇe māraparisāya ahaṃ sakkhī ahaṃ sakkhīti pavattasaddo paṭhavīudrīyanasaddasadiso ahosi. atha māro mahāpurisaṃ āha:

siddhattha tuyhaṃ dānassa dinnabhāve ko sakkhī ti. mahāpuriso tuyhaṃ tāva dānassa dinnabhāve sacetanā sakkhino mayhaṃ pana imasmiṃ ṭhāne sacetano koci sakkhī nāma n' atthi tiṭṭhatu tāva me avasesattabhāvesu dinnadānaṃ vessantarattabhāve pana ṭhatvā sattasatakamahādānassa tāva dinnabhāve ayaṃ acetanā 'pi ghanamahāpaṭhavī sakkhī ti cīvaragabbhantarato dakkhiṇahatthaṃ abhinīharitvā vessantarattabhāve ṭhatvā mayhaṃ sattasatakamahādānassa dinnabhāve tvaṃ sakkhī na sakkhī ti mahāpaṭhavīabhimukhaṃ hatthaṃ pasāresi. mahāpaṭhavī ahan te tadā

This seat does not come to you but it does come to me." Mara 105
was infuriated and, unable to contain the force of anger, hurled his disc weapon at him, but it turned into a canopy of garlands above the being, as he was reflecting on the ten perfections. Now they say that when the disc weapon, with its razor edge, is hurled in anger at other times, it slices the air, splitting a pillar of rock as if it were a young bamboo shoot. But this time it turned into a canopy of garlands and stayed there. Other members of Mara's army hurled rocks, shouting, "These will terrify him away from the seat!" But while the Bodhisatta continued to reflect on the ten perfections, they too fell on the ground like clusters of garlands.

The gods who stood facing them at the outer rim of the universe continually raised their heads and craned their necks as they looked on. They said, "Oh no, Prince Siddhattha is destroyed; what a state his beauty has come to now. What is he going to do?" Then the Great Being spoke to Mara, who remained there: "This seat, earned by all Buddhas on the day of their awakening through the fulfillment of the perfections, comes to me." And he asked, "Mara, who will be a witness to you having made acts of generosity in the past?" Mara said, "These people will be my witnesses." And he stretched out his hand in the direction of Mara's army. Immediately, there was a cry from Mara's army, which rumbled like an earthquake: "I'm a witness, I'm a witness!"

Then Mara addressed the Great Being: "Who will be a witness to you having made acts of generosity in the past?" The Great Being replied: "You have sentient beings as witnesses to your performing acts of generosity in the past. But here in this place there is no sentient being who has been

sakkhīti virāvasatena virāvasahassena virāvasatasahassena mārabalaṃ avattharamānā viya unnadi. tato mahāpurise dinnan te siddhattha mahādānaṃ uttamadānan ti vessantaradānaṃ sammasante sammasante diyaḍḍhayojanasatiko girimekhalahatthi jannukehi patiṭṭhāsi. māraparisā disāvidisā palāyi dve ekamaggena gatā nāma n' atthi sīsābharaṇāni c' eva nivatthavatthāni ca pahāya sammukhasammukhā disāhi yeva palāyiṃsu. tato devasaṅghā palāyamānaṃ mārabalaṃ disvā mārassa parājayo jāto siddhatthakumārassa jayo jayapūjaṃ karissāmā ti nāgā nāgānaṃ supaṇṇā supaṇṇānaṃ devatā devatānaṃ brahmāno brahmānaṃ pesetvā gandhamālādihatthā mahāpurisassa santikaṃ bodhipallaṃkaṃ

a witness to mine. Leaving aside all the generosity I have practiced in earlier lifetimes, let the great and solid earth, who has no sentience, be my witness to the gift of the "seven hundred" I gave in my existence as Vessantara.[22] Drawing his right hand out from the folds of his robe he stretched it out toward the earth, and said: "Are you, or are you not, a witness to my having given the gift of the seven hundreds in my life as Vessantara?" And the great earth resounded, with a hundred, a thousand, and a hundred thousand reverberations, as if to overpower the army of Mara: "I am your witness to that."

The Great Being continued in his reflection on his generosity in his lifetime as Vessantara, and said to himself: "Siddhattha, you have made great acts of generosity, magnificent acts of generosity."[23] And the elephant Girimekhala, who was a 150 *yojanas* tall, went down to his knees. Mara's men fled in all directions, with no two following the same track. They escaped in fright in whatever direction they found themselves in, abandoning their headgear and their clothes as they ran. When the hosts of the gods saw Mara's forces running away they sent messages: nagas to nagas, garudas to garudas, gods to gods, Brahmas to Brahmas. "Mara has been overcome! Siddhattha is the victor! Come on—let's honor him!" And they approached the great man, and the seat of the awakening, with perfumes and garlands in their hands.

In this way they came forward:

agamaṃsu. evaṃ gatesu ca pana tesu

274 jayo hi buddhassa sirīmato ayaṃ
mārassa ca pāpimato parājayo
ugghosayuṃ bodhimaṇḍe pamoditā
jayaṃ tadā nāgagaṇā mahesino.

275 jayo hi buddhassa sirīmato ayaṃ
mārassa ca pāpimato parājayo
ugghosayuṃ bodhimaṇḍe pamoditā
supaṇṇasaṅghā 'pi jayaṃ mahesino.

276 jayo hi buddhassa sirīmato ayaṃ
mārassa ca pāpimato parājayo
ugghosayuṃ bodhimaṇḍe pamoditā
jayaṃ tadā devagaṇā mahesino.

277 jayo hi buddhassa sirīmato ayaṃ
mārassa ca pāpimato parājayo
ugghosayuṃ bodhimaṇḍe pamoditā
jayaṃ tadā brahmagaṇā 'pi tādino.

106 avasesā dasasu cakkavāḷasahassesu devatā mālāgandhavilepanehi pūjayamānā nānappakārā thutiyo vadamānā aṭṭhaṃsu. evaṃ dharamāne yeva suriye mahāpuriso mārabalaṃ vidhametvā cīvarūparipatamānehi bodhirukkhaṃkurehi rattapavāḷadalehi viya pūjayamāno paṭhame yāme pubbenivāsañāṇaṃ majjhimayāme dibbacakkhuṃ visodhetvā pacchimayāme paṭiccasamuppāde ñāṇaṃ otāresi.

This is victory for the glorious Buddha,[24] and defeat 274
for the evil Mara! Filled with joy, the hosts of nagas
proclaimed there the victory of the great sage, in the
circle of the Bodhi Tree.
This is victory for the glorious Buddha, And defeat 275
for the evil Mara! Filled with joy, flocks of garudas
proclaimed there the victory of the great sage,
in the circle of the Bodhi Tree.
This is victory for the glorious Buddha, And defeat 276
for the evil Mara! Filled with joy, hosts of gods
proclaimed there the victory of the great sage,
in the circle of the Bodhi Tree.
This is victory for the glorious Buddha, And defeat 277
for the evil Mara! Filled with joy, hosts of Brahmas
proclaimed there the victory of the great sage,
in the circle of the Bodhi Tree.

And gods of all kinds of appearance in the remainder of 106
the thousand world systems paid homage with garlands, perfumes, and ointments, and sang out their praises.

The sun was still above the horizon as the great man sent Mara's forces on their way. Even the Bodhi Tree seemed to pay him homage: as it made a shower of red shoots and petals on his robes in the first watch of the night, he entered into knowledge of previous existences. In the second watch of the night, the great man purified the divine eye. And in the final watch of the night, he obtained insight into dependent arising. As he continued to turn around in his mind, again and again, forward and backward, the twelve elements of dependent arising and their cause, the ten thousand world

ath' assa dvādasapadikaṃ paccayākāraṃ vaṭṭavivaṭṭavasena anulomapaṭilomato sammasantassa sammasantassa dasasahassilokadhātu udakapariyantaṃ katvā dvādasakkhattuṃ saṃkampi. mahāpurise pana dasasahassilokadhātuṃ unnādetvā aruṇuggamanavelāya sabbaññūtañāṇam paṭivijjhante sakaladasasahassilokadhātu alaṃkatapaṭiyattā ahosi.

107 pācīnacakkavāḷamukhavaṭṭiyaṃ ussāpitānaṃ dhajānaṃ paṭākānaṃ raṃsiyo pacchimacakkavāḷamukhavaṭṭiyaṃ paharanti tathā pacchimacakkavāḷamukhavaṭṭiyaṃ ussāpitānaṃ pācīnacakkavāḷamukhavaṭṭiyaṃ uttaracakkavāḷamukhavaṭṭiyaṃ ussāpitānaṃ dakkhiṇacakkavāḷamukhavaṭṭiyaṃ dakkhiṇacakkavāḷamukhavaṭṭiyaṃ ussāpitānaṃ uttaracakkavāḷamukhavaṭṭiyaṃ paharanti paṭhavitale ussāpitānaṃ pana dhajānaṃ paṭākānaṃ brahmalokaṃ āhacca aṭṭhaṃsu brahmaloke baddhānaṃ paṭhavitale patiṭṭhahiṃsu dasasahassacakkavāḷe pupphūpagarukkhā pupphaṃ gaṇhiṃsu phalūpagarukkhā phalapiṇḍibhārabharitā ahesuṃ khandhesu khandhapadumāni pupphiṃsu sākhāsu sākhāpadumāni latāsu latāpadumāni ākāse olambakapadumāni silātalāni bhinditvā uparūpari sattasatta hutvā daṇḍakapadumāni uṭṭhahiṃsu dasasahassilokadhātu vaṭṭetvā vissaṭṭhamālāguḷā viya susanthatapupphasanthāro viya ca ahosi cakkavāḷantaresu aṭṭhayojanasahassalokantarikā sattasuriyappabhāya pi anobhāsitapubbā ekobhāsā ahesuṃ caturāsītiyojanasahassagambhīro mahāsamuddo madhurodako ahosi nadiyo na-ppavattiṃsu jaccandhā

systems quaked twelve times, right up to the edges of the oceans. While the great man was penetrating through to omniscience, at the break of dawn, the ten thousand world systems rumbled and the entire basis of the ten thousand worlds put on glorious clothes, as if for a festival day.

The light from the flags and banners raised in the eastern 107
part of the circle of the world systems spread as far as the western part of the circle of the world systems. Accordingly, the light from the flags and banners raised in the western, northern, and southern parts of the circle of the world systems spread as far as the eastern, southern, and northern parts of the circle of the world systems too. And the light from the flags and banners raised on the surface of the earth reached as far as the Brahma heavens. And those raised in the Brahma heavens reached right down to the surface of the earth. Flowering trees blossomed; fruit-bearing trees were heavy with clusters of fruits. Flowers growing on tree trunks flourished; and those on the branches, and those on creepers, and lotus blossoms hung suspended in the sky. Lotus stalks with seven flowers burst out, breaking through the stony ground. The ten thousand world systems revolved and seemed like clusters of garlands unloosed and blown around, or like beautifully arranged carpets of flowers. A single radiance filled the eight thousand *yojanas* between the world systems, places where seven suns had never shone before. The waters of the great oceans became fresh and sweet, right down to a depth of eighty-four thousand *yojanas*. The rivers paused in their flow, those who had been blind from birth could see, those who were deaf from birth could hear, and those disabled from birth could walk on their feet. And all

rūpāni passiṃsu jātibadhirā saddaṃ suṇiṃsu jātipīṭhasappī padasā gacchiṃsu andubandhanādīni chinditvā patiṃsu. Evaṃ aparimāṇena sirivibhavena pūjiyamāno nekappakāresu acchariyadhammesu pātubhūtesu sabbaññūtañāṇaṃ paṭivijjhitvā sabbabuddhānaṃ avijahitaṃ udānaṃ udānesi:

278 anekajātisaṃsāraṃ
sandhāvissaṃ anibbisaṃ
gahakārakaṃ gavesanto
dukkhā jāti punappunaṃ.
279 gahakāraka diṭṭho 'si
puna gehaṃ na kāhasi
sabbā te phāsukā bhaggā
gahakūṭaṃ visaṃkhitaṃ
visaṃkhāragataṃ cittaṃ
taṇhānaṃ khayam ajjhagā ti.

108 iti tusitapurato paṭṭhāya yāva ayaṃ bodhimaṇḍe sabbaññūtappatti ettakaṃ ṭhānaṃ avidūrenidānaṃ nāmā ti veditabbaṃ.

chains and bonds became loose, and just fell to the ground.

Honored in this way, he penetrated through to omniscient knowledge in boundless glory and reverence, while manifold miracles were taking place. As all Buddhas have done before him, he sang out a song of triumph:

> "I sought the builder of the house and rushed along 278
> several births, but without any success. Suffering is birth, again and again.
>
> "Oh builder of the house, you have been seen. Do not 279
> build a house again! All the beams are broken, and the ridgepole is shattered. The heart has gone beyond compounded things, it has attained the destruction of all craving."[25]

All the incidents from the departure from the Tusita heaven 108
to the attainment at that spot in the circle of the Bodhi Tree should be known as the near origin.

santikenidāna

109 santikenidānaṃ pana bhagavā sāvatthiyaṃ viharati jetavane anāthapiṇḍikassa ārāme vesāliyaṃ viharati mahāvane kūṭāgārasālāyan ti evaṃ tesu tesu ṭhānesu viharanto tasmiṃ tasmiṃ ṭhāne yeva labbhatī ti vuttaṃ kiñcā 'pi evaṃ vuttaṃ atha kho pana tam pi ādito paṭṭhāya evaṃ veditabbaṃ. udānaṃ udānetvā nisinnassa hi bhagavato etad ahosi: ahaṃ kappasatasahassādhikāni cattāri asaṃkheyyāni imassa pallaṃkassa kāraṇā sandhāviṃ ettakaṃ me kālaṃ imass' eva pallaṃkassa kāraṇā alaṃkatasīsaṃ gīvāya chinditvā dinnaṃ suañjitāni akkhīni hadayamaṃsaṃ ubbattetvā dinnaṃ jālikumārasadisā puttā kaṇhājinakumāri-sadisā dhītaro maddidevi-sadisā bhariyāyo ca paresaṃ dāsatthāya dinnā ayaṃ me pallaṃko jayapallaṃko varapallaṃko ca ettha me nisinnassa saṃkappā paripuṇṇā na tāva ito vuṭṭhahissāmī ti anekakoṭisatasahassā samāpattiyo samāpajjanto sattāhaṃ tatth' eva nisīdi yaṃ sandhāya atho kho bhagavā sattāhaṃ ekapallaṃkena nisīdi vimuttisukhapaṭisaṃvedī

THE RECENT ORIGIN

The "recent origin" is called that because of all the times it 109
is said that the Bhagavan stayed "in these spots, and in these places," with statements like, "the Bhagavan was staying at Anathapindika's monastery in the Jeta Grove" or "he was staying in Vesali in the Gabled Hall in the Great Grove." But even though this all gets recounted, the story should be told right from the beginning.

While he was sitting under the Bodhi Tree, the Bhagavan sang his inspired song and then a thought came to him, "I have gone through many lives for four hundred thousand world-cycles and four incalculable epochs for the sake of this seat. For the sake of this seat, I chopped my head off from the neck and gave it away. I gave away my beautifully made-up eyes, and the flesh of my heart. I gave away into servitude sons such as Prince Jali, daughters such as Princess Kanhajina, and wives such as Queen Maddi. This seat is a throne of victory, and the most excellent seat. Sitting here, all hopes have been fulfilled. I will not get up from it yet." And he sat there for seven days, entering into many hundreds and thousands of crore of attainments. And it has been said about this: "And then the Bhagavan sat in one seat for seven days and experienced the bliss of freedom."

Some of the gods started to comment to themselves on this: "Today surely there is a job for Siddhattha. For he has not given up his attachment to the seat of victory." The Teacher saw their thoughts and in order to allay their doubts, he rose up into the sky and demonstrated the twin miracle.[1]

ti. ath' ekaccānaṃ devatānaṃ ajjā 'pi nūna siddhatthassa kattabbakiccaṃ atthi pallaṃkasmiṃ hi ālayaṃ na vijahatī ti parivitakko udapādi.

110 satthā devatānaṃ vitakkaṃ ñatvā tāsaṃ vitakkaṃ vūpasamanatthaṃ vehāsaṃ abbhuggantvā yamakapāṭihāriyaṃ dassesi. mahābodhimaṇḍasmiṃ hi katapāṭihāriyañ ca ñātisamāgame katapāṭihāriyañ ca pāṭikaputtasamāgame katapāṭihāriyañ ca sabbaṃ gaṇḍambamūle yamakapāṭihāriyasadisaṃ ahosi. evaṃ satthā iminā pāṭihāriyena devatānaṃ vitakkaṃ vūpasametvā pallaṃkato īsakaṃ pācīnanissite uttaradisābhāge ṭhatvā imasmim vata me pallaṃke sabbaññūtañāṇaṃ paṭividdhan ti cattāri asaṃkheyyāni kappasatasahassañ ca pūritānaṃ pāramīnaṃ phalādhigamaṭṭhānaṃ pallaṃkaṃ animisehi akkhīhi olokayamāno sattāhaṃ vītināmesi. taṃ ṭhānaṃ animisacetiyan nāma jātaṃ. atha pallaṃkassa ca ṭhitaṭṭhānassa ca antarā caṅkamaṃ māpetvā puratthimapacchimato āyate ratanacaṅkame caṅkamanto sattāhaṃ vītināmesi. taṃ ṭhānaṃ ratanacaṅkamacetiyan nāma jātaṃ.

111 catutthe pana sattāhe bodhito pacchimuttaradisābhāge devatā ratanagharaṃ māpayiṃsu. tattha pallaṃkena nisīditvā abhidhammapiṭakaṃ visesato c' ettha anantanayaṃ samantapaṭṭhānaṃ vicinanto sattāhaṃ vītināmesi. abhidhammikā panāhu: ratanagharan nāma ratanamayaṃ gehaṃ sattannaṃ pakaraṇānaṃ sammasitaṭṭhānaṃ ratanagharan ti yasmā pan' ettha ubho p' ete pariyāyā yujjanti tasmā ubhayam p' etaṃ gahetabbam eva. tato paṭṭhāya pana taṃ ṭhānaṃ ratanagharacetiyan nāma jātaṃ. evaṃ bodhisamīpe yeva cattāri sattāhāni vītināmetvā pañcame sattāhe bodhirukkhamūlā yena ajapālanigrodho ten' upasaṃkami.

The miracle performed at the circle of the great Bodhi Tree, the one shown in a meeting together of his relatives, and the one performed at the meeting at Patikaputta were all the same as this miracle.

And then the Teacher, having allayed the doubts of the 110
gods with this display, reflected: "It is on this seat that I penetrated through to omniscient knowledge." And he spent seven days just gazing, with eyes unblinking, at the seat that had seen the fruition of four incalculable epochs and a hundred thousand eons in which he had fulfilled the perfections. And this became known as the shrine of the unblinking.

Then he created a walking area between the seat and the spot where he had stood. He spent seven days going backward and forward on this jeweled walkway. And this became known as the "jeweled-walkway shrine."

For the fourth seven-day period, gods created a jeweled 111
house, in the northwestern direction. He spent seven days there, sitting cross-legged, contemplating the Abhidhamma and the endless methods by which causal relationships operate, all around. Now the Abhidhamma specialists say about this: "It is called the Jeweled House, as it was the place for meditation on the seven books of exposition of the Abhidhamma." But because they take both interpretations of this, both can be taken.[2]

As he had spent four weeks near the Bodhi Tree, for the fifth week he went away from the roots of the tree and approached

tatrā 'pi dhammaṃ vicinanto yeva vimuttisukhañ ca paṭisaṃvedento nisīdi.

112 tasmiṃ samaye māro devaputto ettakaṃ kālaṃ anubandhanto otārāpekkho pi imassa kiñci khalitaṃ n' āddasaṃatikkanto dāni esa mama vasan ti domanassappatto mahāmagge nisīditvā soḷasa kāraṇāni cintento bhūmiyaṃ soḷasa lekhā kaḍḍhi: ahaṃ eso viya dānapāramiṃ na pūresiṃ ten' amhi iminā sadiso na jāto ti ekaṃ lekhaṃ kaḍḍhi tathā ahaṃ eso viya sīlapāramiṃ nekkhammapāramiṃ paññāpāramiṃ viriyapāramiṃ khantipāramiṃ saccapāramiṃ adhiṭṭhānapāramiṃ mettāpāramiṃ upekhāpāramiṃ na pūresiṃ ten' amhi iminā sadiso na jāto ti dasamaṃ lekhaṃ kaḍḍhi ahaṃ eso viya asādhāraṇassa indriyaparopariyañāṇassa paṭivedhāya upanissayabhūtā dasa pāramiyo na pūresiṃ ten' amhi iminā sadiso na jāto ti ekādasamaṃ lekhaṃ kaḍḍhi tathā ahaṃ eso viya asādhāraṇassa āsayānusayañāṇassa mahākaruṇāsamāpattiñāṇassa yamakapāṭihīrañāṇassa anāvaraṇañāṇassa sabbaññūtañāṇassa paṭivedhāya upanissayabhūtā dasa pāramiyo na pūresiṃ ten' amhi iminā sadiso na jāto ti soḷasamaṃ lekhaṃ kaḍḍhi. evaṃ imehi kāraṇehi mahāmagge soḷasa lekhā ākaḍḍhamāno nisīdi.

the Goat Herders' Banyan Tree. There he meditated on the Dhamma and sat and experienced the bliss of freedom.

Now at that time, the god Mara thought, "All this time I 112
have been following him, watching out for an opportunity, but I haven't seen any slipup in him. Now he has gone beyond my power." And he sat on the main road filled with sulkiness and annoyance. He finally drew sixteen lines on the ground, thinking of sixteen things.

As he drew one line he thought: "I have not fulfilled the perfection of generosity as he has done. I am just not up to him."

He then went on, "I have not fulfilled the perfections of virtue, of renunciation, of wisdom, heroic effort, forbearance, truth, resolve, loving-kindness, or equanimity, as he has. Because of this, I am just not up to him." And with this he had drawn ten lines.

"I just have not fulfilled, as he has, the ten perfections, which serve as supports and bases for experiencing the knowledge of the faculties, and of this world and beyond. I am just not of his level." And he drew an eleventh line.

Then he thought, "I have not fulfilled the ten perfections, which serve as supports and bases for a unique knowledge into people's dispositions and temperaments, the knowledge needed for the attainment of the great compassion, the knowledge needed for the twin miracle, the knowledge needed for the removal of obstacles, and omniscient knowledge."

So, in all, he drew sixteen lines.

And he sat on the main road and drew sixteen lines, one for each thought.

113 tasmiṃ samaye taṇhā aratī ragā ti tisso māradhītaro pitā no na paññāyati kahaṃ nu kho etarahī ti olokayamānā taṃ domanassappattaṃ bhūmiṃ likhamānaṃ disvā pitu santikaṃ gantvā kasmā 'si tāta dukkhi[1] domanasso ti pucchiṃsu. ammā ayaṃ mahāsamaṇo mayhaṃ vasaṃ atikkanto ettakaṃ kālaṃ olokento otāram assa daṭṭhuṃ n' āsakkhiṃ ten' amhi dukkhī dummano ti. yadi evaṃ mā cintayittha mayaṃ etaṃ attano vase katvā ādāya āgamissāmā ti. na sakkā ammā eso kenaci vase kātuṃ acalāya saddhāya patiṭṭhito eso puriso ti. tāta mayaṃ itthiyo nāma idān' eva taṃ rāgapāsādīhi bandhitvā ānessāma tumhe mā cintayitthā ti bhagavantaṃ upasaṃkamitvā pāde te samaṇa paricāremā ti āhaṃsu. bhagavā n' eva tāsaṃ vacanaṃ manasi akāsi na akkhīni ummīletvā olokesi anuttare upadhisaṃkhaye vimuttamānaso vivekasukhañ ñeva anubhavanto nisīdi. puna māradhītaro uccāvacā kho purisānaṃ adhippāyā kesañci kumārikāsu pemaṃ hoti kesañci paṭhamavaye ṭhitāsu kesañci majjhimavaye ṭhitāsu kesañci pacchimavaye ṭhitāsu yan nūna mayaṃ nānappakārehi palobheyyāmā ti ekamekā kumārivaṇṇādivasena sataṃ sataṃ attabhāve abhinimminitvā kumāriyo avijātā sakiṃ vijātā duvijātā majjhimitthiyo mahitthiyo ca hutvā chakkhattuṃ bhagavantaṃ upasaṃkamitvā pāde te samaṇa paricāremā 'ti āhaṃsu. tam pi bhagavā na manas' ākāsi yathā taṃ anuttare upadhisaṃkhaye vimutto. keci paṇācariyā vadanti: tā mahitthibhāvena upagatā disvā bhagavā evam evaṃ etā khaṇḍadantā palitakesā hontū ti

Now at that time, Desire, Aversion, and Passion, Mara's 113
daughters, said, "We have not seen our father. I wonder where he is?" And they looked around and saw him, dejected, drawing lines on the ground in the main road. And they went up to their father and asked him: "Why are you so miserable and unhappy?"

"Dear ones," he replied. "This great ascetic has gone way out of my range. I have been looking for a chance and just could not see a moment to get him. That is why I am so miserable."

—"Now, don't worry. We will go and do something that will bring him into your power."

—"Dear ones, it is just not possible to bring him into my power. This is a man who is immovable in faith."

—"But we are women, dear father! We'll lead him on so that he is ensnared in passion. Just don't worry about it."

And they approached the Bhagavan. "Sir, we are here at your feet to do anything for you."

The Bhagavan did not pay attention to what they were saying and did not even open his eyes to look at them. He just continued to sit, for his mind had become free from the bases of clinging, and he was experiencing the unsurpassable bliss of seclusion.

Then Mara's daughters said: "Men's tastes vary. Some love virgins, some young girls, some middle-aged women, and some older women. Why don't we entice him in all sorts of different forms?" Each miraculously took on the form of hundreds of different women: virgins, women without children, women with one child, women with two children, women in middle age, and older women. And they

adhiṭṭhāsī ti taṃ na gahetabbaṃ na hi satthā evarūpaṃ adhiṭṭhānaṃ karoti bhagavā pana apetha tumhe kiṃ disvā evaṃ vāyamatha evarūpaṃ nāma avītarāgādīnaṃ purato kātuṃ vaṭṭati tathāgatassa pana rāgo pahīno doso pahīno moho pahīno ti attano kilesappahānaṃ ārabbha

280 yassa jitaṃ n' āvajīyati
jitaṃ assa no yāti koci loke
tam buddham anantagocaraṃ
apadaṃ kena padena nessatha

281 yassa jālinī visattikā
taṇhā n' atthi kuhiñci netave
taṃ buddham anantagocaraṃ
apadaṃ kena padena nessathā ti

approached the Bhagavan and said: "Sir, we are here at your feet to do anything for you." But again, the Bhagavan did not pay attention to what they were saying, and continued to sit, with his mind free from the bases of clinging.

Now some teachers say that when he saw them approaching as very old women, with broken teeth and gray hair, he told them they could just stay that way. But this should not be accepted, as no Teacher would make a resolve of that kind. But the Bhagavan did say, "Go away. Why are you trying so hard? It's not right for you to act like this, even with those who have not got rid of their appetites. But the Tathagata has overcome his desire, has overcome his ill will, and has overcome his ignorance too."

And he gave them some verses:

"The Buddha, whose victory over the defilements 280
is complete, in whom there can arise no more
defilements in this world, the Buddha, whose range of
wisdom is infinite, and who leaves no track: by what
track are you going to lead him astray?
The Buddha, in whom there is no hankering, which, 281
like a net, would bring him back to another life, the
Buddha, whose range of wisdom is infinite, and who
leaves no track: by what track are you going to lead
him astray?"[3]

114 imā dhammapade buddhavagge dve gāthā vadanto dhammaṃ kathesi.

tā saccaṃ kira no pitā avoca: arahaṃ sugato loke na rāgena suvānayo ti ādīni vatvā pitu santikaṃ agamaṃsu.

115 bhagavā 'pi tattha sattāhaṃ vītināmetvā mucalindaṃ agamāsi. tattha sattāhaṃ vītināmetvā vaddalikāya uppannāya sītādipaṭibāhanatthaṃ mucalindena nāgarājena sattakkhattuṃ bhogehi parikkhitto asambādhaṃ gandhakuṭiyaṃ viharanto viya vimuttisukhaṃ paṭisaṃvediyamāno sattāhaṃ vītināmetvā rājāyatanaṃ upasaṃkami. tatthā 'pi vimuttisukhapaṭisaṃvedi yeva nisīdi. ettāvatā sattasattāhāni paripuṇṇāni. etth' antare n' eva mukhadhovanaṃ na sarīrapaṭijagganaṃ na āhārakiccaṃ ahosi jhānasukhena maggasukhena phalasukhen' eva ca vītināmesi.

ath' assa tasmiṃ sattasattāhamatthake ekūnapaññāsatime divase tattha nisinnassa mukhaṃ dhovissāmī ti cittaṃ udapādi. sakko devānaṃ indo agadaharīṭakaṃ āharitvā adāsi. satthā taṃ paribhuñji ten' assa sarīravalañjaṃ ahosi. ath' assa sakko yeva nāgalatādantakaṭṭhañ c' eva mukhadhovanaudakañ ca adāsi. satthā taṃ dantakaṭṭhaṃ khāditvā anotattadahe udakena mukhaṃ dhovitvā tatth' eva rājāyatanamūle nisīdi.

116 tasmiṃ samaye tapassu-bhallukā nāma dve vānijā pañcahi sakaṭasatehi ukkalā janapadā majjhimadesaṃ gacchantā attano ñātisālohitāya devatāya sakaṭāni sannirumhitvā

These verses about the destruction of the defilements are also in the Buddha section of the *Dhammapada.* They said: "Our father was right. 'This happy one, the arhat in the world, is not easy to lead astray.'" And they went back to their father. 114

The Bhagavan stayed there for seven days, and then went to the Mucalinda tree. There he spent seven days in the rain, but Mucalinda, the naga king, enfolded him by coiling himself around him seven times as a protection against the cold, so that he could enjoy the bliss of freedom as if he were staying in his scented bedroom. 115

From there he went to the Kingstead tree, and for seven days again enjoyed the bliss of freedom.

With this, he completed seven weeks.

Throughout this time, he did not feel the need to wash his face, attend to his bodily needs, or take in food. He just spent his time in the bliss of *jhāna,* the bliss of the path, and the bliss of the fruits of the path. And then at the end of the seven weeks, on the forty-ninth day, as he was sitting there, a thought arose: "I'll wash my face." Sakka, the king of the gods, brought him a myrobalan fruit. The Teacher ate it, and his bowels were cleared. Then Sakka brought him a toothpick of betel creeper wood, and water for washing his face. The Teacher used the toothpick and washed his face in water that had been brought from Lake Anotatta and sat down again at the foot of the Kingstead tree.

Now at that time two merchants, called Tapassu and Bhalluka, were traveling from the Ukkala region to the Middle Region with a caravan of five hundred carts. They were encouraged by a blood relative, now a god, to stop their 116

satthu āhārasampādane ussāhitā manthañ ca madhupiṇḍikañ ca ādāya patigaṇhātu no bhante bhagavā imaṃ āhāraṃ anukampaṃ upādāyā ti satthāraṃ upasaṃkamitvā aṭṭhaṃsu. bhagavā pāyāsaṃ paṭiggahaṇadivase yeva pattassa antarahitattā na kho tathāgatā hatthesu patigaṇhanti kimhi nu kho ahaṃ patigaṇheyyan ti cintesi. ath' assa cittaṃ ñatvā catuhi disāhi cattāro mahārājāno indanīlamaṇimaye patte upanāmesuṃ. bhagavā te paṭikkhipi. puna muggavaṇṇaselamaye cattāro patte upanāmesuṃ. bhagavā catunnam pi devaputtānaṃ anukampāya cattāro patte paṭiggahetvā uparūpari ṭhapetvā eko hotū ti adhiṭṭhahi. cattāro pi mukhavaṭṭiyaṃ paññāyamānalekhā hutvā majjhimena pamāṇena ekattaṃ upagamiṃsu. bhagavā tasmiṃ paccagghe selamaye patte āhāraṃ patigaṇhitvā paribhuñjitvā anumodanaṃ akāsi. dve bhātaro vāṇijā buddhañ ca dhammañ ca saraṇaṃ gantvā dvevācikaupāsakā ahesuṃ. atha tesaṃ ekaṃ no bhante paricāritabbaṭṭhānaṃ dethā ti vadantānaṃ dakkhiṇahatthena attano sīsaṃ parāmasitvā kesadhātuyo adāsi. te attano nagare tā dhātuyo anto pakkhipitvā cetiyaṃ patiṭṭhāpesuṃ.

117 sammāsambuddho pi kho tato uṭṭhāya puna ajapālanigrodham eva gantvā nigrodhamūle nisīdi. ath' assa tattha nisinnamattass' eva attanā adhigatassa dhammassa gambhīrattaṃ paccavekkhantassa buddhānaṃ āciṇṇo adhigato kho my-āyaṃ dhammo ti paresaṃ dhammaṃ adesetuka-

carts and offer some food to the Teacher. They approached him, carrying rice cake and a honeycomb. They asked him, "Out of compassion for us, sir, may the Bhagavan accept our food." And they stood beside the Teacher. The Teacher's bowl had disappeared on the day that he had accepted the milk-rice, so he wondered about this: "Tathagatas do not accept food with their hands, so how can I accept this?" The Four Great Kings, knowing what he was thinking about, came from the four directions and brought four bowls made of sapphire, and offered them to him. The Bhagavan did not accept them. They then brought him four bowls made of stone, the color of a kidney bean. Feeling compassion for the four gods, he accepted the four bowls, and stacking them up on each other he made a resolve: "May they become one." The four bowls became one of middling size, with the distinctive lines of each showing around the lip. The Bhagavan accepted the food in the newly made bowl of stone and gave his blessings. The two merchant brothers took refuge in the Buddha and his Dhamma and became lay disciples, with two refuges. And after they had said, "Please sir, give us something that we can continue to honor," he gave them a few hairs from his head, which he obtained by stroking his head with his right hand. They set up a shrine in their city, honoring these items inside it.

Then the fully awakened Buddha got up and went to the 117
Goat Herder's Banyan Tree and sat at its roots. While he was there, considering the profundity of the truths he had realized, a thought arose in him, as is the custom for all Buddhas, that "this truth has been realized by me"—but that it could not be set in motion as a Dhamma to be undertaken by others.

mmatākārappavatto vitakko udapādi. atha brahmā sahampati nassati vata bho loko vinassati vata bho loko ti dasahi cakkavāḷasahassehi sakka-suyāma-santusita-sunimmita-vasavatti-mahābrahmuno ādāya satthu santikaṃ gantvā desetu bhante bhagavā dhammaṃ desetu bhagavā bhante dhamman ti ādinā nayena dhammadesanaṃ āyāci. satthā tassa paṭiññaṃ datvā kassa nu kho ahaṃ paṭhamaṃ dhammaṃ deseyyan ti cintento āḷāro paṇḍito so imaṃ dhammaṃ khippaṃ ājānissatī ti cittaṃ uppādetvā puna olokento tassa sattāhakālakatabhāvaṃ ñatvā Uddakaṃ āvajjesi. tassā 'pi abhidosakālakatabhāvaṃ ñatvā bahūpakārā kho pañcavaggiyā bhikkhū ti pañcavaggiye ārabbha manasikāraṃ katvā kahaṃ nu kho te etarahi viharantī ti āvajjento bārāṇasiyaṃ migadāye ti ñatvā tattha gantvā dhammacakkaṃ pavattessāmī ti katipāhaṃ bodhimaṇḍasamantā yeva piṇḍāya caranto viharitvā āsāḷhipuṇṇamāsiyaṃ bārāṇasiṃ gamissāmī ti cātuddasiyaṃ paccūsasamaye pabhātāya rattiyā kālass' eva pattacīvaraṃ ādāya aṭṭhārasayojanamaggaṃ paṭipanno antarāmagge upakaṃ nāma ājīvikaṃ disvā tassa attano buddhabhāvaṃ ācikkhitvā taṃ divasaṃ yeva sāyaṇhasamaye isipatanaṃ agamāsi. pañcavaggiyatherā tathāgataṃ dūrato 'va āgacchantaṃ disvā ayaṃ āvuso samaṇo gotamo paccayabāhullāya āvattitvā paripuṇṇakāyo phītindriyo suvaṇṇavaṇṇo hutvā āgacchati imassa abhivādanādīni na karissāma mahākulappasūto kho pan' esa āsanābhihāraṃ arahati ten' assa āsanamattaṃ paññāpessāmā ti katikaṃ akaṃsu. bhagavā sadevakassa lokassa cittācāraṃ jānana-

And then Brahma Sahampati thought: "Oh no, the world is destroyed! The world is in danger!" Rallying round the gods from the realm of Sakka, the Yama heaven, the Tusita heaven, the Creative heaven, and the Powerful heaven, and Great Brahmas too, from the ten thousand world systems, he approached the Teacher. He implored him to give Dhamma talks on the truth: "Let the Bhagavan teach the truth, sir; let the Bhagavan teach the truth, sir."

The Teacher gave him his assurance. But he wondered, "To whom am I going to teach this Dhamma first?" Then an idea came to him: "The teacher Alara! He'll quickly understand this Dhamma." But he looked and realized that he had died seven days before. He considered Uddaka. And he saw that he too had died, just the day before. So, he turned his mind to the group of five ascetics and said to himself: "These five monks did a lot for me." And he reflected: "I wonder where they live now?" He saw that they were in Varanasi, in the Deer Park. "I will go there, and I will set in motion the wheel of the Dhamma." He spent a few days doing an alms round in the neighborhood of the Bodhi Tree, and thought, "I'll go to Varanasi for the full-moon day of Asalha." Taking his bowl and robe early in the morning at dawn on the fourteenth day of the fortnight, he went on the main road. After about eighteen *yojanas,* he met the ascetic Upaka on the road and told him about his attainment of Buddhahood. Then he arrived at Isipatana in the evening.

The group of five elders saw him approaching. They made an agreement: "Here comes the ascetic Gotama. He is returning after living an indulgent life: he comes here with his body filled out, his faculties relaxed, and his complexion

samatthena ñāṇena kin nu kho ime cintayiṃsū ti āvajjitvā cittaṃ aññāsi. atha ne sabbadevamanussesu anodissakavasena pharaṇasamatthaṃ mettacittaṃ saṃkhipitvā odissakavasena mettacittaṃ phari.

118 te bhagavatā mettacittena phuṭṭhā tathāgate upasaṃkamante upasaṃkamante sakāya katikāya saṇṭhātuṃ asakkontā abhivādanapaccuṭṭhānādīni sabbakiccāni akaṃsu sambuddhabhāvaṃ pan' assa ajānamānā kevalaṃ nāmena ca āvusovādena ca samudācaranti. atha ne bhagavā mā bhikkhave tathāgataṃ nāmena ca āvusovādena ca samudācaratha ahaṃ bhikkhave tathāgato sammāsambuddho ti attano buddhabhāvaṃ saññāpetvā paññattavarabuddhāsane nisinno uttarasāḷhanakkhattayoge vattamāne aṭṭhārasahi brahmakoṭīhi parivuto pañcavaggiye there āmantetvā dhammacakkappavattanasuttaṃ desesi. tesu aññkoṇḍaññathero

golden. We will not pay any respects to him. He deserves a good seat as he is the son of a great and noble family, but we'll only prepare a seat suitable from that point of view." The Bhagavan, with his insight and knowledge of the way the minds of gods and men behave, asked himself, "What are they thinking?" And he knew their thoughts.

He then suffused his heart with loving-kindness, so that it 118
pervaded all gods and men, universally; and then he suffused loving-kindness in them in particular. Their hearts were so pervaded by the Tathagata's loving-kindness that as he approached them, step by step, they could not keep to the decision they had made before. They did all the things that are usual for a guest, giving him great reverence, rising up for him, and suchlike. And as they did not know about his awakening, they carried on calling him by his name or by the word "friend." And then the Buddha spoke. "Monks, do not address the Tathagata by his personal name or by the word 'friend.' I am the fully awakened Buddha, the Tathagata." And then he sat down on the seat that had been prepared and, while the Asalha conjunction was on the wane, surrounded by eighteen crore of Brahma gods, he delivered the discourse on setting in motion the wheel of the Dhamma.

And in the course of his talk, Kondannya came to knowledge through hearing the Dhamma, and as the discourse reached its conclusion, with the Brahma beings from eighteen realms present, he attained stream entry and its fruit. The Teacher stayed there for the rainy reason, and the next day sat in the temple teaching the elder Vaccha. The other four went on their alms round. In the evening the elder Vappa attained stream entry and its fruit. And on

desanānusārena ñāṇaṃ pesento suttapariyosāne aṭṭhārasahi brahmakoṭīhi saddhiṃ sotāpattiphale patiṭṭhāsi.

119 satthā tatth' eva vassaṃ upagantvā punadivase vappatheraṃ ovadanto vihāre yeva nisīdi. sesā cattāro piṇḍāya cariṃsu. vappathero pubbaṇhe yeva sotāpattiphalaṃ pāpuṇi. eten' eva upāyena punadivase bhaddiyatheraṃ punadivase mahānāmatheraṃ punadivase assajitheran ti sabbe sotāpattiphale patiṭṭhāpetvā pañcamiyaṃ pakkhassa pañca pi jane sannipātetvā anattalakkhaṇasuttantaṃ desesi desanāpariyosāne pañca pi therā arahattaphale patiṭṭhahiṃsu. atha satthā yasassa kulaputtassa upanissayaṃ disvā taṃ rattibhāge nibbijjitvā gehaṃ pahāya nikkhantaṃ ehi yasā ti pakkositvā tasmiṃ yeva rattibhāge sotāpattiphale punadivase arahatte patiṭṭhāpetvā apare pi tassa sahāyake catupaṇṇāsa jane ehibhikkhupabbajjāya pabbājetvā arahattaṃ pāpesi. evaṃ loke ekasaṭṭhiyā arahantesu jātesu satthā vutthavasso pavāretvā caratha bhikkhave cārikan ti saṭṭhiṃ bhikkhū disāsu pesetvā sayaṃ uruvelaṃ gacchanto antarāmagge kappāsiyavanasaṇḍe tiṃsa jane bhaddavaggiyakumāre vinesi. tesu sabbapacchimako sotāpanno sabbuttamo anāgāmī ahosi. te pi sabbe ehibhikkhubhāven' eva pabbājetvā disāsu pesetvā sayaṃ uruvelaṃ gantvā aḍḍhuḍḍhāni pāṭihāriyasahassāni dassetvā uruvelakassapādayo sahassa-

the following day in a similar way Bhaddiya attained the stream and its fruit, and on the next Mahanama, and on the next Assaji. And on the fifth day he called them all together and gave the "Discourse on Non-Self."[4] At the conclusion of the discourse, all five attained the fruits of arhatship.

The Discourse on Setting in Motion the Wheel of Truth

Then the Teacher saw a strong supporting condition for Yasa, 119
a man from a noble family. In the night, as he was leaving home to take the going forth, he said to him, "Come, Yasa." That night he attained the fruits of stream entry, and on the next day he reached arhatship.[5] And he admitted the other fifty-four of his companions into the order with the formula, "Come, monk," and enabled them to reach arhatship.

In this way, there were now sixty-one people who had become arhats. After the rainy season and the festival with which it closes were over, he sent out the sixty in different directions, with the words: "Go wandering, monks, and travel." And he himself started for Uruvela where, in the middle of his journey, in the Kappasiya Forest, he met and trained thirty young Bhadda nobles. Of these, the less proficient became stream-enterers and the most proficient never-returners. He called them all with the "Come, monk" formula and sent them, too, into the regions around, while he went on to Uruvela.

There he performed three thousand five hundred miracles, and so trained three brothers, matted-haired ascetics, Uruvela Kassapa and others, who had a thousand matted-

jaṭilaparivāre tebhātikajaṭile vinetvā ehibhikkhubhāven' eva pabbājetvā gayāsīse nisīdāpetvā adittapariyāyadesanāya arahatte patiṭṭhāpetvā tena arahantasahassena parivuto bimbisārarañño dinnaṃ paṭiññaṃ mocessāmī ti rājagahanagarūpacāre laṭṭhivanuyyānaṃ agamāsi.

120 rājā uyyānapālassa santikā satthā āgāto ti sutvā dvāda-
sanahutehi brāhmaṇagahapatikehi parivuto satthāraṃ
upasaṃkamitvā cakkavicittatalesu suvaṇṇapaṭavitānaṃ
viya pabhāsamudayaṃ vissajjentesu tathāgatassa pādesu
sirasā nipatitvā ekamantaṃ nisīdi saddhiṃ parisāya. atha
kho tesaṃ brāhmaṇagahapatikānaṃ etad ahosi: kin nu kho
mahāsamaṇo uruvelakassape brahmacariyaṃ carati udāhu
uruvelakassapo mahāsamaṇe ti. bhagavā tesaṃ cetasā ceto-
parivitakkam aññāya theraṃ gāthāya ajjhabhāsi:

282 kim eva disvā uruvelavāsi
pahāsi aggiṃ kisako vadāno
pucchāmi taṃ kassapa etam atthaṃ:
kathaṃ pahīnaṃ tava aggihuttan ti.

thero pi bhagavato adhippāyaṃ viditvā

283 rūpe ca sadde ca atho rase ca
kāmitthiyo cābhivadanti yaññaṃ
etaṃ malan ti upadhīsu ñatvā
tasmā na yiṭṭhe na hute araṃjin ti.

hair followers. And he accepted them into the order, with the formula "Come, monk." And he established them in arhatship with his teaching "The Fire Discourse."[6] So, surrounded by a thousand arhats, he went to the Latthi Forest pleasure park, in the neighborhood of Rajagaha, as he had given a promise to King Bimbisara that he would set him free.

When the king heard from the keeper of the grove that the 120
Teacher had come, he went to visit him with an entourage of a hundred and twenty thousand Brahmans and householders and fell down at the feet of the Tathagata, on whose soles appeared the beautifully detailed wheel, as if spread out like a canopy of gold.[7] Then he sat down to one side, with his entourage.

Then this question arose among the Brahmans and householders: "Does the great Teacher practice the holy life under Uruvela Kassapa, or does Uruvela Kassapa practice it under him?"

The Bhagavan recognized the concerns that were circling in their minds, and spoke of the elder in verse:

"What have you seen, you who live in Uruvela, that 282
you have abandoned the fire and speak of yourself as a
poor man? I ask you, Kassapa, this question:
What led you to abandon the fire sacrifice?"

And the elder, seeing what the Bhagavan intended, replied:

"Some value sights and sounds and tastes. Some value 283
sense pleasures and women, and some the sacrifice.
But I see this as a stain, so long as there are attachments. Because of this, there is no delight for me in
sacrifice or oblations."

121 imaṃ gāthaṃ vatvā attano sāvakabhāvappakāsanatthaṃ tathāgatassa pādapiṭṭhe sīsaṃ ṭhapetvā satthā me bhante bhagavā sāvako 'haṃ asmī ti vatvā ekatālaṃ dvitālaṃ titālan ti yāva sattatālappamāṇaṃ sattakkhattuṃ vehāsaṃ abbhuggantvā oruyha tathāgataṃ vanditvā ekamantaṃ nisīdi. taṃ pāṭihāriyaṃ disvā mahājano aho mahānubhāvā buddhā evaṃ thāmagatadiṭṭhiko nāma arahā ti maññamāno uruvelakassapo pi diṭṭhijālam bhinditvā tathāgatena damito ti satthu guṇakathaṃ yeva kathesi. bhagavā n' āhaṃ idānim eva uruvelakassapaṃ damemi atīte pi esa mayā damito yevā ti vatvā imissā aṭṭhuppaṭṭiyā mahānāradakassapajātakaṃ kathetvā cattāri saccāni pakāsesi. magadharājā ekādasahi nahutehi saddhiṃ sotāpattiphale patiṭṭhāsi ekaṃ nahutaṃ upāsakattaṃ paṭivedesi.

122 rājā satthu santike nisinno yeva pañca assāsake pavedetvā saraṇaṃ gantvā svātanāya nimantetvā āsanā vuṭṭhāya bhagavantaṃ padakkhiṇaṃ katvā pakkāmi. punadivase yehi ca bhagavā diṭṭho yehi ca adiṭṭho sabbe pi rājagahavāsino aṭṭhārasakoṭisaṃkhā manussā tathāgataṃ daṭṭhukāmā pāto 'va rājagahato laṭṭhivanaṃ agamaṃsu. tigāvutamaggo nappahosi. sakalalaṭṭhivanuyyānaṃ nirantaraṃ phuṭaṃ[2] ahosi. mahājano dasabalassa rūpaggappattaṃ attabhāvaṃ passanto tittiṃ kātuṃ nāsakkhi. vaṇṇabhū nām' esā

Speaking this verse, and in order to make his status as a 121
disciple known, he placed his head in the Tathagata's foot-rest. "The Bhagavan is my teacher, and I am his disciple." And he rose seven times into the air, once, twice, three times, and so on, until he was up to the height of seven palm trees, and, coming down again, he saluted the Tathagata in respect and sat to one side. Seeing this miracle, people around said, "Oh the power of Buddhas is terrific! He was so fixed in his views, and now Uruvela Kassapa is known as an arhat! He has broken the net of views, tamed by the Tathagata." And they sang the praises of the Teacher. The Bhagavan responded: "Although I tame Uruvela Kassapa today, in the past it was he who tamed me." And he related "The Great Narada Kassapa Jataka," and explained the four noble truths.[8] The king of Magadha, with a hundred and ten thousand followers, attained stream entry and its fruits, and ten thousand of his people declared themselves lay disciples.

The king sat with the Teacher and told to him five wishes. 122
He asked to go for refuge and, inviting the Bhagavan for a meal the following day, rose from his seat, made a reverential circle around him, and left. On the following day, all the people of Rajagaha, numbering eighteen crore, with both those who had seen the Buddha and those who had not, left Rajagaha early in the morning and went to the Reed Grove, wishing to get a glimpse of the Tathagata. The road, three *gāvutas* long, could not hold them. The entire Reed Grove was overflowing. And when people saw the beautiful form of the one with ten powers, they could not control their delight. It was called the Place of Praise, for at such places all the characteristic marks and attributes of the Tathagata and his

evarūpesu hi ṭhānesu tathāgatassa lakkhaṇānubyañjanādippabhedā sabbā 'pi rūpakāyasirī[3] vaṇṇetabbā. evaṃ rūpaggappattaṃ dasabalassa sarīraṃ passamānena mahājanena nirantaraṃ phuṭe[4] uyyāne ca magge ca ekabhikkhussā 'pi nikkhamanokāso n' āhosi. taṃ divasaṃ kira bhagavā chinnabhatto bhaveyya taṃ mā ahosī ti sakkassa nisinnāsanaṃ uṇhākāraṃ dassesi. so āvajjamāno taṃ kāraṇaṃ ñatvā māṇavakavaṇṇaṃ abhinimminitvā buddha-dhammasaṅgha-paṭisaṃyuttathutiyo vadamāno dasabalassa purato otaritvā devānubhāvena okāsaṃ katvā

284 danto dantehi saha purāṇajaṭilehi vippamuttehi
siṅgīnikkhasavaṇṇo rājagahaṃ pavisi bhagavā.
285 mutto muttehi saha purāṇajaṭilehi vippamuttehi
siṅgīnikkhasavaṇṇo rājagahaṃ pavisi bhagavā.
286 tiṇṇo tiṇṇehi saha purāṇajaṭilehi vippamuttehi
siṅgīnikkhasavaṇṇo rājagahaṃ pavisi bhagavā.
287 dasāvāso dasabalo dasadhammavidū dasahi c' upeto
so dasasataparivāro rājagaham pāvisi bhagavā ti

auspicious bodily form are to be praised. Such was the crowd of people looking at the beautiful form of the one with ten powers, in the overflowing park and in the road, there was no room for even one monk to leave. And they say that on that day, King Sakka's throne became hot as an alarm to him: "The Bhagavan might be deprived of food. This should not happen." He had a look and, realizing the problem, magically assumed the form of a young Brahman youth, singing the praises of the Buddha, his Dhamma, and his Sangha.

Through his divine power, he came down right in front of the one with ten powers, and spoke these verses:

"He has tamed himself, and his complexion shines 284
like burnished gold. With him are those who used to
be matted-hair ascetics, now all tamed and freed. The
Bhagavan has come to Rajagaha.
"He has delivered himself, and his complexion shines 285
like burnished gold. With him are those who used to
be matted-hair ascetics, now all delivered and freed.
The Bhagavan has come to Rajagaha.
"He has crossed over, and his complexion shines like 286
burnished gold. With him are those who used to be
matted-hair ascetics, who have now crossed over,
all freed.
The Bhagavan has come to Rajagaha. "His house 287
is tenfold, his powers are tenfold, and his insight is
tenfold.[9] His entourage is ten hundreds: the Bhagavan
has come to Rajagaha."

123 imāhi gāthāhi satthu vaṇṇaṃ vadamāno purato pāyāsi.
mahājano māṇavakassa rūpasiriṃ disvā ativiya abhirūpo
ayaṃ māṇavako na kho pan' amhehi diṭṭhapubbo ti cintetvā
kuto ayaṃ māṇavako kassa vā ayan ti āha. taṃ sutvā māṇavo

288 yo dhīro sabbadhī danto buddho appaṭipuggalo
arahaṃ sugato loke tass' āhaṃ paricārako ti

124 gāthaṃ āha. satthā sakkena katokāsaṃ maggaṃ paṭipajjitvā
bhikkhusahassaparivuto rājagaham pāvisi.
125 rājā buddhapamukhassa saṅghassa mahādānaṃ datvā
ahaṃ bhante tīṇi ratanāni vinā vattituṃ na sakkhissāmi
velāya vā avelāya vā bhagavato santikaṃ āgamissāmi
laṭṭhivanuyyānañ ca nāma atidūre idam pan' amhākaṃ veḷu-
vanaṃ nāma uyyānaṃ n' ātidūre gamanāgamanasampannaṃ
buddhārahaṃ senāsanaṃ idaṃ me bhagavā patigaṇhatū ti
suvaṇṇabhiṃkārena pupphagandhavāsitamaṇivaṇṇauda-
kaṃ ādāya veḷuvanuyyānaṃ pariccajanto dasabalassa hatthe
udakaṃ pātesi. tasmiṃ ārāmapaṭiggahaṇe buddhasāsanassa
mūlāni otiṇṇānīti mahāpaṭhavī kampi. jambudīpasmiṃ
hi ṭhapetvā veḷuvanaṃ aññaṃ paṭhaviṃ kampetvā gahi-
tasenāsanaṃ nāma n' atthi. tambapaṇṇidīpe pi ṭhapetvā
mahāvihāraṃ aññaṃ paṭhaviṃ kampetvā gahitasenāsanaṃ
nāma n' atthi. satthā veḷuvanārāmaṃ paṭiggahetvā rañño

With these verses he came in front of the Teacher, singing 123
his praises. And the crowd saw the glorious appearance of the young man and commented: "This is an unusually good-looking young man. We've never seen one like that before." They asked him: "Where are you from, young man? Whose family are you from?"

And the young man listened to them and said:

"I am a servant: for the one in the world who is strong, 288
self-controlled in every way, a Buddha, unequaled
among men, an arhat, a happy one."

And he sang this verse. And the Teacher walked on the path 124
that had been opened up by Sakka and entered Rajagaha, with a retinue of monks.

The king gave a great feast for the Sangha, with the Buddha 125
at its head, and said: "Sir, I cannot live without the three gems. I wish to visit the Bhagavan at all times, even if it is the time to visit or if it is not. But the Reed Grove is too far away and the royal park, Bamboo Grove, is nearby, easy to get in and out of, and a worthy place for the Buddha to stay. May the Bhagavan accept it from me!" And he took water that was crystal fresh and had been scented with flower petals in a golden water jar and poured it over the hand of the one with ten powers, dedicating the Bamboo Grove. And at the dedication of the grove, the great earth quaked, by this establishment of the roots of the Buddha's Dhamma. In no other place in the whole of Jambudipa was there an earthquake at the reception of a residence, except for the Great Vihara in Lanka. The Teacher accepted the Bamboo Grove monastery and offered joyful blessings, rose from his seat, and then left

anumodanaṃ katvā uṭṭhāy' āsanā bhikkhusaṅghaparivuto veḷuvanaṃ agamāsi.

126 tasmiṃ kho pana samaye sāriputto ca moggallāno cā ti dve paribbājakā rājagahaṃ upanissāya viharanti amataṃ pariyesamānā. tesu sāriputto assajitheraṃ piṇḍāya paviṭṭhaṃ disvā pasannacitto payirupāsitvā ye dhammā hetuppabhavā ti gāthaṃ sutvā sotāpattiphale patiṭṭhāya sahāyakassa moggallānaparibbājakassā 'pi tam eva gāthaṃ abhāsi. so 'pi sotāpattiphale patiṭṭhahi. te ubho pi sañjayaṃ oloketvā attano parisāya saddhiṃ satthu santike pabbajiṃsu. tesu mahāmoggallāno sattāhena arahattaṃ pāpuṇi sāriputtatthero addhamāsena ubho pi ca ne satthā aggasāvakaṭṭhāne ṭhapesi. sāriputtattherena arahattapattadivase yeva sāvakasannipātam akāsi. tathāgate pana tasmiñ ñeva veḷuvanuyyāne viharante suddhodanamahārājā putto kira me chabbassāni dukkarakārikaṃ caritvā paramābhisambodhiṃ patvā pavattavaradhammacakko rājagahaṃ nissāya veḷuvane viharatī ti sutvā aññataraṃ amaccaṃ āmantesi: ehi bhaṇe purisasahassaparivāro rājagahaṃ gantvā mama vacanena pitā vo suddhodanamahārājā daṭṭhukāmo ti vatvā puttam me gaṇhitvā ehī ti āha. so evaṃ devā 'ti rañño vacanaṃ sirasā sampaṭicchitvā purisasahassaparivāro khippam eva saṭṭhiyojanamaggaṃ gantvā dasabalassa catuparisamajjhe nisīditvā dhammadesanavelāya vihāraṃ pāvisi. so

for the Bamboo Grove with his retinue of the order of monks.

Now at that time, two wandering ascetics, Sariputta and 126
Moggallana, were staying at Rajagaha, searching after the deathless. Sariputta saw the elder Assaji on his alms round. His heart became clear with faith, and he attended him. He heard from him the verse beginning, "Whatever phenomena arise with a cause..." and attained stream entry and its fruits.[10] He recited the verse to his companion in the going forth, Moggallana, and he too attained stream entry and its fruits. They both went to practice the holy life with the Teacher, with the approval of their own teacher, Sañjaya. Of the two, great Moggallana became an arhat in a week, and Sariputta in two weeks. The Teacher appointed the two as his chief disciples. On the day that the elder Sariputta attained arhatship, the Teacher called a meeting of his disciples.

Now, while the Tathagata was staying at the Bamboo Grove, the great king Suddhodana had heard the news. "They now say that my son has made an end to his practice of the austerities and has found the unsurpassable and highest awakening. He has set in motion the wheel of his Dhamma, and is staying in Rajagaha, at the Bamboo Grove." He spoke to one of his ministers: "My friend, go to Rajagaha with a retinue of a thousand men, and deliver this message to my son: 'Your father, the great king Suddhodana, wishes to see you.'"

The man said, "Certainly, your highness," and showed his agreement by bowing his head low. As quickly as he could, he covered sixty *yojanas,* with a retinue of a thousand men. He entered the monastery and found the one with ten powers sitting in the midst of his four assemblies, giving a talk on

tiṭṭhatu tāva rañño pahitasāsanan ti parisante ṭhito satthu dhammadesanaṃ sutvā yathāṭhito 'va saddhiṃ purisasahassena arahattaṃ patvā pabbajjaṃ yāci.

127 bhagavā etha bhikkhavo ti hatthaṃ pasāresi. sabbe taṃ khaṇaṃ yeva iddhimayapattacīvaradharā vassasatikatherā viya ahesuṃ. arahattaṃ pattakālato paṭṭhāya pana ariyā nāma majjhattā 'va hontī ti rañño pahitasāsanaṃ dasabalassa na kathesi. rājā n' eva gatako 'va āgacchati na sāsanaṃ sūyatī ti ehi bhaṇe tvaṃ gacchā ti ten' eva niyāmena aññaṃ amaccaṃ pesesi. so 'pi gantvā purimanayen' eva saddhiṃ parisāya arahattaṃ patvā tuṇhī ahosi. rājā eten' eva niyāmena purisasahassaparivāre nava amacce pesesi. sabbe attano kiccaṃ niṭṭhapetvā tuṇhībhūtā tatth' eva vihariṃsu. rājā sāsanamattakam pi āharitvā ācikkhantaṃ alabhitvā cintesi: ettakā janā mayi sinehabhāvena sāsanamattam pi na paccāhariṃsu ko nu kho me vacanaṃ karissatī ti sabbaṃ rājabalaṃ olokento kāḷudāyiṃ addasa. so kira rañño sabbatthasādhako abbhantariko ativissāsiko bodhisattena saddhiṃ ekadivase jāto sahapaṃsukīḷito sahāyo. atha naṃ rājā āmantesi: tāta kāḷudāyi ahaṃ mama puttaṃ passitukāmo nava purisasahassāni pesesiṃ ekapuriso pi āgantvā sāsanamattaṃ ārocetvā 'pi n' atthi dujjāno kho pana jīvitantarāyo ahaṃ jīvamāno 'va puttaṃ daṭṭhuṃ icchāmi sakkhissati nu kho me puttaṃ dassetun ti sakkhissāmi deva sace pabbajituṃ labhissāmī

the Dhamma.[11] So he thought, "Let the king's message wait a bit." And he stood just beyond the assemblies and listened to the Teacher's talk.

And as he stood there, the minister attained arhatship, with all his retinue, and asked to be accepted as a renouncer. The Bhagavan said, "Come, monks," and stretched out his 127
hand. And at just that moment bowls and robes, as if for elders of a hundred years' standing, were miraculously created.

Now at the time when they attain arhatship, noble ones are in a state of "middleness," and so they did not deliver the message from the king. The king thought, "The one who went still hasn't come back, and my message has not been heard." And he called another minister, in exactly the same way as before: "Dear friend, please go." And the same thing happened as before; and he too, once he had attained arhatship, was silent. The king sent nine ministers in all, each with a retinue of a thousand, in just the same way. And they all neglected their task—and stayed there and remained silent.

The king could not find anyone who would even deliver the message for him. He reflected on this. "I have sent so many on this business, and through their lack of affection they have not even delivered a message. Who will carry out my request?" And he looked around the king's forces and saw Kaludayi. The story goes that he was the minister who carried out the king's every wish; he knew all his inner workings and was very trustworthy. He had also been born the same day as the Bodhisatta, had played with him as a child, and was his friend. Then the king addressed him: "Dear Kaludayi, I would like to see my son, and have sent nine

ti. tāta tvam pabbajitvā vā apabbajitvā vā mayhaṃ puttaṃ dassehī ti. so sādhu devā ti rañño sāsanaṃ ādāya rājagahaṃ gantvā satthu dhammadesanavelāya parisapariyante ṭhito dhammaṃ sutvā saparivāro arahattaphalaṃ patvā ehibhikkhubhāve patiṭṭhāsi. satthā buddho hutvā paṭhamaṃ antovassaṃ isipatane vasitvā vutthavasso pavāretvā uruvelaṃ gantvā tattha tayo māse vasanto tebhātikajaṭile vinetvā bhikkhusahassaparivāro phussamāsapuṇṇamāya rājāgahaṃ gantvā dve māse vasi. ettāvatā bārāṇasito nikkhantassa pañca māsā jātā. sakalo hemanto atikkanto udāyittherassa āgatadivasato sattaṭṭhadivasā vītivattā. so phaggunipuṇṇamāsiyaṃ cintesi: atikkanto hemanto vasantasamayo anuppatto manussehi sassādīni uddharitvā sammukhaṭṭhāne maggā dinnā haritatiṇasañchannā paṭhavī supupphitā vanasaṇḍā paṭipajjanakkhamā maggā kālo dasabalassa

thousand men, but not one has come back, not even with any news about him. I am getting on and there might be a threat to my life. I just want to see my son while I am alive. Will you be able to get me to see him?" "Your highness, I will, even if I take the going forth."

"Dear boy, whether you take the going forth or you do not, just get me to see my son."

He said, "Certainly, your highness." And he went to Rajagaha, taking the message.

Standing there, he heard the Teacher giving a talk, surrounded by his assembly, and, with his retinue, he attained arhatship. And he was admitted into the order with the formula, "Come, monk." The Teacher spent the first rainy season after he had become a Buddha in Isipatana. Then he went to Uruvela and stayed there three months. He converted three brothers who were matted-hair ascetics. On the full-moon day of the month of Phussa* he went with a thousand monks to Rajagaha and stayed two months there. In all, since the time when he had left Varanasi, five months had passed. The entire cold season had passed, and it was seven or eight days since the arrival of Udayi, the elder. And on the full-moon day of Phagguni,† Udayi thought: "The cold season has passed. It is springtime. People grow their crops and set out on journeys. The earth is covered in fresh grass, the woods are filled with beautiful flowers, and roads are passable. It is time for the Bhagavan to show friendship to his family."

* January.
† March.

ñātisaṃgaham kātun ti. atha bhagavantaṃ upasaṃkamitvā

289 aṅgārino dāni dumā bhadante
phalesino chadanaṃ vippahāya
te accimanto 'va pabhāsayanti.
samayo mahāvīra bhagīrasānaṃ.
290 nātisītaṃ nātiuṇhaṃ nātidubbhikkhachātakaṃ
saddalā haritā bhūmi esa kālo mahāmunī ti

128 saṭṭhimattāhi gāthāhi dasabalassa kulanagaragamanatthāya gamanavaṇṇaṃ vaṇṇesi. atha naṃ satthā kin nu kho udāyi madhurassarena gamanavaṇṇaṃ vaṇṇesī ti āha. bhante tumhākaṃ pitā suddhodanamahārājā passitukāmo karothā ñātakānaṃ saṃgahan ti. sādhu udāyi karissāmi ñātakānaṃ saṃgahaṃ bhikkhusaṅghassa ārocehi gamiyavattaṃ pūressantī ti. sādhu bhante ti thero ārocesi. bhagavā aṅgamagadha-vāsīnaṃ kulaputtānaṃ dasahi sahassehi kapilavatthuvāsīnaṃ dasahi sahassehī ti sabbeh' eva vīsatisahassehi khīṇāsavabhikkhūhi parivuto rājagahā nikkhamitvā divase divase yojanaṃ gacchati. rājagahato saṭṭhiyojanaṃ kapilavatthuṃ dvīhi māsehi pāpuṇissāmī ti aturitacārikaṃ pakkāmi.

He approached the Bhagavan and said:
"The trees glow now like embers. They have shed 289
their covering of leaves; it is the time for fruit. They
shine like flames: It is the time, great hero, for the
season of delights.
It is not too cold; it is not too hot. There is no hunger 290
or hardship in the land. The earth is green with grass.
This is the moment, great Teacher."[12]

Then the Teacher asked him, "Udayi, why do you sing the 128
praises of the delights of travel, with such a melodious voice?"

"Sir, your father, the great king Suddhodana, wishes to see you. Make peace with your family."

"Very well, Udayi, I will show friendship to my family. Inform the community of monks, and they will act in accordance with the rules for travel."

"Certainly, sir." The elder informed them, and the Bhagavan set off from Rajagaha with twenty thousand monks who had all eliminated the pollutants, ten thousand people from Anga and Magadha, and ten thousand from Kapilavatthu. By traveling one *yojana* in one day they made the journey from Rajagaha, sixty *yojanas* in all, in two months.

129 thero pi bhagavato nikkhantabhāvaṃ rañño ārocessāmī ti vehāsam abbhuggantvā rañño nivesane pāturahosi. rājā theraṃ disvā tuṭṭhacitto mahārahe pallaṃke nisīdāpetvā attano paṭiyāditassa nānaggarasabhojanassa pattaṃ pūretvā adāsi. thero uṭṭhāya gamanākāraṃ dassesi. nisīditvā bhuñjathā ti. satthu santikaṃ gantvā bhuñjissāmi mahārājā ti. kahaṃ pana satthā ti. vīsatibhikkhusahassaparivāro tumhākaṃ dassanatthāya cārikaṃ nikkhanto mahārājā ti. rājā tuṭṭhamānaso āha: tumhe imaṃ paribhuñjitvā yāva mama putto imaṃ nagaraṃ pāpuṇāti tāv' assa ito 'va piṇḍapātaṃ pariharathā ti. thero adhivāsesi. rājā theraṃ parivisitvā pattaṃ gandhacuṇṇena ubbaṭṭetvā uttamabhojanassa pūretvā tathāgatassa dethā ti therassa hatthe patiṭṭhāpesi. thero sabbesaṃ passantānaṃ yeva pattaṃ ākāse khipitvā sayam pi vehāsaṃ abbhuggantvā piṇḍapātaṃ āharitvā satthu hatthe ṭhapesi. satthā taṃ paribhuñji. eten' upāyena thero divase divase āhari. satthā 'pi antarāmagge rañño yeva piṇḍapātaṃ paribhuñji. thero pi bhattakiccāvasāne divase divase ajja ettakaṃ bhagavā āgato ajja ettakan ti baddhaguṇapaṭisaṃyuttāya ca kathāya sakalarājakulaṃ satthu dassanaṃ vinā yeva satthari sañjātappasādaṃ akāsi. ten' eva naṃ bhagavā etadaggaṃ bhikkhave mama sāvakānaṃ bhikkhūnaṃ kulappasādakānaṃ yadidaṃ kāḷudāyī ti etadagge ṭhapesi.

Deciding he would let the king know that the Bhagavan 129
had set out, the elder rose in the sky and appeared at the king's palace. The king was delighted at the elder's arrival and got him to sit on a beautiful couch. He filled his bowl with the finest food, which had been prepared for himself, and offered it to him. The elder rose from his seat and showed a sign that he was leaving.

"But stay here to eat your food."

"Great king, I will eat with the Teacher."

"Where is the Teacher?"

"He has already set out. He is making the journey with an entourage of twenty thousand monks, to see you."

The king was overjoyed. "Then you eat here until my son reaches the city, and then go on alms round with him."

The elder assented. The king had the bowl cleaned with perfumed powder and filled it with the most delicious food. "Give this to the Tathagata," he said, handing him the bowl with his hands. The elder, with everyone looking on, hurled the bowl into the sky and rose up in the air to follow it. Taking the food to the Teacher, he offered it into his hands and the Teacher ate it. So, the Teacher ate alms food from the king for each stage of his journey; each day the elder gave him food in this way. And every day, when the elder had finished his meal, he was ableto say: "Today the Bhagavan has come so far; today he is here..."

He extolled the qualities of the Teacher to everyone in the royal court, and so inspired faith to grow in them, even though they had not seen him yet. Because of this, the Bhagavan then accorded him the highest esteem: "Kaludayi is the best of my disciples who can inspire faith in families."[13]

130 sākiyā 'pi kho anuppatte bhagavati amhākaṃ ñātiseṭṭhaṃ passissāmā ti sannipativā bhagavato vasanaṭṭhānaṃ vimaṃsamānā nigrodhasakkassa ārāmo ramaṇīyo ti sallakkhetvā tattha sabbaṃ paṭijagganavidhiṃ kāretvā gandhapuppha-hatthā paccuggamanaṃ karontā sabbālaṃkārapatimaṇḍite daharadahare nāgaradārake ca dārikāyo ca paṭhamaṃ pahiṇiṃsu tato rājakumāre ca rājakumāriyo ca tesaṃ anantaraṃ sāmaṃ gandhapupphacuṇṇādīhi pūjayamānā bhagavantaṃ gahetvā nigrodhārāmam eva agamaṃsu. tatra bhagavā vīsatisahassakhīṇāsavaparivuto paññattavara-buddhāsane nisīdi. sākiyā nāma mānajātikā mānatthaddhā. te siddhatthakumāro amhehi daharataro amhākaṃ kaniṭṭho bhāgineyyo putto nattā ti cintetvā daharadahare rājakumāre āhaṃsu: tumhe vandathā mayaṃ tumhākaṃ piṭṭhito nisīdissāmā ti tesu evaṃ nisinnesu bhagavā tesaṃ ajjhāsayam oloketvā na maṃ ñātayo vandati handa dāni ne vandāpessāmī ti abhiññāpādakajjhānaṃ samāpajjitvā vuṭṭhāya ākāsaṃ abbhuggantvā tesaṃ sīse pādapaṃsuṃ okiramāno viya gaṇḍambamūle yamakapāṭihāriyasadisaṃ pāṭihāriyaṃ akāsi.

131 rājā taṃ acchariyaṃ disvā āha: bhagavā tumhākaṃ jāta-divase kāḷadevalassa vandanatthaṃ upanītānaṃ pāde vo parivattitvā brāhmaṇassa matthake patiṭṭhite disvā 'pi ahaṃ

The Sakiyans met together to talk about the arrival of the Bhagavan, and when they would be able to see their kinsman. They gave some thought to where the Bhagavan would stay. They agreed that the Banyan Grove was a very delightful place and made all the arrangements for his care there. Then they went out to receive him, with garlands and flowers in their hands, having sent out young boys and girls, all in finery, to welcome him first. Then followed the princes and princesses from noble families, and then they themselves led the Bhagavan to the Banyan Grove, honoring him with perfumes, flowers, powders, and suchlike. There, the Bhagavan sat down on a seat specially prepared for the Buddha, surrounded by twenty thousand arhats, who had eradicated the pollutants. The Sakiyans are a proud race, with stubborn minds. They thought, "Prince Siddhattha is younger than we are, he is like a younger brother, a son, or a nephew." They said to the young people in their families: "You go and pay homage to him. We will sit behind you." 130

When they were all seated, the Bhagavan looked and realized their intention. "These relatives of mine do not pay me due reverence. I will get them to do that." And he attained the higher knowledges, using *jhāna* as his basis, and rose into the sky. Then, as if scattering the dust from his feet on their heads, he performed a miracle that was the same as the twin miracle performed at the root of the Ganda's Mango Tree.

The king saw this wonder and said, "When you were brought to Kaladeva to pay homage to him on the day of your birth, I watched as you turned around and placed your feet on the Brahman's head and I paid homage to you. This was my first homage to you. Then, on the auspicious day of 131

tumhe vandiṃ ayam me paṭhamavandanā vappamaṅgaladivase jambucchāyāya sirisayane nisinnānaṃ vo jambucchāyāya aparivattanaṃ disvā ’pi pāde vandiṃ ayaṃ me dutiyā vandanā idāni imaṃ adiṭṭhapubbaṃ pāṭihāriyaṃ disvā ’pi tumhākaṃ pāde vandāmi ayaṃ me tatiyā vandanā ti. rañño pana vandite bhagavantaṃ avanditvā ṭhātuṃ samattho nāma eko sākiyo pi n’ āhosi sabbe vandiṃsu yeva. iti bhagavā ñātake vandāpetvā ākāsato otaritvā paññatte āsane nisīdi. nisinne bhagavati sikhāppatto ñātisamāgamo ahosi. sabbe ekaggacittā hutvā nisīdiṃsu. tato mahāmegho pokkharavassaṃ vassi tambavaṇṇaṃ udakaṃ heṭṭhā viravantam gacchati temitukāmo ’va temeti atemitukāmassa sarīre udabindumatto pi na patati. taṃ disvā sabbe acchariyabbhutacittajātā aho acchariyaṃ aho abbhutan ti kathaṃ samuṭṭhāpesuṃ. satthā na idānim eva mayhaṃ ñātisamāgame pokkharavassaṃ vassa ti atīte pi vassīti imissā aṭṭhuppattiyā vessantarajātakaṃ kathesi. dhammadesanaṃ sutvā sabbe uṭṭhāya vanditvā pakkamiṃsu eko pi rājā vā rājamahāmatto vā sve amhākaṃ bhikkhaṃ gaṇhathā ti vatvā gato nāma n’ atthi. satthā punadivase vīsatisahassabhikkhuparivuto kapilavatthuṃ piṇḍāya pāvisi. taṃ na koci gantvā nimantesi vā pattaṃ vā aggahesi. bhagavā indakhīle ṭhito ’va

the plowing festival, sitting under the shade of the rose-apple tree, I saw the shadow of the rose-apple tree did not move and paid homage to your feet. That was my second homage to you. Now, I have witnessed this wonder, which no one has seen before, and I pay homage to your feet. This is my third homage to you." When the king had paid such deep reverence to the Bhagavan, not one of the Sakiyans could continue to omit to do so, and so they all paid homage too. The Bhagavan, now he had managed to get his relatives to pay homage, came down from the sky and sat on the seat that had been prepared for him. The meeting place was filled to capacity with his relatives, sitting for the Bhagavan. All sat with their minds unified. Then a great rain cloud poured down a rain of lotus blossoms, and streams of copper-colored water gushed down with a great roar, and those who wanted to be wet became wet, but not even a drop of water fell on those who wanted to stay dry. Everyone was overcome with wonder at seeing such an extraordinary event, and said, "What a miracle! What an amazing thing!"

The Teacher said, "It is not just now that a shower of lotuses poured down on my relatives. Once before it did, too." And he related to them "The Vessantara Jataka," in connection to this. When they had heard this talk on the Dhamma, they all got up, paid him deep reverence, and left. But not one of them—not a prince, nor a minister—invited him for a meal on the following day.

The next day, the Teacher went on the alms round in Kapilavatthu, surrounded by his retinue of twenty thousand monks. And not one person came to pay their respects to him, invite him for a meal, or take his bowl. Standing by

āvajjesi: kathan nu kho pubbabuddhā kulanagare piṇḍāya cariṃsu kiṃ uppaṭipāṭiyā issarajjanānam gharāni agamaṃsu udāhu sapadānacārikaṃ cariṃsū ti. tato ekabuddhassā 'pi uppaṭipāṭiyā gamanaṃ adisvā mayā 'pi dāni ayam eva vaṃso ayaṃ me paveṇi paggahetabbā āyatiñ ca me sāvakā 'pi mamañ ñeva anusikkhantā piṇḍacāriyavattaṃ paripūressantī ti koṭiyaṃ niviṭṭhagehato paṭṭhāya sapadānaṃ piṇḍāya cari. ayyo kira siddhatthakumāro piṇḍāya caratī ti dvibhūmakatibhūmakādisu pāsādesu sīhapañjare vivaritvā mahājano dassanavyāvaṭo ahosi.

132 rāhulamātā 'pi devī ayyaputto kira imasmiṃ yeva nagare mahantena rājānubhāvena suvaṇṇasivikādīhi vicaritvā idāni kesamassuṃ ohāretvā kāsāyavatthavasano kapālahattho piṇḍāya carati sobhati nu kho ti sīhapañjaraṃ vivaritvā olokayamānā bhagavantaṃ nānāvirāgasamujjalāya sarīrappabhāya nagaravīthiyo obhāsetvā vyāmappabhāparikkhepasamupabbūḷhāya asītānubyañjanāvabhāsitāya dvattiṃsamahāpurisalakkhaṇapatimaṇḍitāya anopamāya buddhasiriyā virocamānaṃ disvā

291 siniddhanīlamudukuñcitakeso
suriyasunimmalatalābhinalāṭo
yuttatuṅgamudukāyatanāso
raṃsijālavitato narasīho ti

the post placed at the city gate, he wondered, "How did earlier Buddhas wander for alms in their native cities? Did they go first to the houses of the rich and powerful, without a set system? Or did they go step by step on a steady alms round?" He saw then that no Buddha had ever gone to houses favoring a hierarchical order. "This is the lineage and custom that I should accept. And my disciples, learning this way from me, will fulfill the training of undertaking an alms round." And he embarked on a steady course, starting at the dwelling on the edge of the city. "They say that Siddhattha the prince is doing an alms round!" As word got around, people in two-story and three-story houses threw open their windows, just to have a look.

Rahula's mother, the Queen Rahulamata, also opened her 132
window in the palace. "They say that my husband, who used to roam around town in regal splendor, with golden trappings, has cut his hair, shaved off his beard, and wears yellow robes, begging on the alms round. Does this look good?" She watched him and saw the Bhagavan, in the unparalleled and vast majesty of a Buddha. He was adorned with the thirty-two marks of a great person, and the eighty minor marks, in all their detail, showed up on his body; he lit up the city streets with a halo that suffused his whole body with radiance, sending out rays of different colors.

> "His hair is glossy, dark, soft, and curly. His forehead 291
> is like the sun; it is broad and has no stain or cloud.
> His nose is beautifully proportioned, and soft too.
> Around him is a mass of rays: he is a lion among men."

133 evamādikāhi aṭṭhahi narasīhagāthāhi nāma abhitthavitvā tumhākaṃ putto piṇḍāya caratī ti rañño ārocesi. rājā saṃviggahadayo hatthena sāṭakaṃ saṇṭhapento turitaturitaṃ nikkhamitvā vegena gantvā bhagavato purato ṭhatvā āha: kiṃ bhante amhe lajjāpetha kimatthaṃ piṇḍāya caratha kiṃ ettakānaṃ bhikkhūnaṃ na sakkā bhattaṃ laddhun ti saññaṃ karitthā ti. cārittaṃ etaṃ mahārājā amhākan ti. nanu bhante amhākaṃ mahāsammatakhattiyavaṃso nāma vaṃso tattha ca ekakhattiyo pi bhikkhācāro nāma n' atthī ti. ayaṃ mahārāja rājavaṃso nāma tava vaṃso amhākaṃ pana dīpaṃkaro koṇḍañño pe kassapo ti ayaṃ buddhavaṃso nāma ete ca aññe ca anekasahassasaṃkhā buddhā bhikkhācārā bhikkhācāren' eva jīvikaṃ kappesun ti antaravīthiyaṃ ṭhito 'va

292 uttiṭṭhe na-ppamajjeyya
dhammaṃ sucaritaṃ care
dhammacārī sukhaṃ seti
asmiṃ loke paramhi ca

134 imaṃ gātham āha. gāthāpariyosāne rājā sotāpattiphale patiṭṭhāsi.

With these words she sang the "Lion among Men" verses and 133
informed the king. "Your son is begging for food on the alms round." The king rushed out in great agitation, gathering the folds of his clothes as he ran. He went up to the Bhagavan and stood in front of him. "Why, sir, are you bringing shame to us? What on earth are you doing an alms round for? Why do you signal to the world, 'There is not the food to feed all these monks?'"

—"Great king, this is the way of our lineage."

—"But is not the great Kshatriya tradition of Mahasamma our lineage? In this lineage there has not been one noble who went around begging for alms."

—"That is the case for a royal lineage. But this is the lineage of Dipankara, Kondannya, Kassapa, and all the rest: the lineage of Buddhas. These and many other Buddhas, in their thousands, all went on alms rounds, and did so for their basic sustenance."

Standing in the middle of the street, he spoke this verse:

"Don't be neglectful when you go on the alms round 292
Practice it well, and the Dhamma too. The one who
follows it carefully is happy, In this world and in the
next."

And at the conclusion of the verse, the king attained 134
stream entry and its fruit.

293 dhammaṃ care sucaritaṃ
na naṃ duccaritaṃ care
dhammacārī sukhaṃ seti
asmiṃ loke paramhi cā ti.

135 imaṃ pana gāthaṃ sutvā sakadāgāmiphale patiṭṭhāsi. dhammapālajātakaṃ sutvā anāgāmiphale patiṭṭhāsi.

136 maraṇasamaye setacchattassa heṭṭhā sirisayane nipanno yeva arahattaṃ pāpuṇi. araññavāsena padhānānuyogakiccaṃ rañño n' āhosi. sotāpattiphalaṃ sacchikatvā yeva pana bhagavato pattaṃ gahetvā saparisaṃ bhagavantaṃ mahāpāsādaṃ āropetvā paṇītena khādanīyena bhojanīyena parivisi. bhattakiccapariyosāne sabbaṃ itthāgāraṃ āgantvā bhagavantaṃ vandi ṭhapetvā rāhulamātaraṃ. sā pana gaccha ayyaputtaṃ vandāhī ti parijanena vuccamānā 'pi sace mayhaṃ guṇo atthi sayam eva me santikaṃ ayyaputto āgamissati āgataṃ eva naṃ vandissāmī ti vatvā na agamāsi.

137 bhagavā rājānaṃ pattam gāhāpetvā dvīhi aggasāvakehi saddhiṃ rājadhītāya sirigabbhaṃ gantvā rājadhītā yathāruciṃ vandamānā na kiñci vattabbā ti vatvā paññatte āsane nisīdi. sā vegena gantvā gopphakesu gahetvā pādapiṭṭhiyaṃ sīsaṃ parivattetvā yathājjhāsayaṃ vandi. rājā rājadhītāya bhagavati sinehabahumānādiguṇasampattiyo kathesi: bhante mama dhītā tumhehi kāsāyāni nivatthānī ti sutvā tato paṭṭhāya kāsāvavatthā jātā tumhākaṃ ekabha-

"Do things well when you go on the alms round. Do 293
not do things sloppily. The one who follows it carefully
is happy, in this world and in the next."[14]

135 Hearing this verse, the king attained the state of once-returner and its fruit (and later, he listened to "The Great Guardian of the Dhamma Jataka" and attained the state of never-return and its fruits).[15]

136 And at the time of his death, he lay down as a white parasol was held above him and attained arhatship. There was no need for him to live a life of ardent spiritual practice in the forest. Only when he had realized stream entry and its fruit did he take the Buddha's bowl. Then he led the Bhagavan and his retinue back to the great palace and fed them with food, both crunchy and soft. At the conclusion of their meal, all of the female household came to pay homage to the Bhagavan, with the exception of Rahulamata. She had been encouraged by her women, who said to her, "Go and pay your respects to your husband." But she had responded: "If there is any virtue in me, my husband will come to me. Then I will offer him my homage." And she had not gone.

137 The Bhagavan had the king carry his bowl for him and entered the princess's grand apartment with his two chief disciples. He told them, "Let the royal daughter pay homage just as she pleases, and don't say a thing," and he sat down on the seat that had been prepared. She rushed up and took hold of him by the ankles, rolling her head on his feet worshiping him just as she wanted. The king spoke to the Bhagavan of her great attainments, her affection, and her manifold excellences. "Sir, my daughter heard that you were taking

ttikabhāvaṃ sutvā ekabhattikā ’va jātā tumhehi mahāsayanassa chaḍḍitabhāvaṃ ñatvā paṭṭikamañcake yeva nipannā tumhākaṃ mālāgandhādīhi viratabhāvaṃ ñatvā viratamālāgandhā ’va jātā attano ñātakesu mayaṃ paṭijaggissāmā ti sāsane pesite ekañātikam pi na olokesi evaṃ guṇasampannā me bhagavā dhītā ti. anacchariyaṃ mahārāja yaṃ idāni tayā rakkhiyamānā rājadhītā paripakke ñaṇe attānaṃ rakkheyya esā pubbe anārakkhā pabbatapāde vicaramānā aparipakke ñāṇe attānaṃ rakkhī ti vatvā candakinnarajātakaṃ kathetvā uṭṭhāyāsanā pakkāmi.

138 dutiyadivase nandassa rājākumārassa abhisekagehappavesanavivāhamaṅgalesu vattamānesu tassa gehaṃ gantvā kumāraṃ pattaṃ gāhāpetvā pabbājetukāmo maṅgalaṃ vatvā uṭṭhāy’ āsanā pakkāmi. janapadakalyāṇī kumāraṃ gacchantaṃ disvā tuvaṭaṃ kho ayyaputta āgaccheyyāsī ti vatvā gīvaṃ pasāretvā olokesi. so ’pi bhagavantaṃ pattaṃ gaṇhathā ti vattuṃ avisahamāno vihāraṃ yeva agamāsi. taṃ anicchamānaṃ yeva bhagavā pabbājesi. iti bhagavā kapilapuraṃ gantvā tatiyadivase nandaṃ pabbājesi.

up the robe, from that moment she herself only wore yellow robes. When she heard you were surviving on only one meal a day, she too had only one meal a day. And when she heard you had given up using comfortable beds, she also slept only on a bed of planks. When she heard that you had given up wearing garlands and perfumes, she stopped taking delight in garlands and scents too. Even when her relatives sent her messages that they would look after her, she did not consider any of their offers. Truly, with all these excellences, Bhagavan, she is my daughter."

—"Great king, it is not so strange that the princess should protect herself, when her wisdom is ripe and she has you as a guardian. Even when she wandered in the mountains, without a protector, with wisdom that was not yet ripe, she protected herself." And he told "The Moon Kinnara Jataka" and, rising from his seat, he made his departure.[16]

On the second day, when the ceremonies of initiation, 138
housewarming, and marriage for Prince Nanda were taking place, the Bhagavan went to the young man's house. But he wished him to take the going forth, so, giving blessings to him, he asked him to carry his bowl for him, and left. A beautiful girl of the country saw the prince leaving and said, "Dear husband, come back soon." She stretched out her neck and gazed at him. Nanda was too timid to ask the Bhagavan to take his own bowl, and the Bhagavan received him, even though he was unwilling, into the Sangha.

On the third day, the Bhagavan ordained Nanda.

139 sattame divase rāhulamātā kumāraṃ alaṃkaritvā bhagavato santikaṃ pesesi: passa tāta etaṃ vīsatisahassasamaṇaparivutaṃ suvaṇṇavaṇṇaṃ brahmarūpivaṇṇaṃ samaṇaṃ ayaṃ te pitā etassa mahantā nidhiyo ahesuṃ ty-āssa nikkhamanato paṭṭhāya na passāma gaccha naṃ dāyajjaṃ yāca: ahaṃ tāta kumāro abhisekaṃ patvā cakkavattī bhavissāmi dhanena me attho dhanam me dehi sāmiko hi putto pitu santakassā ti. kumāro ca bhagavato santikaṃ gantvā pitu sinehaṃ paṭilabhitvā haṭṭhatuṭṭho sukhā te samaṇa chāyā ti vatvā aññam pi bahuṃ attano anurūpaṃ vadanto aṭṭhāsi. bhagavā katabhattakicco anumodanaṃ katvā uṭṭhāy' āsanā pakkāmi. kumāro pi dāyajjaṃ me samaṇa dehi sāyajjaṃ me samaṇa dehī ti bhagavantaṃ anubandhi. bhagavā kumāraṃ na nivattāpesi. parijano pi bhagavatā saddhiṃ gacchanto nivattetuṃ n' āsakkhi. iti so bhagavatā saddhiṃ ārāmam eva agamāsi.

140 tato bhagavā cintesi: yaṃ ayaṃ pitu santakaṃ dhanaṃ icchati taṃ vaṭṭānugataṃ savighātaṃ hand' assa bodhimaṇḍe paṭiladdhaṃ sattavidhaṃ ariyadhanaṃ demi lokuttaradāyajjassa naṃ sāmikaṃ karomī ti āyasmantaṃ sāriputtaṃ āmantesi tena hi tvaṃ sāriputta rāhulakumāraṃ pabbājehī ti.pabbajite pana kumāre rañño adhimattadukkhaṃ upajji. taṃ adhivāsetuṃ asakkonto bhagavato nivedetvā sādhu bhante ayyā mātāpitūhi ananuññātaṃ puttaṃ na pabbājeyyun ti varaṃ yāci. bhagavā tassa taṃ varaṃ datvā punadivase rājanivesane katapātarāso ekamantaṃ nisinnena raññā bhante tumhākaṃ dukkaracārikakāle ekā devatā maṃ

On the seventh day, Rahulamata dressed up her son and 139
sent him to the Bhagavan. "See that man surrounded by
twenty thousand monks, and with such a golden skin, and
an appearance like a Brahma god: that is your father! He had
great wealth and treasure, which we have not seen since he
renounced. Go now, and ask for your inheritance, saying, I
am your son, father. I would like the anointment of a univer-
sal monarch. I need wealth, so please give wealth to me.
The son is the heir to the father." The prince went up to the
Bhagavan and felt great affection for his father. Delighted,
he said, "Sir, happy is your shadow!" And he made many
statements that were fitting for the time. The Bhagavan had
finished his meal, gave a blessing, and got up from his seat.
The son followed the Bhagavan, saying, "Please give me my
inheritance, give me my inheritance, sir." The Bhagavan did
not turn the prince away so the attendants could not turn the
prince back. The Bhagavan entered the monastery with him.
Then the Bhagavan thought, "The treasure he would like 140
from his father leads to rebirth and is connected to suffer-
ing. But I can give him the sevenfold noble treasure, which
I found under the Bodhi Tree, and make him the heir to a
transcendent inheritance."[17]

He addressed the Venerable Sariputta: "Sariputta, ordain Prince Rahula in the going forth." And as the prince took the going forth, a great grief arose in the king.[18] Unable to bear it any longer, he pleaded for a favor: "Dear sir, it would be good if they do not ordain children without the consent of the father and the mother." The Bhagavan granted him his wish. On the following day, when he had eaten his morning meal at the king's palace, the king sat to one side and spoke to him.

upasaṃkamitvā putto te kālakato ti āha tassā vacanaṃ asaddahanto na mayhaṃ putto bodhiṃ appatvā kālaṃ karotī ti taṃ paṭikkhipin ti vutto idāni kiṃ saddahissatha ye tumhe pubbe pi aṭṭhikāni dassetvā putto te mato ti vutte na saddahitthā ti imissā aṭṭhuppattiyā mahādhammapālajātakaṃ kathesi. kathāpariyosāne rājā anāgāmiphale patiṭṭhahi.

141 iti bhagavā pitaraṃ tīsu phalesu patiṭṭhāpetvā bhikkhusaṅghaparivuto puna-d-eva rājagahaṃ gantvā sītavane vihāsi. tasmiṃ samaye anāthapiṇḍiko gahapati pañcahi sakaṭasatehi bhaṇḍaṃ ādāya rājāgahe piyasahāyassa seṭṭhino gehaṃ gantvā tattha buddhassa bhagavato uppannabhāvaṃ sutvā balavapaccūsasamaye devatānubhāvena vivaṭena dvārena satthāraṃ upasaṃkamitvā dhammaṃ sutvā sotāpattiphale patiṭṭhāya dutiyadivase buddhapamukhassa saṅghassa mahādānaṃ datvā sāvatthiṃ āgamanatthāya satthu paṭiññaṃ gahetvā antarāmagge pañcacattārīsayojanaṭṭhāne satasahassaṃ satasahassaṃ dāpetvā yojanikāya yojanikāya vihāre kāretvā jetavanaṃ koṭisanthārena aṭṭhārasahiraññakoṭīhi kiṇitvā navakammaṃ paṭṭhapesi. so majjhe dasabalassa gandhakuṭiṃ kāresi. taṃ parivāretvā asītimahātherānaṃ pāṭiyekkasannivesane āvāse ekakuḍḍakadvikuḍḍakahaṃsavaṭṭakadīghasālamaṇḍapādivasena sesasenāsanāni pokkharaṇiyo ca caṅkamanarattiṭṭhā-

"Sir, while you were practicing the austerities a god visited me, and told me, 'Your son is dead.' I did not believe what he said, and answered: 'My son will not die until he has attained awakening.'" The Buddha replied, "What should you believe now? In times past, you were even shown bones and told your son had died, and still you did not believe them." And he told the "Great Guardian of the Dhamma Jataka." And at the conclusion of the story, the king attained the stage of never-return, and its fruits.

The Bhagavan had established his father in the three fruits. 141
He returned to Rajagaha and stayed at the Cool Grove. At that time, the householder Anathapindika paid a visit to his friend, a leading businessman from Rajagaha, and took with him five hundred wagonloads of goods. He heard of the arising of a Bhagavan, and very early in the morning he approached the Teacher, going through the gate that was opened by the great power of the gods. He heard the Dhamma and attained stream entry and its fruits. On the following day, he gave a great feast to the order of monks, with the Buddha at its head. He elicited a promise from the Teacher that he would visit Savatthi. He then had monasteries built all along the route of forty-five *yojanas* that led there and spent a hundred thousand on each one. He then bought Jeta Grove for eighteen thousand crore of gold, by laying them one against the other to carpet the whole surface of the park, and organized new building work there. In the center, he had built the perfumed apartment of the Buddha, and around it, in the beautiful site, he had a wonderful monastery built, at a cost of another eighteen thousand crore of gold. It had separate apartments for the eighty great elders, other

nadivāṭṭhānāni cā ti aṭṭhārasakoṭipariccāgena ramaṇīye bhūmibhāge manoramaṃ vihāraṃ kārāpetvā dasabalassa āgamanatthāya dūtaṃ pesesi. satthā dūtassa sāsanaṃ sutvā mahābhikkhusaṅghaparivāro rājagahā nikkhamitvā anupubbena sāvatthinagaraṃ pāpuṇi.

142 mahāsetthī pi kho vihāramahaṃ sajjetvā tathāgatassa jetavanaṃ pavisanadivase puttaṃ sabbālaṃkārapatimaṇḍitaṃ katvā alaṃkatapaṭiyatteh' eva pañcahi kumārasatehi saddhiṃ pesesi. so saparivāro pañcavaṇṇavatthasamujjalāni pañcadhajasatāni gahetvā dasabalassa purato ahosi. tesaṃ pacchato mahāsubhaddā-cūlasubhaddā ti dve seṭṭhidhītaro pañcahi kumārisatehi saddhiṃ puṇṇaghaṭe gahetvā nikkhamiṃsu. tesaṃ pacchato seṭṭhibhariyā sabbālaṃkārapatimanditā pañcahi mātugāmasatehi saddhiṃ puṇṇapātiyo gahetvā nikkhami. sabbesaṃ pacchato sayaṃ mahāseṭṭhi ahatavatthanivattho ahatavattheh' eva pañcahi seṭṭhisatehi saddhiṃ bhagavantaṃ abbhuggañchi. bhagavā imaṃ upāsakaparisaṃ purato katvā mahābhikkhusaṅghaparivuto attano sarīrappabhāya suvaṇṇarasasekapiñjarāni viya vanantarāni kurumāno anantāya buddhalīḷhāya appaṭisamāya buddhasiriyā jetavanavihāraṃ pāvisi. atha naṃ anāthapiṇḍiko pucchi:

guest houses of single-walled and double-walled buildings, long halls decorated with geese and quails, pavilions, lotus ponds, walking areas, and places for meditation in the day and the night. Then he sent a message inviting the one with ten powers to visit. When the Teacher heard the invitation from the messenger, the Teacher set off from Rajagaha with a large retinue of monks, and in gradual stages reached the city of Savatthi.

Then the great businessman arranged a ceremony to 142
bless the great monastery. On the day of the arrival of the Tathagata he sent his son, dressed in finery, his festival clothes, along with five hundred boys, all dressed in festival clothes. He went ahead with the one with ten powers, and took his entourage, carrying five hundred banners of shiny cloth of five different colors. Mahasubhadda and Culasubhadda, the merchant's two daughters, followed behind them. They were accompanied by five hundred girls carrying water jars, filled to brimming. And behind them walked the merchant's wife, dressed in the finest clothes, attended by a hundred women carrying bowls filled to the brim. Behind them all the great merchant himself came, dressed in new clothes, along with five hundred businessmen and traders, also dressed in new clothes, and met the Bhagavan.

The Bhagavan saw this assembly of lay disciples in front of them, and entered the monastery with his great retinue of monks with the unsurpassable grace of a Buddha. It was as if the radiance of his body turned the forest groves into clusters of feathers, scattered with essence of gold. And then Anathapindika asked, "Sir, what course of action should I follow for this monastery?"

kath' āham bhante imasmiṃ vihāre paṭipajjāmī ti. tena hi gahapati imaṃ vihāraṃ āgatānāgatassa bhikkhusaṅghassa dehī ti. sādhu bhante ti mahāseṭṭhi suvaṇṇabhiṃkāraṃ ādāya dasabalassa hatthe udakaṃ pātetvā imaṃ jetavana-vihāram āgatānāgatassa cātuddisassa buddhapamukhassa saṅghassa dammī ti adāsi. sātthā vihāraṃ paṭiggahetvā anumodanaṃ karonto

294 sītaṃ uṇhaṃ paṭihanti
tato vāḷamigāni ca
siriṃsape ca makase ca
sisire cā 'pi vuṭṭhiyo.
295 tato vātātape ghore
sañjāte paṭihaññati.
leṇattañ ca sukhatthañ ca
jhāyituñ ca vipassituṃ
vihāradānaṃ saṅghassa
aggaṃ buddhena vaṇṇitaṃ.
296 tasmā hi paṇḍito poso
sampassaṃ attham attano
vihāre kāraye ramme
vāsay' ettha bahussute.
297 tesaṃ annañ ca pānañ ca
vatthasenāsanāni ca
dadeyya ujubhūtesu
vippasannena cetasā.
298 te tassa dhammaṃ desenti
sabbadukkhāpanūdanaṃ
yaṃ yo dhammaṃ idh' aññāya
parinibbāti anāsavo ti

—"Householder, you just have to donate it to the Sangha of monks, whether those here, or those that come in the future."

—"Very good, sir." And the great merchant took up a golden jar and poured water on the hands of the one with ten powers, in dedication. "I give this monastery at Jeta Grove to the order of monks from the four directions, with the Buddha at their head."

The Teacher accepted the monastery and gave a blessing.

"They keep away cold and heat, Wild beasts and 294
serpents, insects, and winter rain.

When high wind and fearsome heat persist it keeps 295
them away. It is a place of refuge and a happy place,
to practice both calm and insight. The gift of a
monastery to the Sangha of the Buddha is praised as
the highest.

Because of this, let a wise man, who considers his 296
own well-being, build delightful monasteries, and
let monks, who are well-versed in the teaching, stay
there.

With a mind cleared through faith, let him give to 297
those who are upright among them: food and drink,
clothes, and a place to rest.

They teach him then the Dhamma that gives freedom 298
from all unhappiness. Realizing the truth, here
and now, he is freed from the pollutants and finds
complete peace."

143 vihārānisaṃsaṃ kathesi. anāthapiṇḍiko dutiyadivasato paṭṭhāya vihāramahaṃ ārabhi. visākhāya pāsādamaho catuhi māsehi niṭṭhito. anāthapiṇḍikassa pana vihāramaho navahi māsehi niṭṭhāsi. vihāramahe pi aṭṭhāras' eva koṭiyo agamaṃsu iti imasmiṃ yeva vihāre catupaṇṇāsakoṭisaṃkhaṃ dhanaṃ pariccaji.

144 atīte pana vipassissa bhagavato kāle punabbasumitto nāma seṭṭhi suvaṇṇiṭṭhakasanthārena kiṇitvā tasmiṃ yeva ṭhāne yojanappamāṇaṃ saṅghārāmaṃ kāresi. sikhissa bhagavato kāle sirivaḍḍho nāma seṭṭhi suvaṇṇaphālasanthārena kiṇitvā tasmiṃ yeva ṭhāne tigāvutappamāṇaṃ saṅghārāmaṃ kāresi. vessabhussa bhagavato kāle sotthiyo nāma seṭṭhi suvaṇṇahatthipadasanthārena kiṇitvā tasmiṃ yeva ṭhāne aḍḍhayojanappamāṇaṃ saṅghārāmaṃ kāresi. kakusandhassa bhagavato kāle accuto nāma seṭṭhi suvaṇṇiṭṭhakasanthāren' eva kiṇitvā tasmiṃ yeva ṭhāne gāvutappamāṇaṃ saṅghārāmaṃ kāresi. koṇāgamanassa bhagavato kāle uggo nāma seṭṭhi suvaṇṇakacchapasanthārena kiṇitvā tasmiṃ yeva ṭhāne aḍḍhagāvutappamāṇaṃ saṅghārāmaṃ kāresi. kassapassa bhagavato kāle sumaṅgalo nāma seṭṭhi suvaṇṇiṭṭhakasanthārena kiṇitvā tasmiṃ yeva ṭhāne soḷasakarīsappamāṇaṃ saṅghārāmaṃ kāresi. amhākaṃ bhagavato kāle anāthapiṇḍiko seṭṭhi kahāpaṇakoṭisanthārena kiṇitvā tasmiṃ yeva ṭhāne aṭṭhakarīsappamāṇaṃ saṅghārāmaṃ kāresi. idaṃ kira ṭhānaṃ sabbabuddhānaṃ avijahitaṭṭhānam eva.

He sang the praises of the monastery. And on the following day, Anathapindika started a festival of dedication for the monastery. The festival for the dedication of Visakha's palace took four months. But the dedication of Anathapindika's monastery took nine to finish. And for this ceremony, the expenses came to eighteen crore. So just for this monastery, he spent fifty-four crore. 143

Now long ago, in the time of the Buddha Vipassi, the merchant Punabbasumitta had bought this land by making a carpet of golden pieces all over it. In the time of the Bhagavan Sikhi, a merchant called Sirivaddho bought this place with a spread of golden plough blades and established there a monastery, three *gāvutas* in length. He had built in the very same spot a monastery extending over a *yojana*. In the time of the Bhagavan Vessabhu, a merchant called Sotthiya had bought this piece of land by placing over it elephant feet made of gold and built in just the same spot a monastery extending half a *yojana*. In the time of the Bhagavan Kakusandha, a merchant called Accuta bought this land by placing gold bars over it and built a monastery in the same spot that extended for a *gāvuta*. In the time of the Bhagavan Konagamana, a merchant called Ugga bought this land by placing golden turtles all over it and built a monastery extending sixteen *karīsas*.[19] And in the time of our Bhagavan, Anathapindika bought this land by laying out a crore of small golden coins and built on the very same spot a monastery extending eight *karīsas*. So, they say this spot has never been neglected by any of the Buddhas. 144

145 iti mahābodhimaṇḍe sabbaññūtappattito yāva mahāparinibbānamañcā yasmiṃ ṭhāne bhagavā vihāsi idaṃ santikenidānaṃ nāma tassa vasena sabbajātakāni vaṇṇayissāma.

146 nidānakathā niṭṭhitā.

In this way, the time from the attainment of awakening in the circle of the Bodhi Tree up to his final entry into nibbana is included in "The Recent Origin." And now, through this power, we'll go on to tell all the birth stories ... 145

The story of the origins has finished. 146

ABBREVIATIONS

Texts in Pali are in the Pali Text Society editions

AN	*Aṅguttaranikāya*
BV	*Buddhavaṃsa*
CB	*The Chronicle of the Buddhas* (Horner 1975), cited by verse number and section (e.g., *CB* 1.13)
Cp	*Cariyāpiṭaka*
Dhp	*Dhammapada*
DN	*Dīghanikāya*, individual *suttas* cited by number with *D* (e.g., *D* 16)
J	Jataka, individual stories from The Jātaka (Fausbøll 1877–1896) cited by number (e.g., *J* 547)
MN	*Majjhimanikāya*, individual suttas cited by number with *M* (e.g., *M* 36)
PTS	Pali Text Society
Sn	*Suttanipāta*
SN	*Saṃyuttanikāya*
Th	*Theragāthā*
Thī	*Therīgāthā*
Vin	*Vinaya*

NOTES TO THE TEXT

The Far Origin

1 *namassanādino* Ck] *namassanādito* PTS (see *DP* 2.509–10).
2 *anapekkho* Vipassana Research Institute] *anapekho* PTS.
3 *catūhi satasahassehi BV*] *cattārisatasahassehi* PTS.
4 *manussatthabhāvasmiṃ ... katvā nipajji*: This section is largely commentarial and has not been translated.
5 *assattharukkhamūlamhi BV*] *assatthassa mule* PTS.
6 *yāni* conject. PTS] *yaṃ* PTS. *yā BV.*
7 *dasahassina BV*] *dasahassīna* Ck.
8 *kismiṃ ci BV,* Cv] *kismici* PTS.
9 *paripūraya BV,* Ck, Cs] *paripūriya* Cv.
10 *ubhatokoṭisu*] *ubhato koṭisu* Ck, Cs, Cv.
11 *abhivandisum BV*] *abhivandiyuṃ* Ck, Cs, Cv.
12 *kassaci varasahapattiyo BV*] *kassacī varasamāpattiyo* Ck, Cs, Cv.
13 *mukhaṃvivaṭamatte* (see Fausbøll 1877–1896: 1.279)] *mukhaṃ vivaṭamatte* PTS.
14 *tejasiṃ BV*] *tejasī* PTS] *tejasi* Cs.
15 *bhikkhāyupagataṃ BV*] *bhikkhāya upagataṃ* PTS.
16 *sūlehi vijjhayante pi koṭṭiyante pi satthihi Cp*] *sūlehi pi vijjhayanto koṭṭayante pi sattihi* PTS.
17 *mātāpitā na me dessā na pi me dessaṃ mahāyasaṃ* PTS] *mātāpitā na me dessā atthānaṃ me na desiyo Cp*].

The Near Origin

1 *muñcitvā* Ck, Cs] *muccitvā* PTS.
2 *kayaṃ* Ck] *kāmaṃ* PTS.
3 *suññā ti* Ck, Cs, Cv] Fausbøll's suggests *suññāni.*
4 *ajjhottaramānā* Cs, Cv] *ajjhottharamānāṃ* PTS.
5 *pūjiyamāno*] *pūjayamāne* Ck, Cs, Cv.

The Recent Origin

1 *dukkhi* Ck] *dukkhī* PTS.
2 *phuṭaṃ* conject.] *puṭam* PTS.
3 *rūpakāyasirī* conject.] *rūpakāyasiriṃ* Ck, Cs, Cv.
4 *phuṭe* with Cv] *puṭe* PTS.

NOTES TO THE TRANSLATION

The Far Origin

1 This is the traditional verse homage and background (*maṅgala*) that often prefaces a large work. In Pali, the eleven verses form one long sentence, which has been broken down into six sentences in English.

2 The *Apaṇṇaka jātaka* (The True Story Jataka) the first story in the collection (*J* 1).

3 *Mahiṃsāsaka* is the theory of one of the early Buddhist schools, whose teachers developed their own theories on time and Buddhist philosophy.

4 The Great Monastery (Mahavihara) in Anuradhapura, in what is now Sri Lanka, was the home of the "elders," who felt they were maintaining the oldest traditions of the word of the Buddha. Monastics from there are regarded as the authors of the commentaries.

5 "Vessantara" is a reference to the most famous Jataka, "The Vessantara Jataka" (*J* 547), treated as the final human life of the Bodhisatta. It is the last in the Pali Jataka collection. After this rebirth he waits in the Tusita heaven for his final rebirth, in which, as a human being again, he will become a Buddha: this is described in the second section of this work.

6 *Buddhavaṃsa* (The Lineage of the Buddhas) is quoted throughout the early part of the text. The verses may be found, with different translations, in *Chronicle of the Buddhas* (Horner 1975).

7 The ten sounds include the six that follow in the text as well as the sounds of a different kind of drum, lutes, cymbals, and songs.

8 Most of the verses that follow may be found in *Chronicle of the Buddhas (Buddhavaṃsa)* in Horner 1975, translated by her. The order is largely but not exclusively sequential.

9 The seven treasures are those of a universal monarch (*cakkavattin*): the wheel, the elephant, the horse, the jewel, the woman, the treasurer, and the adviser. All are endowed with great excellence, and some have miraculous powers. Reference to them indicates we are in an ideal city whose king conquers by justice, not force. See *cakkavattin* in the Glossary.

10 Knowledge of the three Vedas is part of the training of a Brahman priest. The three Vedas are the *Ṛg Veda, Yajur Veda,* and *Sama Veda,* sacred texts of the Brahmans. The marks refer to a system of divination wherein each mark (*lakkhaṇa*) on the body denotes some aspect of one's fortune. Later in this text the Bodhisatta is reborn with thirty-two such auspicious marks.

11 "Taking rebirth in a new bodily form" refers to the *paṭisandhi-citta,* the consciousness that takes rebirth in a new conception.

12 "The cool" is nibbana (*nibbāna*), Pali for "nirvana." See nibbana in the Glossary.

13 This is a characteristic Jataka style: the verse shows the comment of the Buddha "in the present" on actions that took place in earlier lives.

14 Becoming (*bhava*) and nonbecoming (*vibhava*) refer to continued existence or the lack of it, respectively. The wish for either becoming or nonbecoming is said to be eradicated at arhatship.

15 The threefold fire of the Brahmanic sacrifice became greed, hatred, and delusion for Buddhists: the Buddha liked to adapt traditional Brahmanic imagery and create new meanings for their terms.

16 Defilements are *kilesa,* the last vestiges of greed, hatred, and delusion, which are eradicated finally at awakening, or arhatship. See *kilesa* in the Glossary.

17 Pollutants (*āsavas*) are the inflows that bring about a distortion of view, a craving for existence, or a wish not to exist. See *āsava* in the Glossary.

18 The five faults here are those likely in wild terrain, such as ground that is too hard or soft, trees growing in the middle of the way, and weeds.

19 The phrase "with the mind concentrated in this way" is used throughout the canon to describe the way the mind, purified by the four *jhānas* (deep meditations), becomes malleable and can apply itself to different powers. See *jhāna* in the Glossary. "The Discourse on the Fruits of Recluseship" (*D* 2; *DN* I.77). Eight such powers are listed; they include supernatural abilities such as hearing and seeing the gods, being able to master matter, recollecting past lives, and knowing the minds of others. The highest is seeing the origin of the pollutants in the mind. Presumably this last is not seen fully here, or else the practitioner would be enlightened.

20 The ascetic clothes he discards would need cleaning and perhaps

mending or replacement by donors. The bark garment, however, has twelve advantages, such as the fact that one can easily discard and renew it oneself; it is light and easy to wash and mend.

21 The eight faults of the leaf hut mostly involve its need for maintenance and its susceptibility to being overrun with insects and lice. The tree's ten advantages include the absence of the need for cleaning, sweeping, or upkeep, and the fact that one can easily move on.

22 The eight attainments, or *samāpattis,* are the four *jhānas* and the four formless meditations. See *samāpatti* in the Glossary. The five higher knowledges, or meditative powers (*abhiññās*), are products of *jhāna* practice. They are elements three through seven of the powers described in the *Sāmaññaphala sutta.* Attainment of the sixth higher knowledge, the destruction of the pollutants, the last described in the *Sāmaññaphala sutta,* would imply arhatship. This text sometimes says that Sumedha has attained six, though as he is not enlightened he cannot have developed the last one fully. See also *abhiññā* in the Glossary.

23 A long commentary follows, omitted here, explaining the various numbers of advantages and disadvantages connected with different aspects of ascetic practice (Fausbøll 1877–1896 I.7–10).

24 "His first setting in motion the wheel of the Dhamma" refers to the Buddha's first discourse, "The Discourse on Setting in Motion the Wheel of the Dhamma," *Dhammacakkappavattana-sutta, SN* V.420–423.

25 Thirty-two miracles appear together only at these events. They are all described when the Bodhisatta takes his vow (*The Buddha's Path* [11]).

26 The thirty-two bodily marks on a "great man" indicate one whose destiny is to become a universal monarch or a Buddha. Later in this work the marks are discerned on the baby Gotama. There are usually thought to be eighty-nine or, as in this text, eighty "minor" marks of the great man. These include features like extended ear lobes.

27 The *parichatta* is a coral tree in the Heaven of the Thirty-Three Gods (Tāvatiṃsa).

28 Modern taxonomy is not always easy to align with ancient species, but these flowers appear to correspond to the Pali terms. For a good general study of flora and fauna in Pali texts, see Dhammika 2015.

29 The three types of becoming: in the sense sphere, the *rūpa* (the meditation sphere where there is still some sense of body and a visual image), and the *arūpa* (formless meditation sphere). See *rūpa* and *arūpa* in the Glossary.

30 The commentaries also see eight factors as being necessary for Buddhahood: being human; being male; having a root cause and supporting conditions; seeing a living Buddha (in earlier lifetimes); becoming a monk; achieving the noble qualities of the higher knowledges (*abhiññās*); needing to investigate the ten perfections required for Buddhahood; and having extreme dedication (*adhikāra*) and a wholesome desire (*chandatā*) for Buddhahood. See Bodhi 1978: 251–254.

31 Upatissa is the family name for Sariputta, the historical Buddha's chief disciple, who sits on his right. Kolita is the family name for Mahamoggallana, the other chief disciple, who sits on his left.

32 This is the first time the hero of this work is called the Bodhisatta. The term is also used for other aspirants to Buddhahood. The hero keeps this name until his awakening, when he becomes a Buddha. See Bodhisatta under "Epithets for a Buddha" in the Glossary.

33 A mythical creature, part man and part snake. See naga in the Glossary.

34 All the following signs in verses 93–116 are described in the "present," but they are used in a general and historical sense too, as phenomena that occurred before, for all Buddhas.

35 Visakha (Visākhā) is the full moon of May, a time, it is held, when all Buddhas make their aspiration.

36 Formless gods have practiced one of the four formless *arūpa* meditations in earlier lives and are reborn without a physical form.

37 The four levels are: control in monastic rules, control in the senses, purity of livelihood, and reliance only on the basic requisites of a monk.

38 Each of the ten perfections has three manifestations: basic, intermediate, and most excellent. So, basic giving (*dāna*) is the giving of one's possessions, intermediate is the offering of one's own limbs, and the most excellent is the relinquishing of one's own life (Bodhi 1978: 299–301).

39 Mount Meru is the central mountain of the world; the Cakkavala Mountains encircle the ocean around Mount Meru.

40 One *yojana* is the distance one could travel with a yoke of oxen; about seven to nine miles. See *yojana* in the Glossary.

41 The five precepts are to undertake to abstain from taking life, taking what is not given, sexual misconduct, lying, and becoming intoxicated. These form the underpinnings of the lay ethical code. The ten precepts are slightly changed and are followed by laypeople during full-moon days at a temple. They include undertaking not to have sexual intercourse at all for that period, as well as not wearing jewelry and not eating after noon.

42 The four "fruits" (*phalas*) of freedom are the results of achieving each of the stages of awakening: stream entry, in which doubt and some defilements are stopped; once-return, in which the meditator will experience only one more rebirth; never-return, which denotes a final lifetime; and finally, arhatship, in which all attachments and defilements are eradicated. See *phala* in the Glossary.

43 The four analytic insights (*paṭisambhidās*): insight into meaning, the Dhamma, the language used for both, and the details and workings of all three in practice. See *paṭisambhidā* in Glossary.

44 The three knowledges are divine vision, the recollection of one's past lives, and eradication of the pollutants—that is, awakening. See *tevijjā* in the Glossary.

45 Cubits (*hatthas*): one *hattha* is similar to a cubit; about a forearm's length, or eighteen inches. See *hattha* in the Glossary.

46 For "universal monarch," see *cakkavattin* in the Glossary.

47 The "three baskets" of the teaching are the *Vinaya* (the monastic code), *Sutta* (the discourses about the Buddha and his followers), and *Abhidhamma* (the philosophical and psychological system of the "higher" teaching, or Dhamma).

48 In "The Vessantara Jataka" (*J* 547) the Bodhisatta does give away his children and is desperate to do so, but he feels bitterly grief-stricken. The point here is that this Buddha felt no such grief when he was asked for his children in the comparable rebirth in his past lives. This is typical of the hyperbole that sometimes characterizes Buddhist texts from this period.

49 This verse is also found, for instance, in *J* 447 and *J* 510, and in "The Songs of the Elders," spoken by Dhammika (*Thī* 303).

50 Sakka (Indra) is the king of the Heaven of the Thirty-Three Gods. Beings there have physical bodies, but of a beautiful and refined kind. They listen to heavenly music, taste divine food, and discuss

the Dhamma as the result of generosity, investigation, virtue, and faith in their earlier lives. Their life spans are very long. When any being in the worlds below is about to perform some great act of generosity, their king feels his throne becoming hot. He often goes to aid the being involved through a divine intervention.

51 The five kinds of joy are widely known from Buddhist practice, as they arise on the route to the first *jhāna.* They intensify, progressing from a mild raising of hairs on the body in the first, to a drenching in the fifth, whereby the body feels like a mountain stream.

52 A single *amuṇa* equals about four bushels; *kahāpanas* are small coins. See also *Sivi jātaka* (*J* 499).

53 To "take refuge" is to make one's personal refuge the triple gem of the Buddha, the Dhamma, and the Sangha. This is undertaken daily by many Buddhists.

54 The spirits (*yakkhas*) are benign here. For *yakkha,* see the Glossary.

55 The *jhāna* of cessation is the attainment of cessation (*nirodhasamāpatti*), a state beyond the formless-sphere meditations, experienced only by arhats.

56 A chant to all these Buddhas is popular throughout Southeast Asia.

57 The nonpercipient (*asaññī*) realm, where beings have no consciousness at all, is where those who have practiced formless meditation and misunderstood it in some way are reborn, for very long time spans indeed. The Pure Abodes are where beings who will attain enlightenment from this refined heaven, not as humans. A Bodhisatta is never born in either of these: the first realm wastes time and the second prevents the last human rebirth necessary for Buddhahood.

58 Most of these are the eponymous heroes of Jatakas in which the Bodhisatta shows generosity: *Akitti jātaka* (*J* 480), *Saṅkha jātaka* (*J* 442), *Mahāsudassana jātaka* (*J* 95), *Nimi jātaka* (*J* 541), *Visayha jātaka* (*J* 340), *Sivi jātaka* (*J* 499), and *Vessantara jātaka* (*J* 547). Govinda does not feature in a Jataka but appears in the *Mahāgovinda sutta* (*D* 19) as a past rebirth of the Buddha. The prince Canda cited here is possibly the Bodhisatta's rebirth as Canda in the *Khaṇḍahāla jātaka* (*J* 543), although in that story he does not particularly demonstrate generosity; rather, he shows fairness.

59 In the *Sāsa jātaka* (*J* 316), the Bodhisatta is a generous hare who offers himself as food to the god Sakka, thinking he is a wandering

Brahman. Sakka saves him, and daubs the hare's image on the full moon so all will remember his selfless giving.

60 The text conflates two meanings of the word "naga." Some of these characters are underwater creatures and some are elephants, for whom naga is also sometimes used. In *Campeyya jātaka* (*J* 506), *Bhūridatta jātaka* (*J* 543), and *Saṅkhapāla jātaka* (*J* 524) he is an underwater naga who is held prisoner but does not use his innate supernatural powers to retaliate. In the *Chaddanta jātaka* (*J* 514) he is a virtuous elephant. The *Mahāsīlava jātaka* (*J* 51) describes the Bodhisatta as a virtuous and just king, Silava, but it is possible the *Sīlavanāga jātaka* (*J* 72) is referred to here, in which he is a good elephant. He is Prince Alinasattu in the *Jayaddisa jātaka* (*J* 513).

61 See *Somanassa jātaka* (*J* 505), *Hatthipāla jātaka* (*J* 509), and *Ayoghara jātaka* (*J* 510). In *Cūlasutasoma jātaka* (*J* 525) the Bodhisatta is a king who renounces.

62 In "The Barley-Meal Sack Jataka," *Sattubhasta jātaka* (*J* 402), the Bodhisatta is born as the wise man Senaka, who, like a modern detective, sees from clues such as the outline of a snake in a Brahman's bag evidence that the Brahman has an unfaithful wife. He is also a wise man in *Vidhurapaṇḍita jātaka* (*J* 545), *Kuddāla jātaka* (*J* 70), and *Araka jātaka* (*J* 169). Govinda, a royal adviser, is mentioned in the last note (*D* 19). The rebirth as the ascetic Bodhi probably refers to the *Cullabodhi jātaka* (*J* 443).

63 In "The Great Janaka Jataka," *Mahājanaka jātaka* (*J* 539), the Bodhisatta swims in the ocean for seven days after a shipwreck and is rescued by the goddess of the sea.

64 In "The Teacher of Forbearance Jataka," *Khantivāda jātaka* (*J* 313), the Bodhisatta is an ascetic who teaches forbearance. He is violently attacked by a king and demonstrates this teaching.

65 *Mahāsutasoma jātaka* (*J* 537), in which the Bodhisatta refuses to break his word to a cannibal king and saves a hundred others.

66 The *Mūgapakkha* or *Temiya jātaka* (*J* 538): the Bodhisatta resolves to feign deafness and dumbness to avoid the terrible karmic consequences of being a king and having to execute many others.

67 This is a puzzling attribution. In "The Single King Jataka," *Ekarāja jātaka* (*J* 303), the Bodhisatta is certainly a just king who renounces, but there is no emphasis on loving-kindness itself.

68 *Lomahaṃsa jātaka* (*J* 94): the Bodhisatta is an ascetic who practices self-mortifications and realizes they do not work; then he lets go

and attains peace. There is no mention of children teasing, but perhaps that element of the story is now lost.

69 *Cariyapiṭaka* (The Basket of Conduct) gives a brief account of some of the past lives involved in developing the perfections (see Horner 1975).

The Near Origin

1 These are the sense-sphere heavens, in ascending order: those of the Four Kings, the Thirty-Three Gods, the Yama gods, and the Tusita gods, followed by those of the gods who delight in creation (*Nimmānaratī*) and gods who have power over the creations of others (*Paranimittavasavattī*). The last is the highest sense-sphere heaven before the Brahma meditative heavens.

2 This geography is explained in *Vin* I.197.

3 A *paccekabuddha* is one who finds full awakening for himself but does not teach a full path. In some Jatakas they do teach others, including the Bodhisatta: see, for instance, *Darimukha jātaka* (*J* 378).

4 According to traditions, all potential Buddhas have a gestation of ten months; all lose their mother after seven days, as apparently all the mothers die of joy.

5 The Asalha festival is held on the full-moon day at the arrangement of the stars (*nakkhatta*) of the June/July full moon, when it is in the twenty-first and twenty-second lunar mansions. This is traditionally the start of the rainy season, when monks and nuns go into retreat. The festival celebrates when this Buddha gave his first discourse.

6 The *uposatha* day: there is one on the day of the full moon, one at the new moon, and one at each of the intermediate points between—so about one each week. The full-moon *uposatha* day is particularly important.

7 Powdered rice, white mustard, jasmine buds, thistle grass, and puffed grain are strewn in welcome. They are mentioned again when the seers who read the marks on the new baby are born (Fausbøll 1877–1896: I.55).

8 The other two stories are Jatakas in the collection that this work introduces: *Ummagga jātaka* (*J* 546) and *Vessantara jātaka* (*J* 547). The second section of this work thus takes place after all the rebirths described in those stories.

9 The four jars are the seventh feature of phenomena that "arise together" with the Bodhisatta.
10 *Nālaka sutta*, which details the sadness felt by the Buddha's uncle, called Asiti there, on realizing he would not hear the teaching of the new Buddha (*Sn* 679–723).
11 A *gāvuta* is a measurement of distance, equal to about two miles. See *gāvuta* in the Glossary.
12 *Mahāpadāna sutta, D* 14.
13 "The Long Discourses of the Buddha," *Dīghanikāya*.
14 Vissakamma is the architect and designer of the gods and is often sent on such errands by King Sakka.
15 The name Rāhula means a fetter or bond.
16 This is just after the year of his conception.
17 See *Sn* 405–442.
18 The story of the Bodhisatta's encounter with these teachers and his dissatisfaction with their teachings is given in "The Discourse on the Noble Search," *Ariyapariyesana sutta* (*M* 26), and "The Greater Discourse to Saccaka," *Mahāsaccaka sutta* (*M* 36).
19 This all seems odd unless you try it in your mind. He is in the east, and when he arrives in that spot after walking around the tree in a circle starting from the south, and stands facing the tree, he will be facing west—the direction he is said to be facing here. But when he has walked up to the tree, and then sits with his back to it, he is facing east.
20 Fourteen cubits would be about twelve feet.
21 The four attributes are the lack of moon on the fourteenth day of waning, thick forest, dark cloud, and midnight.
22 In this life dedicated to perfecting generosity, Vessantara distributes gifts, such as carriages, horses, and elephants, in groups of seven hundred.
23 The recollection of generosity (*cāgānussati*) as a way of cheering the mind is one of the calm (*samatha*) meditations of Pali Buddhism.
24 Although he has not yet attained awakening, this is the first time in the text that the Bodhisatta, or Great Being, or great person, is called the Buddha.
25 *Dhp* 153–154.

The Recent Origin

1 This is the miracle of making a pillar of fire and a pillar of water.

2 Presumably the other interpretation is that it is made with the seven types of jewels, as in "The Great King of Glory Discourse," *Mahāsudassana sutta* (*D* 17).
3 *Dhp* 179–180.
4 "The Discourse on Non-Self," *Anattalakkhaṇa sutta, SN* III.66–68.
5 One who has attained stream entry is called *sotāpanna*. For *sotāpanna* and the experience of stream entry, see the Glossary.
6 "The Fire-Sermon Discourse," *Ādittapariyāya sutta, SN* IV.19–20.
7 Thousand-spoked wheels arising on the soles of the feet are the second of the thirty-two marks that characterize the "great person" (*mahāpurisa*).
8 "The Great Narada Kassapa Jataka" (*Mahānārada Kassapa jātaka*), *J* 544.
9 This may refer to the tenfold path often cited in the *Aṅguttaranikāya*, which takes the eight path factors and adds two more: right knowledge (*sammāñāṇaṃ*) and right freedom (*sammāvimutti*); see *AN* V.244.
10 *Vin* I.40.
11 The composer of this text assumes that the Buddha has by now established the order of nuns, so there are four assemblies: monks, nuns, laymen, and laywomen.
12 See also *Th* vv. 527 and 529.
13 See *AN* I.25.
14 This verse is also at *Dhp* 168–169.
15 *Mahādhammapāla jātaka* (*J* 436).
16 In the "The Moon Kinnara Jataka" (*J* 485), Rahula's mother, Rahulamata, is reborn with her husband, in an earlier rebirth, as a *kinnara*, a mythical deer-like being, and saves him.
17 "Sevenfold noble treasure" refers to the seven factors of awakening, elsewhere compared to the seven treasures of the universal monarch (*SN* V.99).
18 The king at this point has attained only stream entry and once-return, and so still has an attachment to his kingdom and family.
19 A single *karīsa*, here, is the amount of land on which one *karīsa* (about a cubit) of seed can be planted; see *karīsa* in the Glossary.

GLOSSARY

abhiññā meditative powers that become available through calm and insight; there are usually six, the first five being such magical powers as flying, hearing faraway sounds, penetrating the thoughts of others, remembering past lives, and the divine eye, which sees beings passing away and being reborn; the sixth is the destruction of the defilements; the Bodhisatta often achieves the first five in his journey through many existences; he fully achieves the sixth at awakening

arahattā the state of becoming an arhat, a being who is "worthy," has eradicated the defilements, and has attained awakening; arhats achieve enlightenment by hearing the teaching of a Buddha

arūpa formless; the four formless meditations are the second four in the eight attainments

ASALHA the full moon of the eighth month, in the constellation known as Asalha

āsava a pollutant; specifically, an inflow that brings about a distortion of view, a craving for existence, or a wish not to exist

BRAHMA a god from the meditative heavens; gods are reborn in these realms on the basis of practicing *jhāna* and the divine abidings of loving-kindness, compassion, sympathetic joy, and equanimity

cakkavattin a universal monarch; a human ruler who presides over a harmonious kingdom where humans have vast life spans and idealized social conditions

deva a deity, usually from the sense-sphere heavens, who "shines"; such beings are reborn in their heavens on the basis of their faith, morality, generosity, and investigation

DHAMMA the teaching, the path, law; used to describe the teaching of the Buddha; the second refuge in what is known as the triple gem of Buddha, Dhamma, and Sangha; can also be translated variously as truth, law, justice

gāvuta a measure of length, probably around two miles

hattha a measurement based on a forearm's length; despite literally meaning "hand," a *hattha* is more like the ancient cubit, reckoned at around eighteen inches

jhāna one of four deeply alert *samatha* meditations; in these states of calm, the mind becomes "secluded" from the sense-sphere; the mind's hindrances—longing for the senses, ill will, sloth and torpor, restlessness and worry, and doubt—are temporarily overcome as the factors of adverting, exploring, joy, happiness, and equanimity arise for the first *jhāna;* adverting, exploring, joy, happiness are gradually dropped as equanimity deepens and mindfulness increases; the four *jhānas* are the first four of the eight attainments

kamma karma; an action, intention, or volition that produces effects in the future

karīsa a unit of measure equal to a cubit, or about eighteen inches; also the amount of land on which a dry seed can be sown

kilesa an ingrained defilement of the mind that colors and distorts the heart

koṭi a crore, or ten million; used to describe numbers of followers in assemblies or a large unspecified amount of money

magga the path to awakening; there are four stages of awakening, sometimes called the four paths: stream entry, once-return, never-return, and arhatship; progress on the path as a whole is described as eightfold because it has eight factors: right view, intention, speech, action, livelihood, effort, mindfulness, and concentration or meditation

MARA the god of delusion, who tempts meditators from their path

naga (*nāga*) a mythical creature, part human and part snake, who lives underwater or in caves in the ground; a naga has magical powers and can shape-shift and recollect past lives; it guards treasures and wish-fulfilling gems

nibbana (*nibbāna*) nirvana; the highest goal and the cessation of suffering

pārami perfection; a supreme quality or excellence needed to become a Buddha; there are ten: generosity, virtue, renunciation, wisdom, heroic effort, forbearance, truthfulness, resolve, loving-kindness, and equanimity

patisambhidā analytic insight; the four analytic insights are insight into (1) meaning, (2) the teaching and natural law (Dhamma), (3) the language used to describe these, and (4) detailed knowledge of the first three as well as how they work together in practice

phala fruit; when used with the term "path," it refers to the four resultant mental states from the four paths, or stages of awakening; see *magga*

rūpa form or pertaining to form; the *jhānas* (meditations), the first four of the eight attainments, are called *rūpa jhānas,* as they still have some vestiges of form, in the sense of a visual object or bodily experience

SAKKA the king of the Heaven of the Thirty-Three, a sense-sphere deva realm where beings are reborn on the basis of morality, generosity, faith, and investigation; when acts of great merit occur in the human world, Sakka's throne becomes hot, and he is moved to help the participants

samāpatti an attainment; there are eight of these: the four sense-sphere *jhānas,* or meditative stages, and the four formless meditations

samatha calm, peace; there are four stages of calm known as the four *jhānas,* and four that are formless meditations; some *samatha* meditations, however, such as the recollections on the Buddha, the Dhamma, the Sangha, and one's own acts of generosity, do not lead directly to such absorptions, but rather to well-being and happiness in daily life

SANGHA (*saṅgha*) (1) the community of those who have attained stages of the path, and also the community of monks and nuns; (2) the third refuge in what is known as the triple gem: Buddha, Dhamma, and Sangha

sotāpanna (stream-enterer) one who has attained the first stage of the path and so has "entered the stream"; the fruits of stream entry are the freedom and happiness that result from it

supanna (*supaṇṇa*) the garuda bird, a mythical winged creature

sutta a teaching or discourse of the Buddha; the *Suttapiṭaka* is the second "basket" of the Buddha's teaching

tevijjā the three knowledges: (1) the ability to remember past lives; (2) the ability to see the arising and falling away of other beings, or the divine eye; and (3) the eradication of the corruptions

usabha a measure of length, about 140 cubits

VINAYA the monastic code; the *Vinayapiṭaka* is the first of the three "baskets" of the Buddha's teaching

yakkha a spirit, often malign, like a troll or goblin; the term may also refer to spirits in the supernatural world who do not have evil intent

yojana a measure of distance based on how far one can travel with a single yoke of oxen; reckoned to be between seven and nine miles

Epithets for a Buddha

BHAGAVA the Bhagavan, the blessed one

BODHISATTA one "intent on" or "attached to" awakening, who has made a Bodhisatta vow; in Pali Buddhism, the vow entails undertaking to become a Buddha, to find the path, and to teach the path to awakening to others

BUDDHA a human who has found complete awakening and can teach others a path for the eradication of suffering; only one exists at any time and is called "the Buddha"

DASABALA "the one with ten powers"; epithet denoting the Buddha's various skills, such as knowing the full path to awakening and understanding the dispositions of other beings

MAHASATTA Great Being

SATTHA the Teacher

TATHAGATA the "Thus-Gone," who has literally "gone thus" to awakening

BIBLIOGRAPHY

Editions and Translations

Fausbøll, V., ed. 1877–1896. *The Jātaka Together with Its Commentary, Being Tales of the Anterior Births of Gotama Buddha.* 6 vols. London: Trübner and Co. (Published in various reprints as the Pali Text Society edition).

Rhys Davids, T. W., trans. 1880. *Buddhist Birth Stories; or, Jātaka Tales: The Oldest Collection of Folk-lore Extant Being the Jātakakatthavaṇṇanā.* London: Trübner and Co.

———, trans. 1925. *Buddhist Birth-Stories (Jataka Tales): The Commentarial Introduction Entitled Nidāna-kathā, the Story of the Lineage.* Edited by C. A. F. Rhys Davids. New and revised ed. London: Routledge; New York: Dutton.

Horner, I. B., trans. 1975. *The Minor Anthologies of the Pali Canon, Part III: Chronicle of the Buddhas (Buddhavaṃsa) and Basket of Conduct (Cariyāpiṭaka).* Oxford: Pali Text Society.

Jayawickrama, N. A., trans. 1990. *The Story of Gotama Buddha: The Nidāna-kathā of the Jātakaṭṭhakathā.* Oxford: Pali Text Society.

Vipassana Research Institute. 1997. *Chaṭṭha Saṅgāyana,* Pali Tipitaka website. Dhamma Giri, Igatpuri: Vipassana Research Institute. *https://tipitaka.org/chattha.*

Other Sources

Appleton, Naomi and Sarah Shaw. 2015. *The Ten Great Birth Stories of the Buddha: The Mahānipāta of the Jātakatthavaṇṇanā.* 2 vols. Chiang Mai: Silkworm; Bangkok: Chulalongkorn University Press.

Bodhi, Bhikkhu, trans. 1978. "A Treatise on the Pāramis." In *The Discourse on the All-Embracing Net of Views: The Brahmajāla Sutta and Its Commentaries.* Kandy, Sri Lanka: Buddhist Publication Society, pp. 243–317.

Buswell, Robert E. Jr. and Donald S. Lopez Jr. 2014. "Kalpa." In *The Princeton Dictionary of Buddhism.* Princeton: Princeton University Press.

Cone, Margaret and Richard F. Gombrich. 2011. *The Perfect Generosity of Prince Vessantara.* 2nd ed. Bristol, UK: Pali Text Society.

Cowell, E. B., ed. Translated by many hands. 1895–1907. *The Jātaka, or*

Stories of the Buddha's Former Births. 6 vols. Cambridge: Cambridge University Press.

Dhammika, S. 2015. *Nature and the Environment in Early Buddhism*. Online resource. Oxford Centre for Buddhist Studies, https://ocbs.org/wp-content/uploads/2015/09/journalsuppneeb.pdf.

Elsner, Jas. 2021. "Art, Religion and Narrative: A Comparison of Early Christian and Early Buddhist Art." *Codex Aquilarensis* 37: 537–554.

Geiger, Wilhelm. 1943. *Pāli Literature and Language*. Translated by B. Ghosh. Calcutta: Calcutta University.

Gethin, Rupert. 2012. "Was Buddhaghosa a Theravādin? Buddhist Identity in the Pali Commentaries and Chronicles." In *How Theravāda Is Theravāda? Exploring Buddhist Identities*, ed. Peter Skilling et al. Chiang Mai: Silkworm.

Harvey, Peter. 2013. *An Introduction to Buddhism: Teachings, History and Practices*. 2nd ed. Cambridge: Cambridge University Press.

Hinüber, Oskar von. 1996. *Handbook of Pali Literature*. Berlin: Walter de Gruyter.

———. 2015. "Building the Theravada Commentaries: Buddhaghosa and Dhammapāla as Authors, Compilers, Redactors, Editors and Critics." In "Authors and Editors in the Literary Traditions of Asian Buddhism," ed. Cathy Cantwell, Jowita Kramer, Robert Meyer, and Stefano Zacchetti, special issue, *Journal of the International Association of Buddhist Studies* 36/37: 353–388.

Huntington, Susan L. 2012. *Lay Ritual and the Buddhist Art of India: More Evidence against the Aniconic Theory*. Amsterdam: Royal Netherlands Academy of Arts and Sciences.

Jongeward, David. 2018. *Buddhist Art of Gandhara in the Ashmolean Museum*. Oxford: Ashmolean Museum.

Longhurst, A. H. 1938. *The Buddhist Antiquities of Nāgārjunakoṇḍa, Madras Presidency*. Memoirs of the Archaeological Survey of India 54. Delhi: Manager of Publications, Archaeological Survey of India.

Matsumura, Junko. 2010. "The *Sumedhakathā* in Pāli Literature and Its Relation to the Northern Buddhist Textual Tradition." *Journal of the International College for Postgraduate Buddhist Studies* 14: 101–135.

Ñāṇamoli, Bhikkhu, trans. 2009. *The Path of Purification (Visuddhimagga)*. Taiwan: Corporate Body of the Buddha Educational Foundation.

Neelis, J. 2019. "Making Places for Buddhism in Gandhāra: Stories of Previous Births in Image and Text." In *The Geography of Gandhāran*

Art: Proceedings of the Second International Workshop of the Gandhāra Connections Project, University of Oxford, 22nd–23rd March 2018, ed. W. Rienjang and P. Stewart. Oxford: Archaeopress Archaeology, pp. 175–185.

Nyanatusita, Bhikkhu. 2021. *The Path to Freedom: Vimuttimagga.* 2 vols. Hong Kong: Centre of Buddhist Studies.

Reynolds, Frank E. and Charles Hallisey. 1987. "Buddha." In *Encyclopedia of Religion,* ed. Mircea Eliade. New York: Macmillan.

Seeger, Martin. 2018. *Gender and the Path to Awakening: Hidden Histories of Nuns in Modern Thai Buddhism.* Chiang Mai: Silkworm.

Shaw, Sarah, trans. 2006. *The Jātakas: Birth Stories of the Bodhisatta.* New Delhi: Penguin.

Skilling, Peter. 1996. "The Sambuddhe Verses and Later Theravādin Buddhology." *Journal of the Pali Text Society* 22: 151–184.

———. 2008. "Narrative, Art and Ideology: Jātakas from India to Sukhothai." In *Past Lives of the Buddha: Wat Si Chum: Art, Architecture, and Inscriptions,* ed. Peter Skilling et al. Bangkok: River Books, pp. 59–104.

INDEX

ABOUT THE BOOK

Murty Classical Library of India volumes are designed by Rathna Ramanathan and Guglielmo Rossi. Informed by the history of the Indic book and drawing inspiration from polyphonic classical music, the series design is based on the idea of "unity in diversity," celebrating the individuality of each language while bringing them together within a cohesive visual identity.

The Pali and English texts are set in Antwerp, designed by Henrik Kubel from A2-TYPE and chosen for its versatility and balance with the Indic typography. The design is a free-spirited amalgamation and interpretation of the archives of type at the Museum Plantin-Moretus in Antwerp.

All the fonts commissioned for the Murty Classical Library of India will be made available, free of charge, for non-commercial use. For more information about the typography and design of the series, please visit *http://www.hup.harvard.edu/mcli.*

Printed on acid-free paper by Maple Press, York, Pennsylvania.